Ottoman Connections to the Malay World

Ottoman Connections to the Malay World

Islam, Law and Society

EDITED BY

Saim Kayadibi

TOP

The Other Press
Kuala Lumpur

Published by
The Other Press Sdn. Bhd.
607 Mutiara Majestic
Jalan Othman
46000 Petaling Jaya
Selangor, Malaysia
www.ibtbooks.com

The Other Press is affiliated with Islamic Book Trust.

Perpustakaan Negara Malaysia Cataloguing-in-Publication Data

Kayadibi, Saim
Ottoman connections to the Malay World : Islam, law and society / edited by Saim Kayadibi.
Includes index
Bibliography: p. 213
ISBN 978-983-9541-77-9
1. Islam--Malaysia--History. 2. Islam--Turkey--History.
3. Islam--Influence. 4. Islamic law--Interpretation and construction--Malaysia. 5. Malay Archipelago--Civilization--Islamic influences. I. Title.
297.0899923

Printed In Malaysia

Dedicated to
My late father Mehmet
and
my mother Zülfüye

Contents

Acknowledgement ix

Preface xi

1 The religious-intellectual network: the arrival of Islam in the archipelago 1
Nurulwahidah Binti Fauzi - Ali Mohammad -Saim Kayadibi

2 Baba Davud: A Turkish scholar in Aceh 32
Mehmet Özay

3 A preliminary note on the Dayah Tanoh Abee 56
Mehmet Özay

4 Legal developments in the Ottoman state (1299-1926) 85
Ahmed Akgündüz

5 Evolution of the Muslim judicial system 114
Saim Kayadibi

6 Fiqh education at Ottoman madrasahs: A case study of Süleymaniye madrasahs 154
Servet Bayındır

7 Judicial pluralism in the Malaysian legal system 186
Saim Kayadibi

Conclusion 211

Bibliography 213

Index 239

Acknowledgement

All praise is due to Allah, who blessed us with the opportunity to complete this humble book. In advance, I would like to express my deepest thanks and appreciation to all individuals and organizations that contributed, either directly or indirectly, to this book's production. Special thanks must go to the chapter contributors: Prof Dr Ahmet Akgündüz (rector, University of Rotterdam), Dr Mehmet Özay (lecturer, Faculty of Islamic Civilization and Thought, University Technology Malaysia), Assoc. Prof Dr Servet Bayındır (lecturer, Department of Islamic Jurisprudence, Faculty of Theology, Istanbul University), Nurulwahidah Binti Fauzi (Ph.D. student, Department of Islamic History and Civilization, Academy of Islamic Studies, University of Malaya), and Assoc. Prof Dr Ali Mohammad (lecturer, Department of Islamic History and Civilization, Academy of Islamic Studies, University of Malaya).

I would like to take this opportunity to thank Professor Dr Ahmad Hidayat Buang (director, Academy of Islamic Studies, University of Malaya) for his generous support for the research related to this book and also for being a co-researcher; Professor Dr Saffet Köse (lecturer, Department of Islamic Jurisprudence, Selçuk University); the Research Centre of the University of Malaya (IPPP) for research funding; to my dear friend and "abi" Jay Willoughby, who copyedited the book; and to the Islamic

Book Trust staff and its respected director Hj. Koya for his exceedingly helpful cooperation and keen interest in publishing the manuscript. Without his contribution, this book could not have been finalized.

Wa al-salamu 'alaykum wa raḥmatullāhi wa barakātuh

Associate Prof Dr Saim Kayadibi
Kulliyyah of Economics and Management Sciences
International Islamic University Malaysia
July 2011
Gombak, Kuala Lumpur

Preface

Southeast Asia, especially the Malay Archipelago, has enjoyed a long historical connection with Muslim Rumi (Turkish), Ḥaḍramī Arab, and Ottoman traders as can be seen in the two regions' framework of religious, political, and legal cooperation. The Ottomans' pan-Islam policy and the mission of Sultan Abdulhamid II enabled the archipelago to play an active role and thus increase its relationships with Muslim scholars, rulers, and legal heritages elsewhere when it was confronted with European colonialism. The network of Johor-Ottoman and Ḥaḍramī Muslim relationships, as well as the role of Sultan Abu Bakar of Johor, strengthened bilateral connections. The translation of the *Majallah al-Aḥkām* (Ottoman Legal Codes) into Malay also served to develop legal practice of Islamic law in Malay Sharīʻah courts.

The seven articles contained in this collection discuss and analyze selected topics related to the Ottoman and Malay legal structures and development. Chapter 1, "The Religious-Intellectual Network: The Arrival of Islam in the Archipelago" by Nurulwahidah Binti Fauzi, Ali Mohammad, and Saim Kayadibi, elaborates upon the network existing between the *ʻulamā'* and the ruler of Johor during the twentieth century, including its historical background. The researchers indicate that ever since Islam appeared in seventh-century Arabia, Arab society has continued to influence

Asian societies. After Islam's arrival in Southeast Asia, a number of records were found that present a still incomplete picture of the mix of formal and/or non-formal relationships between the Arabs and the Chinese, Indians, Persians, and Turks. The authors focus on Islam's arrival and the Malays' relationship with Muslims, especially the Ottomans and Arab Ḥaḍramīs.

In "Baba Davud: A Turkish Scholar in Aceh," Mehmet Özay presents the scholar Shaikh Davud b. Ismail b. Mustafa ar-Rumi, generally known as Baba Davud or Mustafa ar-Rumi, who was a caliph of the well-known Acehnese religious scholar Abdurrauf as-Singkilī (Teungku Syiah Kuala). One of his works, the *Risālah Masāilal Muhtadi li Ikhwanil Muhtadi,* has been taught at Islamic institutions in Aceh and around the Malay world. It is hoped that his article will make a significant contribution to Ottoman-Malaysian studies. The third chapter, "A Preliminary Note on 'Dayah Tanoh Abee,'" also by Mehmet Özay, describes this centre's famous *zāwiyah* that is located in Seulimum, a subdistrict of the Acehnese capital of Banda Aceh. Its importance is considered to be based on its founding family's origin, the connection between the Sultanate of Aceh Darussalam and the Ottoman empire, and its contribution to Islamizing Southeast Asia.

The Ottomans made a significant contribution to the development of legal matters in Islamic law. With this point in mind, Prof Dr Ahmed Akgündüz enriches the value of this book with his "Legal Developments in Ottoman State (1299-1926)." This important research article, which appears as chapter 4, outlines the course of legal developments before the *Tanẓīmāt* Reforms (699-1255/1299-1839) and during the Post-*Tanẓīmāt* Period (1255-1345/1839-1926).

Chapter 5, Saim Kayadibi's "Evolution of the Muslim Judicial System," investigates this topic by analyzing the effect of those social, cultural, political, and historical elements that shaped the role of both jurists and courts in secular and non-secular environments. In the modern period, most Muslim-majority countries steadily adopted western legal systems and institutions due to the economic and political influence of their colonial masters. Chapter 6, featuring Servet Bayındır's "Fiqh Education at Ottoman Madrasahs: A Case of Süleymaniye Madrasahs," evaluates the science of *fiqh* (Islamic jurisprudence) among the systematic sciences and its place in legal history. The emergence of madrasahs and the importance of Süleymaniye madrasahs among the Ottoman educational institutions, along with their main resources and methods of teaching, are analyzed according to both *furū' al-fiqh* and *uṣūl al-fiqh* individually.

The seventh (and final) chapter, Saim Kayadibi's "Judicial Pluralism in the Malaysian Legal System", investigates this intriguing subject. Malay society, which is well-known for allowing others to live according to their own cultural values and traditions, believes that diversity is a source of cultural and social wealth. This can be seen in Malaysia's extraordinary freedom and richness in both legal and cultural matters, traits that it shares with Ottoman society. Malay society has apparently interiorized the value of diversity, which fosters peace, freedom, tolerance, and strength among different groups. Its legal system has been shaped by external forces: Islamic law (via the Muslims' request) and the legal systems of colonial Europe (by force). In contrast, the country's courts used the Ottoman empire's *Majallah al-Aḥkām al-'Adliyyah,* the Ḥanafī code of Qadri Pasha (later called the *Majallah Aḥkām Johor*), and the *Undang-undang Sivil Islam* as the main sources for judicial rulings. In this article, Kayadibi explores the Malay legal system's evolution in relation to constitutional law, indigenous customary law and tribal legal systems, Sharī'ah and civil court procedures, first contacts with Islamic law, the influence of colonial law, as well as the Ottoman-Malay connection and strong relationships.

It is hoped that this humble work will contribute to the heritage of Malay-Turk relations as well as that of other Muslim nations.

Allah knows best. Praise be to Him, the Lord of the heavens, planets and all that exists.

Saim Kayadibi

1

The religious-intellectual network: the arrival of Islam in the archipelago

***Nurulwahidah Binti Fauzi*[1]**
***Ali Mohammad*[2]**
***Saim Kayadibi*[3]**

Abstract

The expansion of Islam in the Malay state of Johor, especially as it relates to the roles played by Arabs and Ottomans, is an interesting subject in its own right. The resulting network was based upon the efforts of the *'ulamā'* and the ruler, and especially the Muslim Consultant Jurist (*muftī*), to establish religious coordination in Johore. This article analyzes this network during the twentieth century and details its historical background. Emphasis is placed on the role played by the *'ulamā'* role and the challenges they faced at that time, based upon the hypothesis that their contribution to Islam's early expansion and practice in Johor was quite significant.

Introduction

In the historical record, many great civilizations that built empires would definitely boast of playing a significant role in shaping an exemplary government and directly securing the resources needed to fulfil most of its administrative functions. Two of the main agents in this regard would be the *umarā'* (those who manage the government) and the *'ulamā'* (those who manage religious affairs). The former, universally known in Islamic lands as *sulṭān* or *khalīfah*, is the most important figure in an organized government, whereas the latter acts in entrusted with the post of being the leading defender of Islam's principles and laws.

About the *umarā'*, al-Ghazālī once commented that "the whole of the Islamic government contained three elements, the caliph, the sulṭān, and the *umarā'*, who by their approval of the Sulṭan's choice of Caliph in the *bay'a* and by their *fatwās*, expressed the functions of the authority of the sharī'ah."[4] Apart from the head of the government, other elites (e.g., ministers and *'ulamā'* for the Muslims, priests for the Christians, and monks for the Buddhists) were also involved in governing.

The term *'ulamā'*, considered to be a symbol of a country's spiritual strength, means "people who understand." It is derived from *'ālim* (people of knowledge), which comes from the noun form of the verb *'alima* (he who knew).[5] From the meaning itself, it is apparent that the *'ulamā'* are regarded as experts in the field of knowledge, trusted to manage the Islamic legal system, govern the educational system as well as *waqf* (religious foundations) properties, and critique the rulers when they violate Islamic teachings and norms. All of these functions give them a high status in the eyes of society, and thus they deserve to be known as the "inheritors of the prophets".[6]

The bond of this two-way *umarā'*-*'ulamā'* collaboration shaped the nucleus of those connections that would eventually be revealed through Islamic institutions and legislation, as well as those institutions associated with the *muftī*, *qāḍī* (judge), and the Shaykh al-Islām (the superior authority on matters related to Islam). These components can be observed in several Islamic empires in the Malay Archipelago, among them Pasai and Aceh, Patani, and the Malacca Sultanate, which arose in modern-day Indonesia, Thailand, and Malaysia, respectively. All of these eventually came under the control of the Johor Sultanate in Malaya.

Among the sultans who ruled according to the *'ulamā's* guidance were Sultan Alauddin Riayat Shah II (Johor), Sultan

Iskandar Muda Mahkota Alam (Aceh), and Sultan Malik Az-Zahir (Pasai). According to Thomas F. Willer, these *'ulamā'*-influenced rulers were "vestigial, unorganized and poorly equipped religious dignitaries of earlier days, augmented by rural *ulamā'*. Significantly this growing Islamic state structure was dogmatically dominated by ... traditional, syncretic, heterodox and often sufitinged Islam."[7] Clearly, then, the *'ulamā'* had been long-term participants in the royal administration. In fact, this role was seen as one of their obligatory tasks: cultivating and then spreading the seed of Islam throughout the Malay Archipelago.[8]

In order to better understand the forms of interaction built among the *'ulamā'* through the Johor sultanate, this chapter discusses the posited theories of how Islam came to the Malay Archipelago, specifies its development in Johor, and looks at the factors that motivated the Ḥaḍramī Arabs and the Ottoman empire to become involved with the region. The results of these relationships both directly contributed to as well as formed the roles played by members of the *'ulamā'* class.

The theories of pre-Islam in the Malay archipelago: a general argument

After analyzing Islam's arrival in the Malay Archipelago, Fred R. von Mehden[9] concluded that the Middle East's relationship with that region consists of three periods: the first arrival of Islam until the beginning of the nineteenth century, from that century until the Second World War, and the post-war era. This discussion focuses on the events associated with the first phase: Islam's homeland, its originators, and its place in the history. It is an effort to determine who was responsible for establishing what eventually became a network of intellectual and religious transformation among the *'ulamā'* of Johor.

Historians, be they Orientalists or Muslim, have always differed on how Islam reached the archipelago. For example, S.Q. Fatimi contends that Islam came from Arabs (the strongest view); the Indian regions of Cambay, Gujarat, and Malabar; China; and from the Delhi Sultanate and the Ottoman empire.[10] Robert, who agrees with this view, posits the following chronology: the earliest contact (674), taking root around various coastal cities (878), becoming part of the political power structure (1204), and the most developed period (1511).[11] Moquette, R.O. Windtedt, Schrike, Hall, and other Orientalists agree that Islam came to Nusantara through Gujarat. This agreement was based on the finding of a tomb in Pasai, North Sumatra, dated 831H and said to be similar to that of Maulana Malik Ibrahim (d. 822/1419) in Gresik, East Java. Windsted then supported Moquette by arguing that a similar tomb in Bruas, an ancient Malay kingdom in Perak, was said to have originated from the trading relationship as well the spreading of Islam that connected the two areas.[12]

The Dutch historian Pijnappel, who also links Islam's appearance in the Malay Archipelago to Gujarat and Malabar, verified this theory by claiming that the Arabs living in these two places also belonged to the Shāfiʿī *madhhab*. These Arabs were said to migrate and settle in India and, later on, introduced Islam to the Malay Archipelago.[13] Azyumardi, however, has developed several theories, one of which (based upon Arnold) posits that Coromandel Malabar and India were not the sole points of origin; rather, Islam came from the Arabian peninsula.[14] Syed Naquib al-Attas contends that Islam came from the Arabian Peninsula and, to a lesser extent, the Ottoman empire. But even more importantly, it came from the Middle East instead of India.[15] This scholarly debate concluded that regardless of all of the theories presented, the roles and contributions of Arab society cannot be denied.

Arab society seems to have started influencing Asia soon after its appearance in seventh-century Arabia. During the early centuries of its influence in Southeast Asia, however, records were found in separate parts: a mixture of formal or non-formal relationships between several nations, including the Arabs, with China, India, Persia, and Turkey. All formal relationships formed by the Arabs of this time were mostly inclined toward trade. According to Tibbets, Arab traders did not come only after the arrival of Islam, for this regional interaction actually predated Islam.

In fact this relationship, originally based on trading and seafaring, had been its driving force ever since the civilization of Saba' had arisen in Yemen, whose people were said to visit China via the Malacca Straits to trade. Among their ports of call were Mul Jawa (Java), Sribuza (Sriwijaya), Kalah (Kedah), Panhang (Pahang), Jambi, Palembang, and Tiyuman (Tioman).[16] These places were visited because camphor was produced around Barus. This essential trade item was called *alfakur* (Arabic), *kamfara* (Russian), *camfor* (British), *camprige* (French), and *kamfer* (Dutch).[17] The name *Barosai* found on ancient maps was also derived from the word *barus*.[18]

Their obsession with trading and seafaring was largely shaped by the Arab Peninsula's surface and the physical environment: except for the coastal areas, it was arid and barren. Over time, this relatively difficult geographical situation turned its inhabitants into a strong and independent nation, for as M.A. Shaban mentions: "The Arabs, who were able to adapt themselves to the harsh and lives of the Arabian Peninsula, could certainly adapt themselves to a more comfortable life elsewhere."[19]

The above statement illustrates that Arab society had a strong fighting spirit not only on the battlefield, but also in its members' various livelihoods. In the beginning, the Arabs sailed wooden ships to the Malay Archipelago via al-Mukalla Port, then to Malabar, southern India, Sri Lanka, Aceh, Singapore, Johor, and other parts of Malaya.[20] In tandem with the economic and technological developments of later centuries, derived mainly through the opening of the Suez Canal, seafaring technology increased and Southeast Asia's economic attraction was heightened. Eventually, this resulted in an increased flow of migrants (especially Ḥaḍramī Arabs) to the Malay Archipelago.[21]

The existence of Arab trade communities around the Malay Archipelago became more apparent when Arab settlements were spotted along the west Sumatran coast in 674. Thirty-five trading ships from Pasai stopped at Palembang on their way to China in 717. Early Arab-Persian records on the relationship between the Arabs with both Malaya and Indonesia traced it back to the mid-ninth century.[22] This situation was supported by Azyumardi Azra and Arnold, who agreed that although the Arabs were not directly involved in converting the local people for the rulers, the teachings of Islam were spread among the latter after the Arabs began marrying local women and gradually attained political power, which they utilized to spread Islam.[23]

The closeness of economic institutions to the souls of Arab traders was carried to this region along with their Sūfi characteristics. As A.H. Johns relates, members of this group roamed constantly[24] and simultaneously practiced the deep teachings of theosophy, which indirectly convinced the rulers to marry off their children to them.[25] This process directly influenced the cultivation of religion, especially when they were given absolute power to administer religious affairs and the authority to issue *fatwās*, establish *pesantrens* (Islamic boarding schools) and madrasahs, develop a special school curriculum, and produce Islamic literature for public consumption.

Given the above, we can say that at least in this region, Islam spread mainly through trade. Thus, as regards its arrival in Malay Archipelago, it was introduced by Arab, Indian, and Chinese traders and Sūfis. The people welcomed it because it was simpler and better than their original Hindu and Buddhist beliefs. Moreover, the Muslim *mu'allim* (teacher), whether they were spice traders or Sūfis, voluntarily came to the region due to their sincere belief that Islam should be shared at all levels and society and humanity. This relationship shaped the reformation momentum as the number of Arabs living in the Malay Archipelago began to increase during the eighteenth century. Although their earlier bases had mainly been in Indonesia, Dutch colonial invasions caused them to begin moving to nearby Singapore, which at the end of eighteenth century was still ruled by the Sultanate of Johor.

The next section looks at how Islam reached Malaya, especially Johor, through the Ḥaḍramī Arabs and Ottoman Turkey. The reciprocal process of correlation triggered a mutually closed-linked phenomenon that is discussed in the following section.

The development of Islam in Johor: the influence of the Ḥaḍramī Arab colony and Ottoman Turkey

Many Muslim historians and western Orientalists have presented theories and evidence for Islam's establishment in the Malay Archipelago during the seventh century and its progress until the seventeenth century. But its spread to Johor, a state in the historical Malay sultanate of Malacca, is an interesting topic in its own right.

We will not debate how Islam came to Johor; rather, we will focus on how the correlation between the Ḥaḍramīs and the Ottomans during the reign of Sultan Abdulhamid II (1876-1909) progressed from anti-Dutch to pan-Islam sentiments. This triangular relationship can be viewed as a three-corner-chain:

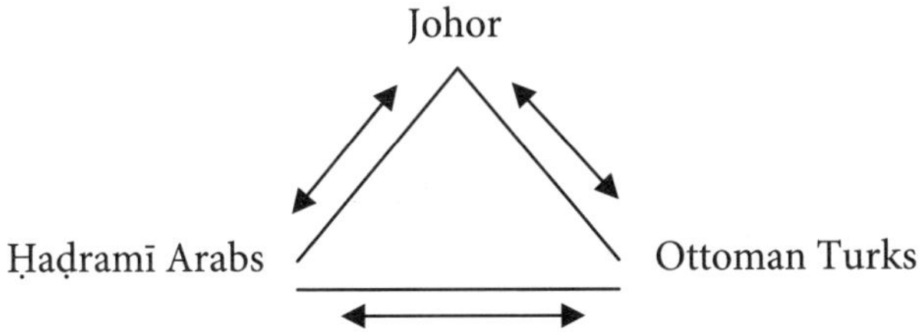

Figure 1: The three-cornered relationship among Johor's three main groups.

The network of Ḥaḍramī Arabs and Johor relations

Early Malay, Arab, and Dutch chronicles mention the Arab presence in archipelago but do not give any details as to which Arab lands they came from, why they migrated to Johor, and how such migration led to the close correlation with Johor's monarchy. In his evaluation of the Arabs' roles and influences as the supporting agent for Islam's arrival, Peter G. Riddel stressed that the main focus should be on the Ḥaḍramī Arabs and their continual relationship with their original homeland.[26] This was due to the fact that existing data related to the Arab presence, prior to ascertaining that it was in Johor, had been recorded to exist among Indonesia's islands during the seventeenth and early eighteenth centuries. These settlements had a Ḥaḍramī majority.

Ismail Hamid, Mahyuddin Hj. Yahya, Hj. Muzaffar Hj. Mohd, and other historians agree that a majority of them were descendants of the Prophet's (ṣ) family (the Ahl al-Bayt) through the Prophet's grandson Ḥusayn. They were members of the 'Alawiyyīn clan that lived in the region of Ḥaḍramawt, Yemen, a leading intellectual region.[27] If they were Ḥasan's descendents, usually they came from Ṭā'if, located near Makkah.[28]

Ḥaḍramawt, which had its own civilization and was divided into two major areas, was located near the trade route connecting India with the Middle East.[29] Its eastern portion contained the large cities of Mukalla and Shihi, which formed the route to the Indian Ocean. Its location just to the south of the Rub' al-Khālī desert encouraged the Ḥaḍramīs to explore the eastern and southern areas for economic and cultural relations. Around the tenth century AC, Ḥaḍramī traders had already reached East Africa, the West Indies, and Southeast Asia.[30]

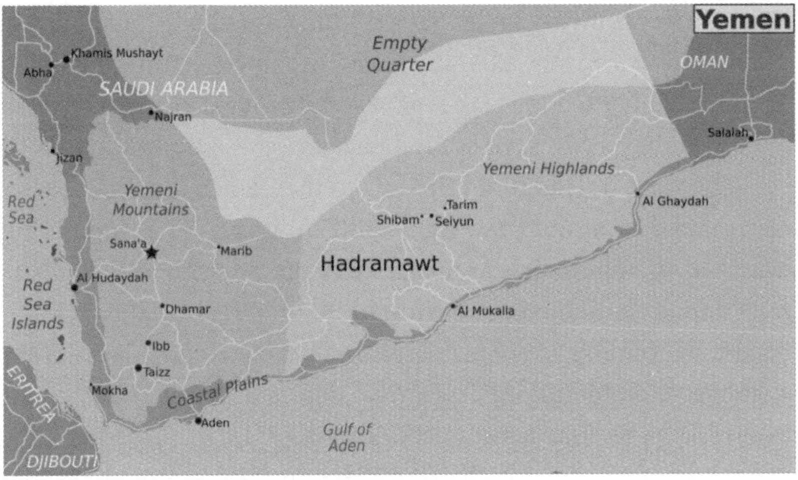

Map of Ḥaḍramawt, Yemen

Local historical literature records many of the events connected with their migration to the Malay Archipelago various islands. For example, *Islam dan Sejarah Asia Tenggara Tradisional* mentions that during the rule of the ʻAbbāsid caliph al-Ma'mūn (813-833) the ʻAlawiyyīn sparked a revolt that was led by Jaʻfar al-Ṣādiq, the Sixth Imām and a member of the Ahl al-Bayt. Among those involved was Sayyid Abdul Malik b. Alawi, a descendant of Muhajirullah Ahmad b. Isa who was born in Qassam (Ḥaḍramawt) and migrated to India with other ʻAlawiyyīn *sayyids*.[31] Since the rebellion failed, they decided to establish a *daʻwah* (missionary) group of 100 people and, around 840, moved to the Sumatran state of Perlak, at that time governed by Meurah Shah Nuwi of Persian descent. He married his young sister Puteri Makhdum Tansuri to one of the missionaries. This couple gave birth to Sayyid Abdul Aziz, who later became Perlak's first king.[32]

The *Sejarah Orang Sayyid di Pahang* also recorded a number of tales concerning the ʻAlawiyyīn's arrival in Indonesia, via India and the Ḥaḍramawt, around the seventeenth century. Among these people were Sayyid Abdullah al-Qudsi, Sayyid Uthman b. Syahab, Sayyid Muhammad b. Ahmad al-Idrus, and Sayyid Hussein al-

Qadri. After studying under Sayyid Muhammad b. Hamid, he who allowed his friends to sail to the Malay Archipelago. Sayyid Uthman b. Syahab inherited the Siak regime, while Sayyid Hussein al-Qadri inherited the government of Pontianak.[33]

The wave of Ḥaḍramī migrants to the islands of Indonesia has been dated to around the eighteenth century.[34] This community was said to appear first around Aceh, and later on at Palembang or Pontianak, Kalimantan. Around 1820 and thereafter, vibrant Ḥaḍramī trading colonies appeared in northern Java. Their colonies around Indonesia can be detected in the 1870 census records.[35] The first census, conducted in 1859, recorded 4,992 Arab men, women, and children living around Java and Madura. A further 2,776 resided outside the Dutch-controlled islands, thereby making a total of 7,768 people. Although the census was conducted among the Arab communities, a majority of their inhabitants were from the Ḥaḍramawt.[36]

The claim for the Arab community's original homeland was strengthened by Robert Day McAmis, who quoted from Mahmud (1960) and Hamid (1983), acknowledging that the Arabs who came to East Africa, northern India, and Indonesia were originally from the Ḥaḍramawt. They were also the ones who brought Islamic culture to China and the western coast of India, and later to Sumatra and Malacca.[37] Hub De Jonge later agreed with this claim and even added that their numbers increased during the second quarter of nineteenth century and the first quarter of twentieth century.[38]

The Dutch, however, resented the Arabs' presence and economic monopoly around the Indonesian islands. The resulting pressure and oppression, along with other factors, led many Arabs to migrate to nearby islands during the nineteenth century. Among the most pressing reasons was the mental pressure applied by the Dutch colonists. As early as the nineteenth century, the Dutch tried to limit the land upon which immigrants could settle;

De Jonge clarified, however, that before the Dutch colonists, the Arabs and Chinese especially, had already settled at certain areas with their own groups.[39]

Several other restrictions were also imposed: the time system, the pass system, and immigration laws. These policies, officially stated to be applied to all immigrant communities equally, were applied selectively. One such harsh policy was limiting the areas in which Arabs could settle, such as Pekojan, Batavia. Van Den Berg observed that this system caused problems for the Arabs because their existing communities became very overcrowded. In addition, they had to apply for travel passes to travel, either by land or sea, outside the district. All such applications were submitted to a very lengthy approval process, which made it hard for merchants to travel in order to deal with business matters.[40]

Unwilling to deal with the situation any longer, some Arabs began to migrate to other locations regions of the archipelago. A majority of them became involved in import-export businesses[41] and shipping. W.R. Roff stated that "the pilgrimage industry in Singapore and other activities associated with it was very largely in the hands of Arabs community."[42] Data from the Straits Settlements in 1901 claimed that thousands of Arabs lived in the archipelago, such as the coast of Glam Village, with other foreign immigrants like the Bugis, Boyanese, Javanese, and Jawi Peranakan.[43] Although this statement listed Glam Village as a Malay Archipelago province, it clearly referred to Singapore. Dutch historian L.W.C. Van Den Berg describes the large-scale activities conducted by Singapore's Arab community in 1886 as "the most flourishing, though not the largest, Arab colony in the Indian Archipelago."[44]

Due to their strong economic position during that time, these Arabs were able to send their children to be educated in Wādi in the Ḥaḍramawt. Those who could not afford to do so would send their children to an Arabic school or madrasah in Malaya.[45]

Armed with a great deal of knowledge, either of the world or the Hereafter, it was not surprising that they became the elites and had good relationships with Muslim communities of Indonesia and Malaya, and especially with the Sultanate of Johor's ruling family and the Ottoman empire.[46]

A study of Singapore's Arab population revealed that its origin can be traced to the sixteenth century, when a certain southern Arab died there in 1584.[47] It is not impossible that the Arab community inhabited the districts around Singapore at such an early date, considering that their population in 1824 was estimated at fifteen people and had increased to 1,226 in 1911. A study by A.M. Al-Sagoff listed some data that support this claim.

Year	**Men**	**Women**	**Total**
1824	-	-	15
1825	10	-	10
1826	17	-	17
1827	18	-	18
1828	-	-	17
1829	29	3	32
1830	28	-	28
1832	61	3	64
1833	96	-	96
1834	55	11	66
1836	33	8	41
1849	121	73	194
1860	63	52	117
1871	275	191	446
1881	551	285	836
1891	503	203	706
1901	523	396	919
1911	708	518	1,226[48]

Table 1: Arabs Residents of Singapore

Their arrival in Johor was linked to those Arab residents who had migrated from Singapore around 1849, as recorded below.

Year	Men	Women	Total
1849	392	307	699
1860	411	325	736
1871	709	636	1,345[49]

Table 2: Arab Residents of Johor

The increasing number of Arabs was due to economic factors as well as official Johor policies during the 1880s and 1890s, when they began to learn from the British policies being pursued in certain Malayan states. Johor adopted liberal land policies to encourage Malays and Arabs from neighbouring lands, which brought new residents and led former residents to return.[50] Whatever their reasons for migration, a majority of these Arabs still carried with them authoritative religious culture and activities that were considered the main and earliest sources of the local Muslim community.[51]

The network of Arab-Ottoman relations

When we look at the relationships of the Johor-Ḥaḍramī Arabs with Ottoman Turkey, a question arises: did any connection between these two groups bring them together as regards how they influenced and responded to the events that took place around the archipelago, especially Johor, around the end of the nineteenth century and the early years of the next?

In reality, the existence of these Arab settlements can be traced back to the Ottomans. The Arabs were one of the largest races to assimilate with the Turks and Kurds, for such major Arab lands as modern-day Syria, Lebanon, Egypt, and Iraq were part of the Ottoman empire.[52] The empire definitely needed their expertise, and the fact that it valued the Arab society in their midst can be seen in the words of Yahya Armajani: "The Turks honored the religion of the Arabs, the language of the Arabs, and the laws which the Arab had established."[53] This recognition and appreciation was proven when the Ottoman sultan of that time gave the *'ulamā'* from the *sayyid* group a special and important position among the aristocratic class and made them his primary reference when it came to resolving the empire's problems.[54]

Sometimes, these Arabs were appointed Shaykh al-Islām, a position established by Selim I (1512-1520) and Süleyman the Magnificent (1520-1566), and which reached its peak of glory under Abul Su'ud (1545-1574), who successfully transformed his era's constitutional law according to the Sharī'ah.[55] History recorded that appointing a member of the *'ulamā'* class to this post gave the latter vast influence and authority.[56] For example, even the sultans had to obey this official's *fatwās*. In Sharī'ah-related matters, the Shaykh al-Islām had veto power and was sometimes able to impose his will over that of the sultan.

If the *'ulamā'* say *olur* (can) or *olmaz* (cannot), the sultan must comply. As for enforcing certain issues, the *'ulamā'* depended upon the sultan's power and the Shaykh al-Islām's support. For example, any sultan who wanted to expand his power and conquer new land had to obtain a fatwa from the Shaykh al-Islām beforehand, and if the latter sentenced an officer to death for treason, the sentence was carried out immediately.[57] These events prove the Shaykh al-Islām's immense influence in leading the Ottoman empire of that time. Various documents record the participation of Arabic *'ulamā'* in the governing structures, among them Sayyid Abul Huda al-Sayyadi, Şeyh Dergahı, and İzzet Pasha.[58] According to Albert Hourani, apart from this official post many Arab *'ulamā'* during the eighteenth century were appointed as deputy *muftī* (*naqīb al-ashrāf*), and madrasah teachers to help the *muftīs* sent from Istanbul.[59]

In regard to Arabic's influence and recognition under the Ottomans, the standard of the language was enhanced. Islamic regulations were taught in Arabic at premier schools in Istanbul and at the level found in Cairo and Damascus. Some Turkish scholars even preferred to write in Arabic. Poetry and secular writings were written in Turkish; however, due to great emphasis placed on persevering culture and ethics, all texts dealing with religion and law, as well as history and biography, had to be written in Arabic. Hajji Khalifa (1609-1657), a high Ottoman official, wrote in both languages, but his most famous work, a general history and bibliography dictionary of Arabic writers, *Kashf al-Ẓunūn,* was written in Arabic.[60]

The influence of Arabic society in legal circles was observed during the emergence of pan-Islam movement under Sultan Abdulhamid II (1842-1918). They received credentials and the sultan's total trust to become agents when the siren of pan-Islam was heard all over the Islamic world. This trust was based on the Ottoman government's centuries-long practice of employing Arab *'ulamā'*. A study of their existence is considered crucial, since they eventually became quite famous among both the Ottoman sultans and Sultan Abu Bakar of Johor, who agreed to employ one of them as the *muftī*, one of the highest positions in the administration of religious matters.

The network of Johor-Ottoman Turkey-Ḥaḍramī Arab relations

History has recorded that the Ḥaḍramī Arabs had a tremendous economic and religious impact on the Malay Archipelago. Azra also mentioned that Turkey's influence began as early as the fourteenth century, when it had started rescuing the pilgrimage routes to Makkah[61] and, during the seventeenth century, as Portugal began to assert itself in the region. It reached its peak at the end of the nineteenth century, with the beginning of pan-Islam movement.[62] In Johor, a mutual relationship existed between the two sultanates through the main agent: those

Ḥaḍramī Arabs who held a special place to spread Islamic values and teachings in Johor.

Based on historical data, a number of important factors contributed to the Ottoman empire's control: (1) the economic power inherent in exporting its fundamental product and importing basic necessities (e.g., grain, rice, and sugar[63] and (2) its close relationship with the region's rulers, which was more of a politico-religious connection designed to gain moral strength in order to deal with the threats coming from colonial Christian Europe.[64] This close tie, just one among many, referred to the relationship during the rule of Sultan Alauddin Riayat Syah al-Kahar (d. 1571).[65] In the *Bustan Al-Salatin*, Nur Al-Din Al-Raniri narrated that this sultan sent the fluent Arabic-speaker Hüseyn Efendi to Istanbul as his envoy. In June 1562, after performing hajj and evading a Portuguese attempt to block him, this Acehnese emissary was presented to the sultan and presented his ruler's request for military assistance against the Portuguese. The sultan agreed and helped Aceh build its army to such an extent that it was able to conquer Aru and Johor in 1564. This two-way relationship deepened when Sultan Riayat Shah al-Qahar was awarded the title of *sultan* when he was gifted with a silver *russet nafiri* (trumpet). The Ottoman sultan even granted permission to Aceh's ships to raise the Ottoman flag.[66] This close relationship allowed Aceh to sustain its independence for 300 years.

During the nineteenth century, the Ottoman empire also became involved in stimulating the anti-imperialist struggle throughout the archipelago. For example, Ottoman assistance was sought during Dato' Bahaman's revolt in Pahang and it supported Sultan Taha Safiuddin's Jambi resistance at the end of the nineteenth century.[67] The same can be said in Singapore, when articles called upon the Muslims to resist the British while the European powers were attacking Turkish colonies in the Balkans in 1867.[68]

Pan-Islam and the mission of Sultan Abdulhamid II

Pan-Islam movements during the end of the nineteenth century engendered great change in Johor's political relationships. Under the auspices of Jamāl al-Dīn al-Afghānī, this movement sought to unite all Muslim countries, whether Shīʿī or Sunnī, under one caliph. Its adherents hoped that this would give the Muslims enough strength to drive out the Europeans and undo all that they had done to degrade Islamic civilization.[69]

The change in the Arabs' thought that took place during the middle of the nineteenth century was actually initiated by the colonists themselves. The pan-Islam movement wanted to find the most appropriate solution to the colonial situation, which had been around since the sixteenth century, when western European countries started invading other lands in an effort to realize their ideology of imperialism.[70] Their main purpose in the Malay Archipelago was to obtain the raw materials needed to meet Europe's industrial needs, find new markets for their products, and convert Muslims to Christianity.[71]

The impact of this movement resulted in a pan-Islamic establishment,[72] which saw Jamāl al-Dīn al-Afghānī and Muḥammad ʿAbduh as pioneers of the *kaum muda* (New Generation) movement in Malaya.[73] This movement eventually split into two conflicting sides: *kaum muda* (Young Generation) and *kaum tua* (Old Generation), caused by ideas coming from the Middle East,[74] and later brought about the effort of uniting the *ummah* in the struggle against movements that tried to destroy Islam.[75]

Apart from this, the chaos that engulfed the Ottoman empire during the nineteenth century caused Abdulhamid II to support pan-Islam by spreading the call for the Muslim world to unite under one caliph. In fact, he issued a decreed that stated: "We must strengthen the ties with Muslims of other hemisphere. We must get closer with stronger bonds. This is because there is no hope for the future other than this union."[76] Anthony Reid said: "For the Muslims of South-East Asia, the Ottoman Caliphate in the far Turkey represented a dream, a wish to shelter under one Islamic power during the time of declining Islamic politic. There was an important period which witnessed how that dream brought about real political effect."[77]

There existed a continuation of meaning between these two comments, when Muslim throughout the Islamic regions bonded either politically or religiously, which later happened between the Johor Sultanate and Ottoman Turkey. Initially, Abdulhamid II sought to take a proactive attitude toward the sufferings of Ḥaḍramī Arab Muslims in Indonesia by sending an ambassador to Batavia at the end of the nineteenth century. Turkish diplomats promised the Muslims, especially these Ḥaḍramīs, that they would fight for them to enjoy the same rights and at the same level as those enjoyed by the Europeans. In addition, Turkey would also seek to liberate the Muslims in the Dutch East Indies from Dutch oppression.[78]

The opening of a Turkish consulate in Singapore (1864) and Batavia (1883) brought the Johor Sultanate and Ottoman Turkey closer to each other and established an intellectual connection with Johor.[79] This relationship, which began during the reign of Sultan Abu Bakar (r. 1885-1895) and continued until Sultan Ibrahim's death (1922), was conducted through Syeikh Muhammad al-Sagoff, a well-known Ḥaḍramī entrepreneur who was affiliated with the Turkish consulate in Singapore. This diplomatic relationship was presented as a two-way relationship between the British and the Ottoman empires.

This situation highlighted Sultan Abu Bakar's wise leadership, for it enabled him to provide the best politico-religious protection of that time. Good relations with Queen Victoria, the colonists' "backbone," resulted in his being recognized as sultan through an agreement signed on 13th January 1886.[80] His effort to build a solid relationship with the Ottoman empire was officially recognized when both he and various government officials obtained the Primary Standard of the Government of Turkey. Other elements of this success consisted of forming long-lasting familial ties and an ongoing intellectual connection.

Al-Sagoff, who was instrumental in establishing this Ottoman-Johor bond, was also seen as one of the foremost Ḥaḍramī Arab figures at the international level as well. His credibility was most obvious when he and several Arab leaders, among them Syed Omar b. Ali al-Junied[81] and Syed Mohamed b. Abdul Rahman al-Koff,[82] became business pioneers in Singapore as early as 1824. Although they were seen as entrepreneurs, their profound knowledge of religious matters also qualified them to be ranked among the *'ulamā'* as well.

Being a well-known merchant, he was required to travel in Europe and the Middle East.[83] One of the wealthy Arabs who had a close relationship with Abu Bakar as well as Abdulhamid II, he was eventually appointed consul in Singapore during the 1880s, replacing Syed Muhammad.[84] His efforts to make Abdulhamid II's wish a reality finally bore fruit in 1879, when the two rulers were scheduled to meet in Istanbul. The sealed relationship was narrated in *Hikayat Johor*: "In the end His Majesty finally met with His Most Esteemed Majesty Sultan Abdulhamid Khan in Constantinople. He was most well-received and celebrated as His Honorable Sultan of Turkey was very-well pleased to see a king from the East who was so well-borne in his manner and his conduct of Islamic matters."[85] He also received the title of Honorary Consul-General for Turkey in Singapore and was accepted into the Osmaniyah Order in Turkey by the sultan himself.[86]

The network of relationships was further strengthened when Abu Bakar awarded the "Bintang Kebesaran Dato' Seri Paduka Mahkota Johor" medal to various Turkish dignitaries, among them General Ahmad Ali Basya, Munir Basya, Hakkie Bek, Ahmad Fakhri Bek, Ibrahim Bek, and Md. Said Bek in 1892. On 22 February of the following year, Abdulhamid II (1842-1918) bestowed the "First Degree Award of the Turkish Government" upon Abu Bakar.[87]

When the Turkish government's policy was realized, Abdulhamid II strengthened diplomatic ties through the above-mentioned award as well as through Hatice Hanım and Ruqayyah Hanım, two women of Circassion descent[88] who symbolised the long-lasting relationship between the two nations. Hatice Hanım was married to Abu Bakar, while Ruqayyah Hanım was matched with Engku Abdul Majid, his younger brother. This event was recorded in the *Hikayat Johor* as follows:

> When Her Most Honorable Majesty Sultanah Fatimah passed away, Madam Hatice, the other wife of The Most Honorable Almarhum Sultan Abu Bakar, was privileged as sultanah in a royal ceremony on 3 Ramadhan 1321, corresponding with 28 February 1894, at the Zaharah Palace, under the command of The Most Esteemed Sultan Abu Bakar.[89]

This marriage resulted in no children. Engku Abdul Majid and Ruqayyah, however, were blessed with two children: Ungku Abdul Aziz, who became the fifth Minister of Johor, and Ungku Abdulhamid, Head of Translation Bureau (father of Ungku Abdul Aziz, former vice chancellor of the University of Malaya). After her husband's death, Ruqayyah married Sayid Abdullah al-Attas, a wealthy merchant from Betawi, Jakarta. The marriage was blessed with a son, Syed Ali al-Attas (father of Syed Hussein and Syed Naquib, two eminent local scholars). After the couple divorced, she married Dato' Jaafar. From this union, seven children were born, including Onn (the founder of UMNO and father of the third Prime Minister, Hussein Onn).[90]

This direct friendship was so deeply grounded that the connection between these two sultanates was not limited to political relationships only; rather, it extended to the final paying of respects to Abu Bakar's family at his funeral ceremony. This evidence can be found in Na Tien Pet's poem "Syair Almarhum Baginda Sultan Abu Bakar di Negeri Johor," which narrated how the Ottoman sultan had told his consulate representative to attend his counterpart's funeral service after the latter's death in London on 4 June 1896.[91] His poem stated: "Hence when the deceased was cleansed, shrouded, and prayed for, as in Islamic custom, it was handed over to the doctor's care to be mummified, to be carried back to Johor…"[92]

His successor, Sultan Ibrahim, continued to strengthen this political relationship, and his son Sultan Abu Bakar was awarded the First Rank Insignia by Abdulhamid II.[93] The event was recorded in the *Hikayat Johor II* as:

> On 15th of Muharram 1316 corresponding with 4th of June 1898, the royal kith and kin and governments officials and Chinese merchants and many more assembled at the palace hall under the government ceremonials custom, because His Royal Majesty Most Esteemed Sultan Ibrahim was to be bestowed with a star award from Sultan Abdulhamid Khan the Second, brought by The Honorable Dato' Seri Amar Diraja (Dato' Abdul Rahman bin Andak from Istanbul), along with greetings from Sultan Turkey to The Most Noble Sultan Ibrahim, who commanded that all other star awards from the English and Turkey to be sent back, and thus the relationship between the kings were lengthened.[94]

At the outset of Sultan Ibrahim's reign, reforms in the religious administration were implemented. For example, the *'ulamā'* of the Johor Religious Department were ordered to mention Ibrahim's name in the second sermon of the Friday congregational and Eid prayers along with that of the Ottoman sultan, who was considered the patron of Islam. This honour was one way to acknowledge the latter's role a caliph of the Muslim world. This practice ended when Kemal Atatürk, founder of the Republic of Turkey, abolished the caliphate. The names of Sultan Ibrahim and his descendants, however, are mentioned to this day.

Ottoman Turkey's patronage of this Islamic sultanate was severed during the First World War, when the empire sided with Germany;[95] however, the *'ulamā'* continued on with the remnants of Ottoman intellectual life. Some parts of Ottoman civilization were successfully transferred to Johor. One example is the *Majallah al-Aḥkām al-'Adliyyah,* a Turkish legal code related to social interactions that was used in Johor's courts as an Islamic ordinance system. This religious legacy highlights how the *'ulamā'* from among the Ḥaḍramī Arabs influenced Johor's religious and educational administration institutions as the Ottoman empire was collapsing.

Conclusion

To conclude, the Ottoman-Ḥaḍramī Arab relationship experienced several phases of renewal in regard to the intellectual reformation in Johor. It was initially generated by the *umarā'* and was continued by the *'ulamā'*, one of whom held the office of *muftī.* Although the influence of those members of the *'ulamā'* class who were appointed to government positions were highlighted, the roles played by independent *'ulamā'* cannot be discounted, for the connections between them eventually generated a close bond. Although serving in different capacities, their presence in the government's institutions enabled both groups play a vital role in developing the region's various societies through spreading Islam and Islamic knowledge.

Those members of the *'ulamā'* who served as muftīs were seen to have an important role in the society. For example, Sheikh Abdul Rauf Ali al-Fansuri was the second most important person after Sultanah at a time when matters of government and religion were administered separately. She governed and administered, and he assisted her in his capacity as Qāḍī al-Malik al-ʿĀdil (*muftī*) and the leader of the realm's religious affairs.[96] This is just one indication of the *'ulamā's* important role in the government. In addition, their status as members of the State Council made it possible for the law to be carried out based on Islamic ruling. Throughout the twentieth century, debates on the contributions of Johor's muftis were highlighted, as were those of their contributions that helped shaped an intellectual relationship among the Muslims of Johor and the surrounding lands.

Notes

1. PhD student Nurulwahidah Binti Fauzi, Department of Islamic History & Civilization, Academy of Islamic Studies, University of Malaya. Email: comely_84@yahoo.com
2. Assoc. Prof Dr Ali Mohammad, Department of Islamic History & Civilization, Academy of Islamic Studies, University of Malaya. Email: alimohd@um.edu.my
3. Assoc. Prof Dr Saim Kayadibi, associated with the Faculty of Economics and Management Sciences, Department of Economics, International Islamic University Malaysia, Kuala Lumpur. Email: saim@iium.edu.my and skayadibi@yahoo.com
4. Dwight E. Lee, "The Origin of Pan-Islamism," *The American Historical Review,* 47 (1942): 282.
5. The word *'ulamā'* is also derived from *shaykh, mudarris,* or *ataupun* (honour), like *'umdah al'-ulamā' wa al-mudarrisīn* (those who are foremost among the *'ulamā'* and the just judges). See Mahmoud Yazbak, "Nabulsi Ulama in the Late Ottoman Period, 1864-1914," *International Journal of Middle East Studies,* 29 (1997): 74.
6. John L. Esposito, *Islam in Asia, Religion, Politics, and Society* (New York: Oxford University Press, 1987), 13. See also Joseph A. Kechichian, "The Role of the Ulama in the Politics of an Islamic State: The Case of Saudi Arabia," *International Journal of Middle*

East Studies, 18 (1986): 54.

7. Thomas F.Willer, "Malayan Islamic Response to British Colonial Policy," *Jurnal Sejarah,* 10 (1973): 82.
8. Muhd Qasim Zaman, "The Ulama in Contemporary Islam: Custodians of Change," *British Journal of Middle East Studies,* 31 (2004): 265.
9. See Fred R. von der Mehden, *Two Worlds of Islam Interaction between Southeast Asia and the Middle East* (Gainesville: University Press of Florida, 1993), 10.
10. For further reading see, S.Q. Fatimi, *Islam Comes to Malaysia* (Singapore: Malaysian Sociological Institute, 1963), 15.
11. Robert Day McAmis, *Malay Muslims: the History and Challenge of Resurgent Islam in Southeast Asia* (UK: William B. Eerdmans Publishing Company, 2002), 12.
12. See R.O Windstedt, "A History of Malaya," *JMBRAS* 13 (1935): 29; B.J.O. Schrieke, *Indonesian Sociological Studies* 1 (1955); D.G.E. Hall, *A History of South East Asia* (London: McMillan, 1964), 190-191.
13. Azyumardi Azra, *Jaringan Ulama Timur Tengah dan Kepulauan Nusantara abad ke 17 dan 18* (Jakarta: Prenada Media, 2004), 2-3.
14. Azyumardi Azra, ibid., 6.
15. Syed Muhammad Naquib al-Attas, *Preliminary Statement on a General Theory of the Islamization of the Malay Indonesian Archipelago* (Kuala Lumpur: Dewan Bahasa dan Pustaka, 1969), 25.
16. Ismail Hamid, *Perkembangan Islam di Asia dan Alam Melayu* (Petaling Jaya: Heinemann Educational Books, 1986), 50-51.
17. Dada Meuraxa, *Sejarah: Masuknya Islam ke Bandar Barus Sumatera Utara* (Bandung: Penerbit Sasterawan, 1963), 12-14.
18. Othman Mohd. Yatim, *Epigrafi Islam Terawal Di Nusantara* (Kuala Lumpur: Dewan Bahasa dan Pustaka, 1990), 11.
19. Ibid., 11.
20. Imam Syed Zain Hussien Al-Habsyi, Owner of an Arabic Bookstore in Wadi Hana, Johor Bharu. Interview on May, 8 2008, at 9:00 am.
21. See also the writings of Robert Day McAmis, *Malay Muslims: The History and Challenge of Resurgent Islam in Southeast Asia* (UK:

Wm. B. Eerdmans Publishing Co., 2002), 10.

22. Robert Day McAmis, ibid., 10-11.
23. Azyumardi Azra, ibid., 12.
24. A.H. Johns, "Sufism as a Category in Indonesian Literature and History," *JSEAH*, 2 (1961): 10-23.
25. Azyumardi Azra, ibid., 15.
26. Peter G. "Riddel, Religious Links between Hadramaut and the Malay-Indonesian World, C.1850 to C. 1950," *Hadrami Traders, Scholars and Statesmen in the Indian Ocean, 1750s-1960s*, ed. Ulrike Frietag and William G. Clarence-Smith, (Leiden: E.J. Brill, 1997), 217.
27. Ḥaḍramawt, an area of 60,000 square km, contains approximately 300,000 people: 50,000 live in the coastal regions, while another 100,000 live in the valley. The rest are Bedouins who travel according to the suitability of the land and environment. Ḥaḍramawt has four main points, viz., Mukallā, Shiḥr, Tarīm, and Seiyūn, the last two of which have the oldest educational institutions (*Rubat*) that educated local and foreign students. Thus, many people have claimed that a majority of the *'ulamā'* came from Ḥaḍramawt and have sufficient knowledge and high leadership qualities that enabled them to join the royal classes whenever they went. See W.H. Ingrams, "Hadramaut: Past and Present," *The Geographical Journal* 92 (1938): 291-297. See also Leo Hirsch, "A Journey in Hadramaut," *The Geographical Journal*, 3 (1894): 196-205.
27. R.B. Serjeant, "Materials for South Arabian History: Notes on New MSS from Hadramaut," *Bulletin of the School of Oriental and African Studies* 13 (1950): 283.
28. Tn. Hj. Muzaffar, ibid., 113.
29. Mahyuddin Hj. Yahya, *Sejarah orang Syed di Pahang* (Kuala Lumpur: Dewan Bahasa dan Pustaka, 1984), 4.
30. Natalie Mobini-Kesheh, *The Hadrami Awakening: Community and Identity in the Netherland East Indies, 1900-1942* (New York: Cornell University, 1999), 143. The main daily focus of the Hadrami Arab society, apart from acquiring religious knowledge, was looking after the linage (genealogy) of their forefathers, in order to preserve

their bloodline, which was claimed to have originated from the Ahl al-Bayt of Prophet Muḥammad, (ṣ) the presence of books on genealogy among these people is a common phenomenon. Until today, the most famous individual involved in recording information about the Ahl al-Bayt was Syed Alwi b. Tahir al-Haddad. See more in R.B. Serjeant, ibid., 283-284.

31. Tn. Hj. Muzaffar, ibid., 104-107.
32. Abd Rahman Hj. Abdullah, *Islam dalam sejarah Asia Tenggara Tradisional* (Kuala Lumpur: Pustaka Hj. Abdul Majid, 2006), 5-8.
33. Mahyuddin Hj. Yahya.
34. Natalie Mobini-Kesheh, ibid., 143..
35. Ibid., 21.
36. Ibid.
37. Robert Day McAmis, ibid., 10.
38. He added that there were still groups of Arabs from the Hijaz who appeared around Indonesia-Malaya Peninsula; however, their numbers were not as high as those from Ḥaḍramawt. Huub De Jonge, ibid., 95.
39. Settlements around Batavia, for example, were mostly monopolized by Chinese immigrants until around 1740, when the so-called Chinese Massacre took place. For more information on this event, see Huub De Jonge, ibid., 96.
40. Huub De Jonge, ibid., 99-100.
41. A report in L. De Vries, "Hadramis in the East Indies," *Ingrams,* 147.
42. W.R. Roff, "The Malay-Muslim World of Singapore at the Close of the Nineteenth Century," *The Journal of Asian Studies* 24 (1964): 80.
43. William R. Roff, ibid., 75-76.
44. Ibid.
45. Ibid., 82.
46. See L. De Vries, ibid., 147.
47. A.M Alsagoff, "The Arabs of Singapore," *Genuine Islam* 6 (1941): 74.
48. Saadiah Bt Said, "Penglibatan Keluarga al-Sagoff Dalam Ekonomi Johor 1878-1926," *Jurnal Jauhar* 2 (1983): 6-7.

49. J.A.E. Morley, "The Arabs and the Eastern Trade," *JMBRAS* 22 (1949): 175.
50. *Singapore Free Press Weekly*, dated 11.4.1885, p. 195. Dato Menteri to the Resident of Muar, dated 12.8.1891. Copies of letters from the Minister and Secretary of Johor Government, 1891-1899.
51. Peter G. Riddel (1997), ibid., 221.
52. Albert Hourani, ibid., 226.
53. Yahya Armajani, ibid., 156.
54. Halil İnalcık, *Studies in Eighteenth Century Islamic History*, ed. Thomas Naff and Roger Owen, vol. 4: *Papers on Islamic History*" (Philadelphia: University of Pennsylvania: The Middle East Center, 1977), 38.
55. Joseph Schacht, *An Introduction to Islamic Law* (London: Oxford University Press, 1964), 91-93.
56. Evliya Çelebi described the positions and strata of Ottoman rule as follows: (a) ulama including *mollas* (the highest position for ulama), (b) judge, *naqib* (the Prophet's descendants who lived in the city), (c) mufti and professor (academic); (d) *kapipullari* (army and soldiers, who hold the title *agha* [e.g., *kethuda-yeri, serdar* of the Janissaries); (e) *kapicibasi* (head of the guard); and (f) *muteferika* (the palace elites). See Halil İnalcık, 38. Those ulama who served in the higher ranks of the Ottoman administration graduated from private schools and then had to work for sultan and within the religious administration for the Ottoman Empire. Prof Dr Mehmet Ipşirli, "The Ottoman Ulama," in Prof Kemal Çicek, *The Great Ottoman Turkish Civilization* 3 (Ankara: Yeni Türkiye, 2000): 339.
57. Yahya Armajani, *Middle East: Past and Present* (New Jersey: Prentice Hall, 1986), 153-154.
58. Consultation with Prof Dr Abu Bakar Ceylin and Prof Dr Hamit Kırmızı, on Jan 16 2010, 4:00 pm.
59. Albert Hourani, ibid., 237.
60. Ibid., 239.
61. Azyumardi Azra, ibid., 36. Auni Hj. Abdullah also supported this by saying that the Ottoman Empire was the largest political power from the 15th to the 19th century. Auni Hj. Abdullah, *Tradisi*

Pemerintahan Islam & Kolonialisme dalam Sejarah Alam Melayu (Kuala Lumpur: Darul Fikir, 2005), 5. Ottoman Sultans did not only act as defenders of the borders of Islam, but also as guardian of Makka and Madina (in the Hijza) as well as Jerusalem and Hebron (in Palestine). He therefore held the honorary title of "the Guardian of the Two Holy Cities." They also guarded the main pilgrimage routes. Their main responsibility was to lead the annual pilgrimage, a highly ritualized affair that indirectly stressed Ottoman sovereignty to the whole world. Every year, thousands of pilgrims came to Makka. During the hajj season of 1804, an estimated 70,000 people living in Europe attended. Most of the pilgrims came from Yemen, middle Africa, and Iraq; but many also came from Cairo and Damascus. See Albert Hourani, ibid., 222.

62. H.E. Wilson, "The Islamization of South East Asia," *Journal of Historical Research (Ranchi)* 15 (1972): 1.
63. Şevket Pamuk, "The Ottoman Empire in the 'Greatest Depression' of 1873-1896," *The Journal of Economic History* 44 (1984): 108.
64. Many Turkish nobles declared themselves to be Ottoman instead of Turks. The most significant reason for doing so was based on religion instead of ethnic or family background. Until the 19th century, the Ottoman elites were no longer seen as that part of Ottoman society that spoke pure Turkish, for their speech had become mixed with Arabic and Persian. See Nikki R. Keddie, "Pan Islam as Proto-Nationalism," *The Journal of Modern History* 41 (1969): 17. Historical records show that the Ottoman Empire had good and close relationships with various Islamic nations (e.g., those located in the Caucasus, Asia Tengah, and the Malay Archipelago) from the 18th century until early 20th century, among them the Acheh and Johor sultanates. For more information, see Judith Nagata, ibid., p.18.
65. Auni, ibid., 6.
66. HaciWan Muhd Saghir Abdullah (ed), *Hadiqatul Azhar Wal Rayahin* (Kuala Lumpur: Khazanah Fataniah, 1998), 144-145.
67. Auni Hj Abdullah, ibid., 93.
68. Ibid., 94.

69. Peter G. Riddell, *Islam and the Malay-Indonesian World: Transmission and Responses* (London: Hurst & Company, 2001), 85. Further readings in Fadhlullah Jamil, *Islam di Asia Barat modern: Penjajahan dan Pergolakan* (Kuala Lumpur: Karisma Publication, 2007), 13-14.
70. According to a number of historians, such as Mauritus Julius Bonn, imperialism is a relationship based on political power in order to form and build a relationship and thereby manage and protect an empire. In the beginning, imperialism was observed in the old empires of Syria, Egypt, Persia, and Rome. It reached its peak at the end of 15th century, led by the British colonialists, who not only brought policies regarding the accession of a region or district, but also as regards various economic aspects and military dominance. See *The Encyclopaedia Americana* 15 (1964): 725.
71. Fadhlullah Jamil, ibid., 13-14.
72. Orientalists have agreed that the main objective of the establishment of the movement was as the "realization of the ideal Islamic ideal, the unity of the world in Islam, the central direction under a leader, Imām, of the world community, and the basic concept from which thought and action sprang was religious rather than racial or national". A quote from Becker, "Panislamismus," *Islamstudien,* 1924-1932.
73. Wiiliam R. Roff, "Kaum Muda-Kaum Tua: Innovation and Reaction amongst the Malays, 1900-1941," K.G. Tregonning, ed., *Papers on Malayan History* (Singapore: University of Singapore, 1962), 162-192.
74. Judith Nagata, "Islamic Revival and the Legitimacy among Rural Religious Elites in Malaysia," *Man: The Journal of the Royal Anthropological Institute* (N.S.), 17, 1 (1982): 44.
75. Mohamad Kamil Ab. Majid, "Gerakan Tajdid: Sejarah Dan Perspektif Masa Kini," *Jurnal Usuluddin,* 4 (1996), 98.
76. Snouck Hurgronje, ibid., 1631.
77. Anthony Reid, "Nineteenth Century Pan-Islamism in Indonesia and Malaysia," *Journal of Southeast Asian Studies* 2 (1967): 274-278.
78. Ibid., 1631.
79. Auni, ibid., 94.
80. Syaharom Husain (ed), *Tawarikh Johor* (Singapore: Al-Hamadiah Press, 1950), 145.

81. A wealthy Arab merchant in Singapore during his time, around 1824 he already owned several plots of land in High Street and a piece of land on the island's North Bridge Road. Later, he bought properties on Victoria Street and Arab Street, as well as the Islamic cemetery on Victoria Street. During the time of his son, he bought land on the Victoria Street and Arab Street, upon which is located the Hospital Tan Tock Seng. See C.B. Buckley, *An Anecdotal History of Old Times in Singapore 1819-1967* (Singapore: University of Malaya Press, 1969), 564.
82. Well-known among Arab families for his business between Singapore and Java, he also owned the familiy's trade ships and fire ships. C.B. Buckley, ibid., 564.
83. C.B Buckley, ibid., 565.
84. Anthony Reid, ibid., 271-272.
85. Mohd Said b. Hj. Sulaiman, *Hikayat Johor* (Johor: Johor Government Publishing Office, 1930), 58.
86. Syed Mohsen al-Sagoff, *The al-Sagoff Family in Malaysia* (Singapore: Mun Seong Press, 1962), 11.
87. Mohd Yusof Md. Nor, "Syair Sultan Abu Bakar Dokumentasi Sejarah Negeri Johor," in Obe Seminar Sejarah Dan Budaya Johor, *Yayasan Warisan Johor & Gabungan Persatuan Penulis Nasional Malaysia (GAPENA),* 3-6 May 2000, 10-11.
88. These important and powerful harem women were also known as *Harem i-humayun*. The place was called *harem* because it was a forbidden place to everyone but the appropriate male members of the women's families. Favoured by the mother and wife of the sultan (the *kadin efendis*), they supervised the concubines, most of whom were from the Caucasus. For centuries, the harem women received special treatment because of their beauty, high skills and minds, all of which won them high respect and good reputations. These educated women supervised others, educated new women, received salaries, and could leave after nine years of service to the palace. Some of them married high-class officers and were given by the sultan to kings and governors. Two of the Turkish women given to Sultan Abu Bakar and Engku Abdul Majid b. Temenggung were Circassion women from the

Caucasus and were the most beautiful, educated, and respected among their peers. Refer to Fanny Davis, *The Ottoman Lady: A Social History from 1718 to 1918* (America: Greenwood Press, 1986), 1-5.

89. Mohd Said b. Hj. Sulaiman, *Hikayat Johor* (Johor: Johor Government Publishing Office, 1930), 58.
90. Mohammad Redzuan Othman, *Islam dan Masyarakat Melayu Peranan dan Pengaruh Timur Tengah* (Kuala Lumpur: Penerbit Universiti Malaya, 2005), 90-91.
91. Na Tien Pet (ed) and Noriah Mohamed, *Syair Almarhum Baginda Sultan Abu Bakar di Negeri Johor* (Johor: Yayasn Warisan Johor, 2001), 197-205.
92. Mohd Said b. Hj. Sulaiman, ibid.
93. Selamat Johor Tanda Kenangan Pengingat Kesyukuran Ulang tahun Yang Keempat Puluh Bagi Ke Bawah Duli Yang Maha Mulia Sultan Ibrahim Bertakhta Kerajaan Johor.
94. Muhd Said b. Hj. Sulaiman, *Hikayat Johor II* (Johor: Peninsular Tax And Management Services, 1950), 61.
95. Hj Shaharom Hussain, "Hubungan Johor Dengan Turki," *Jurnal Jauhar* 4 (2002): 55.
96. Hasan Muarif Ambary, "Kedudukan dan Peran Tokoh Sejarah Syeikh Abdulrauf Singkel in Birokrasi dan Keagamaan Kesultanan Acheh," *Makalah Seminar Festival Baiturrahman II*, Banda Acheh, 16 January, 1994, 8.

2

Baba Davud: A Turkish scholar in Aceh

Mehmet Özay[1]

Abstract

This paper introduces Shaikh Davud b. Ismail b. Mustafa Rumi (a.k.a Baba Davud or Mustafa ar-Rumi), an Islamic scholar believed to have lived in Banda Aceh sometime between 1650 and 1750, to the larger Muslim world. This person is important for three reasons: (1) Baba Davud, who lived at the time of the Aceh Darussalam Sultanate (16th-17th Century), became a leading student and a religious caliph of Abdurrauf as-Singkilī (a.k.a. Teungku Syiah Kuala), a well-known Acehnese religious scholar; (2) his *Risalah Masailal Muhtadi li Ikhwanil Muhtadi* has been taught at Islamic institutions in Aceh and around the Malay world; and (3) no scholarly works have been written about him, despite the striking fact that he and Syiah Kuala co-founded the Dayah Manyang Leupue institution, to which he subsequently became affiliated.

In order to analyze him as an Islamic scholar, I provide information on the development of the Islamic sciences and the existence of Islamic scholars among within Aceh's various sultanates. For this reason, the early period of Islam and the region's subsequent Islamization until the seventeenth century are considered significant. In this context, it is vital to emphasize the

Islamic scientific circles in the sultanate during the seventeenth century.

Introduction

This text discusses the life of the Turkish scholar known as Baba Davud or Mustafa ar-Rumi, whose grave is located in the provincial capital city of Banda Aceh. It also attempts to answer several questions, among them "Who is the scholar known as Baba Davud or Mustafa ar-Rumi?", "How did he come to these lands?", and "How did he obtain his education?" As was common in other pre-modern Southeast Asian societies, written culture was not a common practice in Aceh. Thus, even though Aceh has produced many scholars, today only very few of them are known in any detail.[2]

Some issues need to be clarified briefly before this scholar's life and intellectual identity are discussed: the region in which he lived and the regional scholars' role in the local society and the sultans' court. These background topics are discussed below. The development of Muslim educational institutions and the status of foreign and domestic scholars in Aceh are also analyzed, with an emphasis on the relationship between scholars and rulers during Baba Davud's presumed lifetime. Existing documents on his life and scholarly personality, as well as his works and information about his alleged offspring, are also put forward. Unfortunately, the lack of authentic primary sources and detailed information about existing sources is a serious obstacle. In addition, Ottoman-Aceh relations are also discussed due to Baba Davud's Turkish origin. Given that this is first article written about Baba Davud, it is hoped that this work may encourage further studies about him.

Aceh: Doorway to Makkah

The fact that Islam spread to Southeast Asia from Aceh means that Aceh has more than just a geographical importance. Many scholars who travelled throughout the region to spread Islam were educated in its Islamic educational institutions, which explains why it has been known as "Doorway to Makkah" for centuries.[3] This reflects the sultanate's importance in the subsequent Islamization of the region.[4]

Scholars have posited two theories about when Islam arrived in Aceh. Based on Marco Polo's notes during his compulsory stop in Sumatra on the way back to Europe, western orientalists, especially Snouck Hurgronje, think that Islam reached Southeast Asia in the thirteenth century. According to local historians, however, Islam arrived as far back as the first Islamic century.[5] As for how and through whom Islam reached the region, they ascribed this to Muslim merchants' long-standing middle-man role in the Middle East-China trade and, later on, to the emergence of Sūfī movements in the Muslim world.[6]

Muslims came to the Malay Archipelago from the Middle East (Ḥaḍramawt, Oman, Iraq, and Iran); Baluchistan and Sind (Indo-Pak border regions); and Cambay, Gujarat, Coromandel, Malabar, Sri Lanka, and Bengal (Indian coastal regions). The first wave of Arab and Iranian Muslim merchants continued these travels during the eighth-twelfth centuries, and the second wave of Islamization occurred between the thirteenth and eighteenth centuries.[7] Muslims first settled on Sumatra's northern shore, the region known today as Aceh. Over time, the first Islamic sultanate arose from this Islamic community.[8]

The role of scholars in the Aceh Sultanate

As Islam spread throughout Southeast Asia through Aceh's city states, the role of foreign-born Islamic scholars became note-worthy. Scholars and Islamic educational institutions played an important role in the life of Aceh's first sultanate.[9] Accepting the sultans' personal invitations to come to his domain, these scholars settled in Aceh and began laying the groundwork for the educational institutions that would shape the region's cultivation of knowledge.

During the various phases of Islamization, especially between 1550-1650, scholars coming from Egypt, Syria, Arabia, India, and Iran made vital contributions.[10] Local scholars trained in Aceh also played an important role. The sixteenth and seventeenth centuries featured Aceh's most important and best known scholars, namely Hamzah Fansurî, Shamsuddin Sumatranî, Nuruddin ar-Raniri, and Abdurrauf as-Singkilī. Thus this period is considered the region's pinnacle of achievement as regards the understanding of Islam and the production of works in the Islamic sciences. Many other domestic and foreign scholars also spread Islam while travelling in Aceh and different regions of Southeast Asia.[11]

Shaikh Abul Khair b. Shaikh Hajar, Shaikh Moḥammad Yamanī, Shaikh Muhammad Jailani b. Hassan b. Muhammad Hamid ar-Raniri, and other Islamic scholars led Acehnese society in education, social, and political issues.[12] The rulers entrusted these above-name scholars with managerial duties in the palace and allowed them to help train the next generation of rulers. For example, the scholars named above contributed to the education of Iskandar Muda, whose reign (1607 1636) is considered the most glorious period in the Aceh Darussalam Sultanate.[13] Shamsuddin Sumatranî, who dispensed religious guidance to the palace and served as the Shaikh'ul Islam, also participated in politics: he was appointed to meet and conduct negotiations with James Lancaster, a special envoy of Queen Elizabeth I, during the latter's official visit to Aceh in 1602.[14]

To understand the scholars' position in Aceh, it is useful to look at their situation in the region's other important states, such as Perlak, Samudra-Pasai, and the Aceh Darussalam Sultanate. The ruler of Perlak, founded by Mevlana Sayyid Sultan Abdulaziz Shah

(r. 840-846) and usually considered Aceh's first sultanate, invited scholars from Arabia, Iran, and Gujarat to take up residence in his realm. Due to the Islamic educational institutions that they subsequently set up, Perlak was able to play an important role in developing the Islamic sciences. Teungku Muhammad Amin founded Dayah Cotkala, an educational centre resembling a modern university, and implemented therein a multi-functional training program consisting of Islamic knowledge, history, geography, finance, agriculture, astronomy, and other courses. With the rulers' consent and support, graduates were sent to Makkah, Madīnah, Baghdad, and Cairo to specialize in their chosen fields.[15]

A similar occurrence can be seen Samudra-Pasai, one of the region's mpost important sultanates and one that had a strong interest in scholarship and scholars. During the second half of the twelfth century, while Sultan al-Kamil sat on the throne, Mevlana Naina b. Naina al-Malabari and many other scholars came to Samudra. He gave them various positions at the palace and encouraged them to spread their knowledge of Islam wherever they could. He appointed al-Malabari commander of the army and gave Abdurrahman al-Pasi an executive position in the palace.[16]

Scholars advised the rulers on both religious and political matters. For example, Malik az-Zahir, the son of Malik us-Saleh, invited scholars from Makkah, Iran, and India to hold a major scientific debate;[17] he also contributed to the spread of Islamic educational centres throughout the Malay Archipelago.[18] Scholars also had a role in establishing the Aceh Darussalam sultanate. A group of soldiers led by Shaikh Abdullah Kan'an came to Indra Purpa, located near present-day Banda Aceh, and ultimately acted as the catalyst for the region's Islamization and the appearance of the sultanate led by Meurah Johan Shah (1205-1234).[19] These extraordinary examples show the importance accorded to Islamic scholars and Islamic educational institutions by the rulers of Aceh's various sultanates.

A brief overview of the Aceh Darussalam Sultanate

The Perlak sultanate, which arose in the ninth century, was followed by the Beunua, Samudra-Pasai, Pedier (Pidie), Daya, Lingga, Lamuri, and other important sultanates.[20] Perlak survived into the sixteenth century. After the Portuguese captured Malacca in 1511, Ali Mughayat Syah combined the Lamuri and Dar'ul Kamal sultanates to form the Aceh Darussalam sultanate. He subsequently established a federation by uniting the region's various city states.[21]

In a short time, Shah implemented his plan to unify the region so that it could better defend itself against the Portuguese threat: "Ali Mughayat Syah (1514-1530) maintained an alliance against the Portuguese by consultation with many leaders from Aceh as well as with scholars. Pasai, Pedir, Aru and Daya sultanate took place within this alliance."[22] While expanding his territory further in the fight against the Portuguese, he transformed the Aceh Darussalam sultanate into the region's most important Islamic state.[23] Hence, it was one of the leading five major Islamic states during the sixteenth century.[24] It officially ended in only 1903 after the Dutch captured its last ruler: Muhammad Davud (1874-1903).

With the early sixteenth-century arrival of European colonialism in Southeast Asia, led by the Portuguese, the existing small sultanates united in a religious, political, and economic struggle to defend themselves against this invasion.

Relations with the Turks

The roots of the Turkish-Acehnese relationship go back several centuries. Based upon the historical account known so far, it began by making "close relations with the Turks" one of the five basic tenants of the sultanate's foreign policy. This policy, which was initiated by Alaaddin Mughayat Shah, the founder of Aceh

Darussalam sultanate,[25] endured for centuries. The Ottoman empire was actively engaged in the region's anti-Portuguese struggle right from the outset, a period that coincided with the sultanate's early years. As a sign of this sultanate's strong Islamic faith, the caliphate of the Ottoman empire, the most powerful Islamic state of the time, was accepted in the sixteenth century; establishing relations against the Portuguese was thus a natural development.[26]

Subsequent sultans abided by Shah's foreign policy undertakings as a reference and implemented similar policies. Although the Ottoman empire always regarded the requests of the sultanate's ambassadors positively, it appears that the desired help was not always forthcoming. In this context, the first serious Ottoman-Aceh Darussalam relationship began during the reign of Alauddin Riayat Syah al-Kahar (1537-1571). Al-Kahar signed military and trade agreements with Süleyman the Magnificent through the Ottoman governor of Egypt. It is recorded that in exchange for future Ottoman support, the Aceh Darussalam sultanate granted its merchants privileges in Pasai, an extremely important trading centre.[27]

The two parties also formed a political tie: the sultanate adopted the Ottoman flag as its own,[28] although its moon and star were replaced by a sword. Moreover, it appears that relations were established through the individual efforts of scholars and Turkish merchants. When all of these factors are taken into consideration, it is possible to say that the initial military relationship between the Ottomans and the Acehnese eventually expanded into the political, cultural, scientific, and religious realms. Ottoman military experts and craftsmen sent to Aceh were accommodated and subsequently settled down in Bayt al-Maqdis, located somewhere near the palace. A military academy, Bitai, was also established there and staffed, to an unknown degree, by Ottoman experts .[29]

The presence of Turkish scholars in Aceh, along with their Arab and Iranian counterparts, also indicated the existence of close ties.[30] In addition to Europe's colonial presence during the sixteenth and seventeenth centuries, this relationship and arrival of Ottoman and Mongol (Mughal) scholars played an important role in the region's conversion to Islam.[31] For instance, al-Firus al-Baghdadi, the founder of Dayah Tanoh Abee; Teungku Di Bitai, known as the Saint of Bitai;[32] and Haji Ahmet Kasturi[33] are scholars whose names are still well-known today. Baba Davud's family came from the Ottoman empire's domain and settled in Aceh.

The Sultanate's socio-political structure

Acquiring an accurate insight into Baba Davud's environment and status requires us to look at Aceh's socio-political events and developments. During the first half of the seventeenth century, the sultanate enjoyed a very advanced commercial and religious intellectual life.[34] When Sultan Iskandar Muda came to power in 1607, he inherited a strong frontier Islamic state. By combining this structure with his charismatic personality and solid statesmanship, he further enhanced it in terms of social and political strengths. Consequently his reign, in terms of military conquest and cultural development, is regarded as the sultanate's most glorious period and this holds an important place in Aceh's history.[35] Muda, who had a solid belief in Islam, made important progress in terms of the sultanate's political, military, religious, and cultural developments. One of his major accomplishments was to unify the region through military conquests so that the region could present a united front designed to protect themselves against the attempts of Portugal and other colonial powers to establish themselves in the Straits of Malacca.

He also pursued a very active foreign policy, part of which consisted of signing trade agreements with the Dutch and the

British in order to set the terms by which economic and commercial activities would be conducted. In addition, Muda never established his own hegemony in the region. During this period, it was possible to count the Portuguese, Dutch, British, Indians, Arabs, and Iranians among the foreigners who were conducting direct or indirect commercial activities in the region.[36]

> Iskandar Muda was a statesman with great ideals. Muda knew how important the Malacca Straits was as a sea route was in the international trade, especially for the Southeast Asian trade. He developed relations with Keling (India), Iran, Arabia, Ottoman and Western Europe. At the same time relationships were established with countries such as Thailand (Siam) and China (Tionghoa). With these actions Muda wanted to control the Malacca Straits and the Malay Peninsula.[37]

Muda, who did his best to establish Aceh as an Islamic stronghold, designated the rulers as the protectors of culture and tradition; scholars were designated as practitioners of Islamic provisions in the administrative mechanism. They latter were well represented in his court after he ascended the throne.[38] Given this reality, the author of *Bustan'us Salatin* refers to him as the greatest of all the Acehnese sultans who stressed the importance of Islamic education. Seeking to cultivate Islamic education among his subjects and his regional administration units, he built a mosque and, at the same time, initiated the creation of a significant madrasah in the Baiturrahman Mosque (*Bayt al-Rahim* madrasah) complex.[39] This is detailed in the following section.

Muda placed great importance on Islamic scholars and spreading Islamic educational institutions. He appointed Shamsuddin Sumatranî and Shaikh Abdullah as-Shams, the leading scholars of his time, to important posts in the palace. Shamsuddin Sumatranî became the Shaykh al-Islam and advised Muda on political issues.[40] After his death in 1630, Shaikh Abdullah as-Shams took on an important role in the palace as an advisor. It was normal for Aceh's scholars to advise the sultan on matters connected with religion and politics.

In the context of Islamic education, Muda's order to establish a madrasah in the Baiturrahman Mosque complex is one of the best examples. Such institutions divided their courses into eighteen departments, including the positive, social, and religious sciences.[41] This particular academic institution could also be considered a university in the modern sense, as it featured departments of medicine, chemistry, mathematics, logic, law, philosophy, theology, exegesis, Ḥadith, history, literature, public administration, mining, agriculture, and others. In addition, it had its own military academy.[42]

During this period, forty-four Acehnese and foreign scientists lectured at the University of Baiturrahman and similar among them were Shaikh Muhammad Azhari (metaphysics), Abu al-Kahar b. Shaikh b. Hajar (Islamic law), Shaikh Yamani (theology), and Muhammad Jailani b. Hasan b. Hamid (logic and the methodology of canon law).[43] The importance given to knowledge and scholars continued under Muda's successors. For example his stepson and successor Iskandar Tsani (1636-1641) emphasized the Islamic sciences and the continuance of cultural life. Nuruddin b. Ali Hasanji b. Muhammad Hamid ar Raniri, who came to Aceh during his reign, was one of his advisors. At Iskandar Tsani's request, he wrote *Bustan'us Salatin* (The Garden of Kings),[44] which remains the core work on Aceh's history.

After Iskandar Tsani's death, Aceh was ruled by female sultans for about sixty years (1641-1699). During these years Shaikh Abdurrauf as-Singkilī played an important role, for the first female sultan, Iskandar Tsani's widow Safiyatuddin, and those who followed her received his complete support. This man, who moved the Shattariyya order to Indonesia,[45] worked in the palace as the *waliyul mulki* (deputy sultan) and continued to produce scientific works. Among his works were the first Malay interpretation of the Qur'an[46] (according to Bayzavî's commentary) and *Mir'at at-Tullab fi Tashil Ma'rifat Ahkam As Syariah lil malik al wahab*[47] (a book on canon law), both of which are ranked among the most important. As-Singkilî also wrote on theology, canon law (*fiqh*), Ḥadīth, and Sufism.[48]

Baba Davud

Given the explanations above, we can assume that Baba Davud was born and raised some time after 1650. His full name was Davud b. Agha Ismail b. Agha Mustafa al-Javi ar-Rumi.[49] Baba Davud, whose ancestors came to Aceh, was also known as Mustafa ar-Rumi.[50] The name tag al-Javi indicates the possibility of his mother's Malay origin or his birth in Indonesia.[51] There is no definite information about his birth and death dates. However, if it is considered that his teacher Abdurrauf as-Singkilī lived between 1615-1693 and came back to Aceh in 1661 after receiving his education in Arabia, we can assume that he lived some time between 1650-1750.

To date, authentic information about his identity has been found in two main works. The first is that found in the introduction of *Baydawi Tafsīr,* which was translated by as-Singkilî and contributed to by Baba Davud. This source mentions that Baba Davud was a student of as-Singkilî and had the following lineage: Baba Davud b. Ismail; Ismail b. Agha Mustafa; Agha Mustafa b. Agha Ali ar-Rumi.[52] The second work, *Manzarul Ajla Martabatil A'la,* was written by Shaikh Faqih Jalaladdin b. Kamaluddin al-Asyi, one of Baba Davud's students. It refers to Baba Davud as a student of Abdurrauf al-Fansurî.[53]

There are several different opinions of how Baba Davud reached Aceh. According to Azyumardi Azra, he was one of the many soldiers deployed by the Ottomans to help the Aceh sultanate defend itself against the Portuguese.[54] But Abdullah Shagir, a contemporary Malay scholar, criticizes this view and opines that Ismail ar-Rumi (d. 1631/1643), shaikh of the Qādirī order who was sent from Turkey to Aceh during this period, is likely the father of Baba Davud ar-Rumi.[55]

Syaikh Davud b. Ismail b. Mustafa ar-Rumi was also known as Tunku Chik di Leupue (Shaikh of Di Leupu) because of his administrative service in the Dayah, which he founded in collaboration with his teacher Syiah Kuala in Banda Aceh's region called *Di Leupe*. It is reputed that Shaikh Abdurrauf wanted him to manage the Dayah Leupeu.[56]

A copy of the Qur'an, written with a special calligraphy by Shaikh Abdurrauf, was given to Baba Davud. Upon the latter's death, it was transferred to Haji Yahya, the leader of Dayah Leupue and, apparently, transferred from generation to generation among his descendents. Until recently it was in the hands of Teungku Abdulaziz Ujung in Penauyong. Ali Hasjmy noted that he once saw it.[57] It is believed that Syiah Kuala's grandson Mahmud has a photocopy of this Qur'an. Baba Davud is considered as one of Syiah Kuala's leading students because of his role both in establishing the Dayah and completion of translation works.[58]

Due to his Anatolian origin, Baba Davud was also called "Rumi," as this was the usual way for Arabs and Persians to refer to the Byzantine empire.[59] After the Seljuk Turks conquered and established Turkish sovereignty in Anatolia, this name was transferred to them.[60] When Sultan Mehmed the Conqueror captured Istanbul, it was used for the Ottoman Turks as well and continued to be a common designation for their empire even after it became a major world power during the mid-fifteenth century. Therefore, any Muslims coming to Southeast Asia from this land were called "Rum." Azra has remarked:

> In Indonesia and the Malay world there is a special narrative about Rum Sultanate that transferred from generation to generation. In the past, not only Turks, but also Arabs and Iranians played important roles in trade and Islamic education. Though there is no definite evidence about this issue, Turks too, contributed to Islamization of this region at the beginning.[61]

Emperoum, a village located in the centre of Banda Aceh, supports this argument because this name apparently stems from its first inhabitants: a group of Ottoman subjects. *Empe* is an honorific phrase, whereas *Rum* is used for people coming from Anatolia. In this context, *emperoum* was applied to the people who lived in this village as an expression of respect; eventually, it became the village's name.[62]

The Ottoman empire's political and cultural power impacted the whole Muslim world, along with the Islamic sultanate in the Malay Archipelago. Within this framework, the Muslims of the Malay world used to call the Ottoman sultan the "King of Rum" (Raja Rum) in the fifteenth century because of the conquest of Istanbul.[63]

His works and scholarly personality

Baba Davud was one of the important students and successors of as-Singkilî, who is widely regarded as Aceh's greatest scholar. The significance of the former's scholarly personality can be seen in his creation of the Dayah Manyang Leupue, an Islamic education centre, in conjunction with al-Singkilî.[64] Baba Davud helped complete his teacher's *Turjumanul al-Mustafid*, considered the first Malay-language translation and commentary of the Qur'an. This work, which has made important contributions to the development of Islamic knowledge in the Malay world, was first published in Istanbul.[65] The original copy was given to one of Baba Davud's grandchildren in Patani (southern Thailand) and then passed on to Shaikh Ahmed b. Muhammad Zain al-Patani, who published the first edition of this study.

Although his descendents who still live in Patani and Kelantan say that Baba Davud wrote several books, no concrete information about them has ever been discovered. His manuscript work was copied by Shaikh Davud b. Ismail al-Patani from his lineage (a.k.a. Tok Davud Katib), after which his cousin Shaikh Ahmed al-Patani took over. This work was subsequently rewritten by Shaikh Ahmed b. Muhammad Zain al-Patani, Shaikh Davud b. Ismail el-Patani, and Shaikh Idris b. Hussein Kelantanam, all of whom made corrections to the original work.[66] The first copy of this study was published in Istanbul, Makkah, and Cairo.

In addition to contributing to as-Singkilî's works, Baba Davud wrote *Risalah Masailal Muhtadi li Ikhwanil Muhtadi* (The Guide for Right Path for the New Starting Brothers),[67] which was taught for nearly three hundred years as the basic text at religious schools in Aceh and other parts of the Malay world. Written in Javî in the form of a question-answer dialogue, the best method of that time, it imparted elementary religious knowledge to those first year students who did not know Arabic. Interestingly it is still being used today, with no change in its content, to teach issues related to faith, worship, and other subjects.[68] It was taught during the first stage of Islamic education in Aceh, Malaysia, Indonesia, Singapore, and southern Thailand, where Malay is spoken.[69] Considered an important work, it has contributed to the religious education of hundreds of thousands of Indonesian students and is still being used in Aceh's religious schools.[70]

Many famous scholars studied under Baba Davud, among them Nayan al-Baghdadi, son of al-Firus al-Baghdadi (the founder of Dayah Tanoh Abee), and Muhammad Zain.[71] Al-Baghdadi continued his education at the Dayah Leupue di Penaoyung under the supervision of Shaikh Davud b. Ismail b.

Mustafa ar-Rumi (a.k.a. Tunku Chik di Leupue), a leading scholar of the period. When al-Baghdadi earned his certificate, Baba Davud encouraged him to open an Islamic educational centre in Seulimum, 40 kms outside Banda Aceh.[72] Thus, Baba Davud is credited with being the force behind opening Islamic educational institutions there. Shaikh Fakih Celaleddin, a scholar from Aceh, also studied under Baba Davud.[73]

Baba Davud's tomb and offspring

I acquired the first information about Baba Davud while conducting fieldwork in Aceh during September-December 2005. His tomb is located in a small cemetery near Penaoyung, in front of the Di Leupue mosque. After the widespread damage caused by the 2006 tsunami, local residents surrounded his tomb with pieces of wood and wire and marked it with a note: "Makam Ulama Atjeh Anak Murid Tg. Syiah Kuala." During my 2005 visit, intense construction activity was being done by foreign NGOs and a carpenter's workshop had been set up next to the cemetery. Thanks to the local residents, who had not forgotten the past, the location of Baba Davud's tomb was identified.

Today, there are no living descendants of Baba Davud in Aceh. In southern Thailand, however, a famous scholar named Shaikh Davud b. Ismail el-Cavi el-Patani, who lived in Patani, has been put forward as one of his grandsons. Another descendant, Haji Nik Wan Fatma (Kak Mah) bint Haci Wan Abdulkadir Kelantan b. Shaikh Davud b. Ismail el-Patani, died on 26 July 1999 in Kota Baru.[74]

Conclusion

For a long time scholars have tried to determine why Islam became so popular in the Malay Archipelago, and the region's inhabitants have expressed interest in their research. What kind of phases did Islamization pass though until it became firmly established? My research indicates that the indigenous people's adoption of Islam occurred over a long period of time, beginning with the eighth century and continuing to our own time. Islam was introduced by merchants and Sūfis who moved and sometimes settled among the people. The efforts of indigenous scholars also helped this transformation. The development of Islam as a result of individual communication demonstrates its slow but steady penetration.

Aceh, the "Doorway to Makkah," played the primary role in this process. During the first period of Islamic history, its rulers invited scholars from various Muslim lands, especially the Middle East and India. Out of this policy emerged indigenous religious training centres and scholars. Scholars played important roles in the palace, educational institutions, and society. With the start of Islamic missionary (*da'wah*) activities, Islamic educational institutions increased in the region as indigenous scholars produced works on various topics. Thus, this corner of Muslim world created its own civilization and established Islam on a solid foundation.

Scholars who came to Aceh, either on their own or invited by the rulers, planted the roots of their Islamic teaching deeply by establishing Islamic educational institutions. Although many scholars either came to Aceh or were born and raised there, very few of them are known to us today. Baba Davud, who had a Turkish ancestor, shares a similar fate. After all, the only reason he is mentioned at all in various books is because he was a student of Syiah Kuala. Based on these data and the role of scholars in Aceh, this article provides some general information about Baba Davud. Due to the lack of well-organized works on him, more comprehensive and deeper studies on this scholar and his works need to be undertaken.

Notes

1. Dr Mehmet Özay, Senior Lecturer, Faculty of Islamic Civilization and Thought, University Technology Malaysia.
2. A.H. Johns, "Islam in Southeast Asia: Problems of Perspective," C.D. Cowan and O.W. Wolters (ed.), *Southeast Asian History and Historiography:-Essays Presented to D.G.E. Hall* (New York: Cornell University Press, 1976), p. 312; Snouck Hurgronje, *The Acehnese*, tr. A.W.S. O'Sullivan, vol. 1 (Leiden: E.J. Brill, 1906), p. 18; (See: Martin van Bruneissen, "A Note on Source Materials for the Biographies of Southeast Asian 'Ulama.")
3. Snouck Hurgronje, *The Acehnese*, vol. II, p. 19; Anthony Reid, "Indonesian Diplomacy: A Documentary Study of Atjehnese Foreign Policy in the Reign of Sultan Mahmud: 1870-1874," *JMBRAS*, vol. XLII, Part 2, December, 1969, p. 74.
4. Syed Muhammad Naquib al-Attas, *A General Theory of the Islamization of the Malay-Indonesian Archipelago* (Dewan Bahasa dan Pustaka, 1969), p. 7.
5. Henry Yule and Henri Cordier, *The Book of Ser Marco Polo, The Venetian: Concerning The Kingdoms and Marvels of the East*, vol. 2, 3rd ed. (New Delhi: Munshiram Manoharlal, 1920), p. 284; M.B. Hooker (ed.) *Islam in South-East Asia*, 2nd ed. (Leiden: E.J. Brill, 1988), p. 3; W.P. Groeneveldt, *Historical Notes on Indonesia & Malaya—Compiled from Chinese Sources* (Jakarta: C.V. Bhratara, 1960), p. 92; William Marsden, *The History of Sumatra* (Kuala Lumpur: Oxford University Press, 1966), p. 5 (Reprint of the 3rd ed.)
6. Lynda Norene Shaffer, *Maritime Southeast Asia to 1500* (New York: M.E. Sharpe, 1996), p. 101; A.C. Milner, "Islam and the Muslim State," M.B. Hooker (ed.) *Islam in South-East Asia*, p. 44; N.A. Baloch, *The Advent of Islam in Indonesia* (Islamabad: National Institute of Historical and Cultural Research,1980), p. 2.
7. N.A. Baloch, ibid., p. 4; Ira M. Lapidus, *A History of Islamic Societies* (Cambridge: Cambridge University Press, 1999), p. 474; G.W.J. Drewes, "New Light on the Coming of Islam to Indonesia?" (ed.), Ahmad Ibrahim, Sharon Siddique, and Yasmin Hussain, *Readings*

on Islam in Southeast Asia: Social Issues in Southeast Asia (Singapore: Institute of Southeast Asian Studies, 1990), p. 8; Arun K. Das Gupta, *Acheh in Indonesian Trade and Politics: 1600-1641* (New York: Cornell University, 1962), p. 189.

8. H. Abdullah Ujong Rimba, "Daerah Manakah Yang Mula Mula Menerima Agama Islam di Indonesia," *Seminar Sejarah Masuk Dan Berkembangnya Islam Di Aceh Dan Nusantara,* Majelis Ulama Propinsi Daerah Istimewa Aceh Dan Pemerintah Daerah TK. II (Aceh Timur, 1980), p. 3.
9. A.H. Johns, "Islam in Southeast Asia: Problems of Perspective," p. 312; See. Oman Fathurahman and Munawar Holil, *Katalog Naskah Ali Hasjmy Aceh* (*Catalogue of Aceh Manuscripts: Ali Hasjmy Collection*), The 21st Century Center of Excellence Programme "The Center for Documentation and Area-Transcultural Studies (Tokyo: Tokyo University of Foreign Studies, 2007).
10. Tuanku Abdul Jalil, "Pengertian Adat Aceh," *Loka Karya Adat Dan Budaya*, Lho'Seumawe, 8-10 January, 1988, p. 3
11. A.H. Johns, "Malay Sufism," *JMBRAS*, vol. XXX, Part 2, No. 178, August 1957, p. 9.
12. Raden Hoesein Djajadiningrat, *Kesultanan Aceh*, Seri Penerbitan Museum Aceh 2, (Proyek Rehabilitasi dan Perluasan Museum Daerah Istemewa Aceh, 1979), p. 90; Ali Hasjmy, *Aceh dan Pahang* (Aceh: Documentation and Information Center, 1989), p. 43; Syed Muhammad Naquib al-Attas, *A Commentary on the Hujjat Al-Siddiq of Nur al-Din Al-Raniri* (Kuala Lumpur: Ministry of Culture, 1986), p. 5-6.
13. Rusdi Sūfi (ed.), *Biografi Pejuang-Pejuang Aceh*, Dinas Kebudayaan Propinsi Nanggroe Aceh, Darussalam Proyek Pembinaan dan Pengembangan Suaka Peninggalan Sejarah kepurbakalaan (Banda Aceh: Kajian dan Nilai Tradisional, 2002), p. 4.
14. William Marsden, *The History of Sumatra*, p. 436; A.H. Johns, "Malay Sufism," *JMBRAS*, vol. XXX, Part 2, No. 178, August 1957, p. 10.
15. Syahbuddin Razi, "Dayah Cot Kala," *Seminar Sejarah Masuk Dan Berkembangnya Islam Di Aceh Dan Nusantara,* Majelis Ulama

Propinsi Daerah Istimewa Aceh Dan Pemerintah Daerah TK. II (Aceh Timur: 1980), p. 2, 5, 7.

16. Uka Tjandrasasmita, *Aceh Dalam Retrospeksi Dan Refleksi Budaza Nusantara* (Jakarta: INTIM Informasi Taman Iskandar Muda, 1988), p. 70; Ali Hasjmy, *Sejarah Kebudayaan Islam di Indonesia* (Jakarta: Bulan Bintang, 1980), p. 9.
17. M. Hasbi Amuriddin, *The Response of the Ulama Dayah to the Modernization of Islamic Law in Aceh* (Bangi: Penerbit Universiti Kebangsaan Malaysia, 2005), p. 9, 33.
18. Syed Muhammad Naquib al-Attas, *A General Theory of The Islamization of the Malay-Indonesian Archipelago*, 1969, p. 12; T. Ibrahim Alfian, Wadjah Rakjat Atjeh Dalam Lintasan Sedjarah", *Seminar Kebudajaan Dalam Rangka Pekan Kebudajaan Atjeh Ke-II*, (The Second Atjeh Cultural Festival, 20 August-2 September 1972) Dan Dies Natalis Ke XI Universitas Sjiah Kuala, Panitia Pusat Pekan Kebudajaan Atjeh Ke-II, (Banda Aceh: 1972), p. 3-4.
19. Ali Hasjmy, *Sejarah Kebudayaan Islam di Indonesia*, p. 14; Teuku H. Ibrahim Alfian, "Islam Dan Kerajaan Aceh Darussalam" (ed.), Taufik Abdullah, *Sejarah Dan Dialog Peradaban* (Jakarta: LIPI Press, 2006), p. 237; Teungku Anzib Lamnyong, *Adat Aceh*, Manuscript India Office Library in Verhandelingen van het Koninklijk Instituut voor Taal-, Land-, en Velkendunde. Jilid XXIV, Gravenhage: Martinus Nijhoff, 1958 (Aceh: Pusat Latihan Penelitian Ilmu-Ilmu Sosial, 1976), p. 17.
20. Armando Cortesao (ed.), *The Suma Oriental of Tome Pires*, vol. I (New Delhi: Asian Educational Services, 1990), p. 135-136; Mark Dion, "Sumatra through Portuguese Eyes: Excerpts from Joao de barros' Decadas Da Asia, Decada I, Livro IV, Capitulos, p. iii-iv.— For detailed information, see Lukman Thaib, *Acheh's Case: A Historical Study of the National Movement for the Independence of Aceh-Sumatra* (Kuala Lumpur: University of Malaya Press, 2002), p. 1-21.
21. A.H. Johns, "Islam in Southeast Asia: Problems of Perspective," p. 307-308; Ito Takeshi, *The World of the Adat Aceh: A Historical Study of the Sultanate of Aceh*, Ph.D. dissertation, Australian

National University, 1984, p. 12.

22. Ali Hasjmy; T.A. Talsya, *Aceh dan Pahang* (Medan: Pencetak Prakarsa Abadi Press, 1989), p. 24.
23. Morris E. Eugene, *Islam and Politics in Aceh:-A Study of Center-Periphery Relations in Indonesia* (New York: Cornell University, 1983), p. 19.
24. Metin Kunt, "The Later Muslim Empires: Ottomans, Safavids, Mughals," Marjorie Kelly (ed.), *Islam: The Religious and Political Life of a World Community* (New York: Praeger, 1984), p. 117; Ali Hasjmy, *Banda Aceh Darussalam Pusat Kegiatan Ilmu dan Kebudayaan*, dalam Ismail Suny (ed.), *Bunga Rampai Tentang Aceh* (Jakarta: Bhratara Karya Aksara, 1980), p. 5; Anthony Reid, *Witnesses to Sumatra: A Travellers's Anthology* (Kuala Lumpur: Oxford University Press, 1995), p. 54. (Note: These sultanates are the Ottoman Empire, Morocco, Isfahan (Iran), Agra (India), and the Aceh Darussalam Sultanate).
25. Hasjmy, ibid., p. 4.
26. Snouck Hurgronje, ibid., vol. 1, p. 208..
27. Ar-Raniri, ibid., p. 31-32; Azyumardi Azra, *Jaringan Ulama -Timur Tengah dan Kepulauan Nusantara Abad XVII dan XVIII-*, 4th ed. (Bandung: Penerbit Mizan, 1998), p. 52.
28. Mehmed Ziya, *Açe Tarihi* (Istanbul: 1312), p. 85 (This work is in Ottoman Turkish); Anthony Reid, *An Indonesian Frontier: Acehnese and Other Histories of Sumatra* (Singapore: Singapore University Press, 2005), p. 71; İsmail Hakkı Göksoy, *Güneydoğu Asya'da Osmanlı-Türk Tesirleri* (Isparta: Fakülte Kitabevi, 2004), p. 57.
29. Rızaulhak Şah, "Açe Padişahı Sultan Alaaddin'in Kanuni Sultan Süleyman'a Mektubu," Tarih Araştırmaları Dergisi, AÜDTCF, *Tarih Araştırmaları Enstitüsü*, S. 8-9. vol. V, 1967, Ankara Üniversitesi Basımevi, p. 385; İsmail Sofyan (ed.) *Perang Kolonial Belanda Di Aceh: The Dutch Colonial War in Aceh* (Banda Aceh: The Documentation and Information Center of Aceh, 1990), p. 54; Snouck Hurgronje, *The Acehnese*, vol. 1, p. 209; Anthony Reid (ed.), "Islamization and Christianization in Southeast Asia: The Critical Phase, 1550-1650; Anthony Reid, *Southeast Asia in the Early*

Modern Era (Ithaca: Cornell University Press, 1993), p. 162.

30. Siti Zainon Ismail, *Warisan Seni Budaya Melayu-Aceh,* Kaitan Pemerian Teks Sastera dan Realiti Budaya (Selangor: National University of Malaysia, n.d.), p. 130; Snouck Hurgronje, *The Acehnese*, vol. 2, p. 292.
31. Anthony Reid (ed.), "King, Kadis and Charisma in the Seventeenth Century Archipelago"; Anthony Reid, *The Making of an Islamic Political Discourse in Southeast Asia* (Clayton-Victoria, Australia: Aristoc Press Pty, Centre of Southeast Asian Studies, Monash University, 1993), p. 91.
32. Saffet Bey, "Bir Osmanlı Filosu'nun Sumatra Seferi, *Tarihi-i Osmani Encümeni Mecmuası*, 1 Teşrin-i Evvel 1327 (1912 M), p. 605-606.
33. The cemetery of H. Ahmad Kasturi is located in the quarter of ACC Dayan Dawood in Darussalam, Banda Aceh. In addition to his grave, there are other four scholars' graves. The inscription mentions just the names and the birth and death dates "Haji Ahmad Kasturi, Dari Turki, 1316-1389." Beyond this little information, it has not been impossible to reach any other references about Ahmad Kasturi. So, the authenticity of the Latinized inscription remains suspicious.
34. A.H. Johns, "Islam in Southeast Asia: Problems of Perspective", p. 314.
35. Rodolphe de Koninck, *Aceh in the Time of Iskandar Muda* (Banda Aceh: Pusat Dokumentasi Dan Informasi Aceh, 1977), p. 1.
36. J. Paulus (ed.), 'Asal Usul Raja Raja Aceh," *Encyclopedie van N.I.* (Leiden: 1917), p. 27.
37. Paulus, ibid., p. 19; See. Arun Komar Das Gupta, "Iskandar Muda and the Europeans, Ali Hasjmy," *Sejarah Masuk Dan Berkembangnya Islam Di Indonesia*, 3rd ed. (Percetakan Offset: 1993), p. 42-47.
38. Rusdi Sūfī (ed.), *Biografi Pejuang-Pejuang Aceh*, p. 6.
39. Paulus, *Asal Usul Raja Raja Aceh*, p. 30.
40. Richard Winstedt, *A History of Classical Malay Literature* (Kuala Lumpur: Oxford University Press, 1977), p. 143.
41. Ali Hasjmy; T.A. Talsyha, *Aceh dan Pahang* (Aceh: Lembaga Adat Dan Kebudayaan 1989), p. 26.

42. Ali Hasjmy, "Banda Aceh Darussalam Pusat Kegiatan İlmu Dan Kebudayaan," *Seminar Sejarah Masuk Dan Berkembangnya Islam Di Aceh Dan Nusantara,* Majelis Ulama Propinsi Daerah Istimewa Aceh Dan Pemerintah Daerah TK. II (Aceh Timur: 1980), p. 9. (Note: It is believed that the catalogue of Ali Hasjmy's library will provide some more understanding of the intellectual and scientific works available in Aceh centuries ago. See Oman Fathurrahman and Munawar Holil, *Katalog Naskah Pustaka Ali Hasjmy Aceh,* 2007).
43. Nuruddin ar-Raniri, *Bustan'us Salatin, Chapters II and III,* Transcription by Jelani Harun (Kuala Lumpur: Dewan Bahasa dan Pustaka, 2004), p. 339.
44. Ali Hasjmy, *Aceh dan Pahang,* p. 44.
45. D.A. Rinkes, *Nine Saints of Java,* trans. H.M. Froger (Kuala Lumpur: Malaysian Sociological Research Institute, 1996), p. xxxi; Snouck, Hurgronje, *The Acehnese,* vol. 2, p. 18.
46. Syed Muhammad Naquib al-Attas, *A General Theory of the Islamization of the Malay-Indonesian Archipelago,* p. 16.
47. This work was ordered by Sultanah Sri Sultan Taj al-Alam Safiyatuddin.
48. M. Hasmi Amuriddin, *The Response of the Ulama Dayah to the Modernization of Islamic Law in Aceh,* p. 13.
49. Ali Hasjmy mentions not 'el-Javî,' but Ali,' at the end of his full name for Baba Davud. "Shaikh Davud bin İsmail bin Agha Mustafa bin Agha Ali ar-Rumi." See Ali Hasjmy, *59 Tahun Aceh Merdeka* (Jakarta: Bulan Bintang, 1977), p. 117. However, Azyumardi Azra gives his full name as "Davud el-Cavi el-Fansuri bin Ismail bin Agha Mustafa bin Agha Ali ar-Rumi" şeklinde verir. See Azyumardi Azra, *Jaringan Ulama Timur Tengah dan Kepulauan Nusantara Abad XVII dan XVIII,* 1st edition (Jakarta: Penerbit Mizan, 1994), p. 211.
50. Haji Wan Muḥammad Shagir Abdullah, *Penyebaran Islam Dan Silsilah Ulama Sejagat Dunia Melayu,* vol. 5 (Kuala Lumpur: Persatuan Pengkajian Khazanah Klasik Nusantara & Khazanah Fathaniyah, 1999), p. 15.
51. Azyumardi Azra, *Jaringan Ulama Timur Tengah dan Kepulauan Nusantara Abad XVII dan XVIII,* 4th edition (Jakarta: Penerbit

Mizan, 1998), p. 211.

52. The name "Baba Davud" is mentioned on page 683 of the "Turjuman al-Mustafid" manuscript. See MSS 3316, Pusat Manuskrip Melayu, Perpustakaan Negeri Malaysia, Kuala Lumpur; Hamka, "Sebab Aceh Serambi Mekkah," *Seminar Sejarah Masuk Dan Berkembangnya Islam Di Aceh Dan Nusantara*, p. 4; Haji Wan Muḥammad Shagir Abdullah, *Khazanah Karya*, vol. 1, 1991, p. 160.
53. Haji Wan Muḥammad Shagir Abdullah, *Penyebaran Islam Dan Silsilah Ulama Sejagat Dunia Melayu*, vol. 5, p. 24.
54. Azyumardi Azra, *Jaringan Ulama Timur Tengah dan Kepulauan Nusantara Abad XVII dan XVIII*, p. 211.
55. Haji Wan Muḥammad Shagir Abdullah, *Penyebaran Islam Dan Silsilah Ulama Sejagat Dunia Melayu*, p. 24-25.
56. Ahmad Baha Mokhtar, "Syarh Latif Ala Arba'in Ḥadithan li al-Imām al-Nawawi Karangan Syeikh Abd Rauf al-Fansuri: Satu Kajian Teks," Ph.D. dissertation, Jabatan Al-Qur'an dan Al-Hadith (Kuala Lumpur: Akademi Pengajian Islam, Universiti Malaya, 2008), p. 56.
57. Ali Hasjmy, *Kebudayaan Aceh Dalam Sejarah* (Jakarta: Penerbit Beuna, 1983), p. 218.
58. Azyumardi Azra, *Jaringan Ulama Timur Tengah dan Kepulauan Nusantara Abad XVII dan XVIII*, p. 211.
59. Anthony Reid, *An Indonesian Frontier: Acehnese and Other Histories of Sumatra*, p. 69.
60. Cemal Mersinli, "Roma-Rum Kelimeleri," *TTK Bulleten*, vol. 5, No. 17-18, April (Ankara:1941), p. 160
61. Armando Cortesao (ed.), *The Suma Oriental of Tome Pires*, vol. I (New Delhi: Asian Educational Services, 1990), p. 142.
62. Mehmet Özay, *Açe Kitabı* (Istanbul: Fide Yayınları, 2006), p. 111.
63. Azyumardi Azra, *The Transmission of Islamic Reformismt to Indonesia: Networks of Middle Eastern and Malay-Indonesian 'Ulama' in The Seventeenth and Eighteenth Centuries*, Dissertation in the School of Arts and Sciences Columbia University, 1992, p. 103; İ. Hakkı Göksoy, *Güneydoğu Asya'da Osmanlı-Türk Tesirleri*, p. 11.
64. Ali Hasjmy, *Kebudayaan Aceh Dalam Sejarah* (Jakarta: Penerbit Beuna, 1983), p. 382.

65. Sagir Abdullah, *Penyebaran Islam Dan Silsilah Ulama Sejagat Dunia Melayu*, p. 16; Hasbi M. Amiruddin, *The Response of the Ulama Dayah to the Modernization of Islamic Law in Aceh*, p. 13.
66. Sagir Abdullah, *Penyebaran Islam Dan Silsilah Ulama Sejagat Dunia Melayu*, vol. 5, p. 16.
67 See *Masailal Muhtadi li Ikhwanil Muhtadi* in *Pusat Manuskrip Melayu* (Kuala Lumpur: Perpustakaan Negeri Malaysia), MSS 3662.
68. Ali Hasjmy, *Kebudayaan Aceh Dalam Sejarah*, p. 382; Amiruddin, *The Response of the Ulama Dayah to the Modernization of Islamic Law in Aceh*, p. 39
69. Ali Hasjmy, *Kebudayaan Aceh Dalam Sejarah* (Jakarta: Penerbit Beuna, 1983), p. 218.
70. Ali Hasjmy, *Bunga Rampai Revolusi dari Tanah Aceh* (Jakarta: Bulan Bintang, 1978), p. 81.
71. Haji Wan Mohammad Shaghir Abdullah, *Penyebaran Islam dan Silsilah Ulama Sejagat Dunia Melayu*, vol. 7, Siri Ke-8 (Kuala Lumpur: Persatuan Pengkajian Khazanah Klasik Nusantara & Khazanah Fathaniyah, 1999), p. 2.
72. Ali Hasjmy, *Ulama Aceh*, Mujahid Pejuang Kemerdekaan dan Pembangun Tamadun Bangsa 1997, p. 4.
73. Haji Wan Muḥammad Shagir Abdullah, *Penyebaran Islam & Silsilah Ulama Sejagat Dunia Melayu*, vol. 6, p. 41.
74. Haji Wan Muḥammad Shagir Abdullah, *Penyebaran Islam Dan Silsilah Ulama Sejagat Dunia Melayu*, vol. 5, p. 26-27.

3

A preliminary note on the Dayah Tanoh Abee[1]

Mehmet Özay[2]

Abstract

This paper describes the famous Dayah Tanoh Abee[3] *zāwiyah* (DTA) located in Seulimum, a subdistrict of Banda Aceh. Its importance is considered to be based on its founding fathers' origin, the connection between the Aceh Darussalam sultanate and the Ottoman empire, and its contribution to the Islamization of Southeast Asia.[4] This article also analyses the role of the Ottoman empire's geography in this regard. The argument contained herein is grounded on my interview of the DTA's last leader.

Al-Firus al-Baghdadi, the DTA's founder, and six other Islamic scholars migrated from Baghdad, the seat of the former 'Abbāsid empire and site of great symbolic value, to Aceh in 1627. This fact is important, because Baghdad at that time was an Ottoman province. He and his three brothers settled near Banda Aceh and began teaching. The Aceh Darussalam sultanate[5] was ruled by Sultan Iskandar Muda (1607-1636), who was doing his best to build relationships with other Islamic countries, especially those in the Middle East, to bolster economic and military ties and make progress in developing the religious sciences. He therefore encouraged scholars to come to Aceh, visit other Islamic regions, write on Islamic jurisprudence and other subjects, and implement

Islamic law in his sultanate. As a distinguished example of his approach, he appointed Shamsuddin Sumatranî as Syaikh ul-Islam.

Ever since its establishment, the DTA has been a leading centre of such distinctive Sūfi orders as Naqshbandiyyah and Shattariyya. Moreover, the invaluable manuscripts held in its library have given it a distinguished status in Southeast Asia. After finishing their education in the *zāwiyah,* many of the local and regional students embarked upon their own travels to proselytize other Southeast Asian peoples by founding their own religious education centres. During this nearly four-hundred-year process, the DTA became known as one of Southeast Asia's leading religious teaching centres and possessor of its oldest manuscript library.

Introduction

For at least 2,000 years, Aceh has been one of Southeast Asia's busiest entrepots as regards trading activities among Arabia, Iran, India, and China due to its geo-strategic position at the western entrance of the Malacca Straits.[6] This geographical advantage and the ensuing commercial interactions birthed a new direction for the region, especially in Aceh, after Islam appeared in Arabia.

Historically Acehnese Islam, as accepted for the region's other parts, has included Muslim migrants coming from different lands.[7] Religious scholars, who either came to Aceh or were born and raised there as natives, made significant contributions to the region's Islamization, not only by personally teaching but also by writing theological and philosophical works. Given this context, one can say that Aceh's sphere of influence includes all of Southeast Asia. Beyond the personal contribution of each religious scholar, the DTA is more than worthy as the subject matter of a research paper. Therefore, I focus upon the family of al-Firus al-Baghdadi, who came from Baghdad with several other *'ulamā'*, settled down, and established a *zāwiyah* (*dayah*) in Aceh.

The importance of Aceh as the pioneer of Islamic educational centres can be seen in its scholarly output in jurisprudence, philosophy, and Qur'anic exegeses by both indigenous and foreign-born *'ulamā'*,[8] as well as the presence of Sufism long before the coming of the European colonialists. The Acehnese, the first Southeast Asian people to be introduced to Islam, have served as its regional representatives for hundreds of years by initiating Islamic education centres and sending religious scholars throughout the Malay Archipelago. In addition, religious scholars came and stayed for a certain period, or actually settled down, especially during the initial phase of Islamization between the thirteenth and fifteenth centuries. It might be argued that institutionalization took place after this first step.

The DTA appears to be a unique example of the second phase, which started with the seventeenth century. This phase is also important due to its distinguished administration during Iskandar Muda's reign. Commencing from the sultanate of Samudra-Pasai, Aceh enjoyed its golden era under this devout sultan's patronage not only in Indonesia, but also throughout all of Southeast Asia in general. As a result, Aceh was known as Serambi Mekah (the gateway to Makkah).[9] Even today the Acehnese take great pride in this title, for it has given them a unique identity among Indonesia's thirty-three provinces.

During Muda's reign, religious scholars are known to have held such distinguished roles as Shaykh al-Islām and head of the religious court; moreover, they were appointed as statesmen responsible for receiving foreign envoys.[10] A notable point, however, is whether the institutionalization of Islamic education centres and Muda's administration was deliberate or coincidental.

Given the reasons for writing this paper, I will focus on some of the DTA's aspects. From the outset, the DTA assumed its role as one of Aceh's most distinguished *zāwiyahs* and retained this status for nine successive generations, almost 380 years, until its last head passed away in October 2006. Some other mentionable factors are the founding fathers' origins, the uninterrupted continuity of their descendants' leadership, the creation and maintenance of a centuries-old library of authentic Islamic literature, and its function during the anti-Dutch holy war that began in the last quarter of the nineteenth century.

Based on my September-October 2005 interviews in Aceh with Teungku Muhammad Dahlan Al-Fairus al-Baghdadi, the DTA's last leader, the founding fathers arrived from Baghdad in 1627. His predecessors are easily traced back to the above-mentioned year. The importance of Baghdad lies in the fact that this ancient city of Islamic civilization was at that time a provincial capital city of the Ottoman empire. His arrival and subsequent proselytization in Aceh is not the only such example of a Turkish presence in Aceh's history, for it is known that, over time, scholars from other Islamic lands also came.[11]

Even so, this is not exceptional in the case of Aceh for, according to Martin van Bruinessen, more influential Southeast Asian Islamic scholars and other Muslims have remained in the shadows. Although no written documents could be obtained to elucidate the family's origins and "how and what they studied, and what were their relations with the courts"[12] due to some understandable reasons (e.g., many manuscripts the *zāwiyah*'s library were damaged and/or destroyed during and after the Dutch invasion), the succession of the DTA's leadership is a strong proof for the authenticity of the family's origin. It is also impossible to prove whether the family originated in Baghdad or moved there from Anatolia, the empire's central part.

In accordance with the common practices of each religious scholar, the family members doubtlessly administered the *zāwiyah* and contributed to spreading Islam and compiling Islamic literature. This succession enabled the *zāwiyah*'s leaders to create a well-stocked library consisting of old Arabic and Jawi-Melayu works that were both translated and written by various religious scholars. In addition to educating the people, they also played a significant socio-political role, especially after the Dutch declared war on Aceh on 26 March 1873.[13]

Regarding the above-mentioned aspects, this present paper might be regarded as an effort to reconstruct the historical Turkish-Acehnese connection and generate a broader basis for the accumulation of information.

Aceh during the spread of Islam

Both Muslim traders and scholars introduced Islam at various levels, beginning with Sumatra and then throughout Southeast Asia, during the first Islamic century.[14] Many Arab, Persian, and Indian Muslim traders chose the western Indian region of Gujarat as their commercial centre for conducting businesses with the Malay Peninsula and Sumatra.[15] As a result, Islam's spread has been linked directly to these trade relations, which became the "catalyst for conversion."[16] In Pasai, an old gravestone bearing the name of Abdullah b. Muhammad b. Abdulkadir b. Abdul' Aziz b. al-Mansur Abu Jafer al-Abbasi al-Muntasir (d. 1407) from Delhi is just one authentic proof of the presence of a foreign-born Muslim scholar.[17]

The Islamic expansion outward from India can be read as a repetition of the spread of that country's religions and cultures to the Malay Archipelago that had taken place centuries before the appearance of Islam.[18] On the other hand, the Turks' role in this subsequent expansion is worth thinking about. Having entered their own Islamization process in the ninth century, they inevitably ushered in a new direction in Islamic history due to their military power.[19] As a result, Turkish traders appeared around the Indian Ocean in the dying years of the ʿAbbāsid empire, especially in Khurmuz. Under the Seljuk empire they reached Oman's shores and began sailing eastward to conduct large-scale trading missions.[20] This realistic time frame has led researchers to posit that the Turks could have been participants in the region with the Arab, Persian, and Indian traders in the region, although their share did not reach the level enjoyed by the latter groups. Based on this, there is also a probability that both Turkish-origin traders and religious scholars contributed to the region's Islamization.

Due to this, there is a great interest in determining the origins of the *zāwiyah*'s founders. While it cannot be confidently stated that the family is of Turkic origin, it should be emphasized that they came from Baghdad, a major Islamic city that had been under the influence of Turkish Islamic civilization for some time, first during the end of the ʿAbbāsid empire and then during the Ottoman era. Based on this fact, the question of which aspects of this tradition did the family transmit to Aceh should be asked. Presumably, its members brought a distinctive Islamic cultural heritage, which contained a body of tradition that was not of Southeast Asian origin, with them to Aceh as well.

Islam's expansion has caused the relationships among the Middle East, India, and Southeast Asia to differ over time. During all these processes, religious scholars from the Middle East and parts of India migrated to Aceh. This migration can be divided into three distinct phases: (1) the eighth to twelfth centuries, when the Arabs and Persians dominated trade with the Far East; (2) the twelfth to fifteenth centuries, a period of increased commercial activity and cultural relationships during which Sūfis and religious scholars accompanied traders; and (3) the fifteenth to seventeenth centuries, when European colonialists appeared in the region. As soon as they started their invasions of the lands located around the Indian Ocean, the Southeast Asian-Middle Eastern commercial and political relationships reached very significant levels. One reason for this was the involvement of the Ottoman empire.[21]

Trade activities allowed Aceh to embrace religious movements earlier than other Southeast Asian regions. On the other hand, the spread of Islam led to Southeast Asians travelling to Arabia to perform the hajj and a gradual increase in trade activities.[22] Some *'ulamā'* also accompanied the voyages of traders to Southeast Asia to win converts. Especially from 1571 till 1586, *'ulamā'* from various parts of the Islamic world came to Aceh, as can be seen in the arrival of Muhammad Azhari from Makkah, who taught some Islamic sciences in Aceh, as well as Shaikh Abul Khair b. Shaikh Hajar and Shaikh Muhammad Yamani from Makkah as well. Another example is Shaikh Muhammad Jailani b. Hasan b. Muhammad from Gujarat, who helped develop Islamic culture and science by penning significant works of metaphysics and Sufism and teaching Islamic sciences in the region.[23]

Aceh: A place of Islamic education after Malacca

Prior to the Portuguese invasion, northern Sumatra boasted several city states or petty kingdoms. The first city states, such as Perlak and Samudra-Pasai, played a pioneering role in introducing Islam.[24] With the fall of Malacca to the Portuguese on 10 August 1511, Aceh gradually became both a regional trading centre for Muslims as well as for Islamic education and culture.[25] In addition, it was also a gathering place for Islamic scholars who wanted to accompany the traders to new lands.[26] The seizure of Malacca represented Portugal's opening campaign to establish a sea-borne empire by asserting its superior power in the Indian Ocean region. Since Malacca had been a hub of the sea-borne trade among Arabia, Persia, and China for centuries, this invasion was hardly accidental.

After Malacca fell, Muslim traders and scholars moved to other port cities in the region. As a result Aceh, located in northern Sumatra, became a flourishing commercial centre for all groups of traders, especially for Muslims, since it was close to Malacca and geographically suitable for interacting with the lands along the Red Sea, western India's shores, and western Sumatra. Over time, this reality transformed Aceh into the region's most powerful Islamic state.[27] The Portuguese naturally tried to capture Aceh's port cities, which were located on the opposite side of the Straits. Ali Mughayat Syah, the Aceh Darussalam sultanate's first ruler, was fully aware of their intent and sought to foil it by uniting some nearby petty sultanates (1511) to establish his sultanate; later on, he subjugating the city states of Pedir (1521) and Pasai (1524) for the same reason.[28] During the ensuing decades, the sultanate developed large-scale trade with Middle Eastern ports.

Interactions with the Middle East

The above development caused the sultanate to develop as a pioneer entity as regards the economic, political, and military affairs in the Malay world. Along with the contribution of *'ulamā'* migrating from Malacca and other parts of the Muslim world, Aceh gradually became a significant centre of Islamic education and culture.[29] Due to this process, as well as those mentioned above, the sixteenth and seventeenth centuries saw it develop in the cultural and scientific areas as well.[30]

Some references state that religious scholars were in the forefront of introducing and spreading Islam in Aceh. Prominent among them were the prolific Sūfi authors Hamzah Fansurî (Qādiriyyah), Shamsuddin Sumatranî (1575-1630; Naqshbandiyyah), Nuruddin Muhammad b. Ali b. Hasan al-Hamid ar-Raniri (d. 1658;[31] Rifā'iyyah), and Abdurrauf b. Ali al-Cavî al-Fansurî al-Singkilî

(1615-1693; Shattariyya).[32] Although Fansurî and his disciple Sumatranî were representatives of both Ibn al-'Arabī's *waḥdah al-wujūd* (existential monism) and the Qādiriyyah order, they could not establish a school of thought due to ar-Ranirî's reaction.[33] These four distinguished scholars were the chief forces behind improving Islamic thought and practice not only in Aceh, but throughout the Malay Archipelago.[34] Their efforts doubtlessly led to the emergence of a region-wide Malay Islamic civilisation.

Before taking a position in the sultanate, Fansurî furthered his knowledge of the Islamic sciences by visiting Pahang, Banten, Pattani, Jerusalem, Makkah, and Baghdad. While in Baghdad, he encountered Sūfī movements, studied, and became an expert especially on the Qādiriyyah.[35] His disciple Sumatranî eventually became the sultanate's *shaikh'ul Islam* and was entrusted with foreign affairs due to his expertise in politics. In this capacity, he met with James Lancaster, the leading British envoy at that time, who presented a letter for the sultan of Aceh from Queen Elizabeth I in the palace in 1602.[36]

The socio-political structure under Sultan Iskandar Muda (1607-1636)

According to Muhammad Dahlan, a member of the family's ninth generation, al-Firus al-Baghdadi came to Aceh in 1627.[37] It is important to look briefly at socio-political circumstances that existed when he laid the foundation of a religious educational centre in order to better understand the nature of the sultanate, which, it must be remembered, was highly developed in social terms before Muda ascended the throne.[38] In addition, further developments regarding the *'ulamā's* activities also occurred during these years.

Reigning from 1607 until 1636, Muda earned a distinguished place in Aceh's history not only because under his rule the sultanate achieved its highest level of economic and political development, but also because his political priorities consisted of establishing religious education centres and improving the Islamic sciences. It should be emphasized that during his reign, the Islamic worldview encompassed the entire social, legal and moral order. His efforts to develop the sultanate in every field proved that it could be a leading Islamic power and representative of Islamic civilization at the international level at that time. Thus, it had every incentive to pursue close relationships with other Islamic entities.[39]

Muda sought to expand the sultanate's borders by successive conquests of land and especially maritime powers in both Sumatra and the Malay Peninsula. He subsequently mobilized the army to conquer Deli, Kedah, Perak, Johor, and Pahang.[40] This period became known as the "golden era," a time of power and glory, due to these conquests and the sultanate's ensuing control of Sumatra's spice trade.[41]

Although our knowledge of the historical background of Aceh's Islamic educational institutions remains uncertain, it is said that such institutions were established from Muda's reign onward. Among them, the *meunasah*, *rangkang*, and *dayah* deserve to be mentioned.[42] Muda, swathed in glory, contributed a great deal to helping Aceh become a distinguished Southeast Asian centre of religious education by encouraging non-Acehnese religious scholars to come to Aceh.[43] One of the important reasons behind the development of Islamic education in the sultanate was the undertaking by some local scholars to visit Makkah and Madīnah in the seventeenth century, especially during Muda's reign, to improve their knowledge of the Islamic sciences. Some of them stayed in Arabia for years. Some Arab and Indian scholars settled in Aceh and did their best to improve the local level of Islamic education and sciences. In addition, these contacts allowed the Islamic world's intellectual treasure relevant to be transmitted to Aceh.[44] These above-mentioned developments illustrate the close cultural contact between the Muslim world's periphery and centre.

Religious scholars were instrumental in developing the Malay language by penning their own works in that language. Beyond Islam's role as a uniting factor in politics, language also did much to unite the region's people against European colonialism, especially at the end of the sixteenth century.[45]

Iskandar Muda's efforts to develop and implement Islamic law are clear. In this context he is known as a reformer, for he established a system of jurisprudence, the *Adat Meukota Alam* (a combination of traditional Malay [*adat*] and Islamic law),[46] and the Baiturrahman Mosque. This latter institution is a very charming example of historical and religious structures not only in Aceh, but also in Indonesia today.[47]

Other than works about God's nature and the relation between God and human beings, the Sūfis underwent a developing phase at this time, similar to those occurring in other parts of the Islamic world.[48] A noted example is the *waḥdah al-wujūd* thought, which was strongly supported by Iskandar Muda. On another note, the philosophical arguments started by Fansurî were continued by his disciple Sumatranî; the sultan showed his support for the latter by appointing him *Syaikh ul-Islam*,[49] a position second to that of the sultan.[50]

The al-Firus al-Baghdadi family

One of this essay's main goals is to look into the origin of the *zāwiyah*'s founding fathers. Although this institution's existence, continuity, and function are known, only a small amount of the detailed data deals with its origin. My 2005 interviews with its leader revealed that the family originally came from Baghdad in

1627. According to their family tree in the first page of a book on the Shattariyya in the DTA library, Shaikh Nayan al-Firus al-Baghdadi belonged to its first generation.[51]

Leaving Baghdad with three of his brothers and some others, he and his brothers eventually settled in a village called Tanoh Abee, Sagou XXII Mukim. Al-Firus, the eldest brother, established a *zāwiyah* and became its first leader. Now it is called by the same name in *Seulimum*, where is about 50 km from the capital city, Bandar Aceh. The others went to the northern Aceh village of Tiro.[52] It is assumed that these religious scholars accompanied a group of traders travelling from western India to Southeast Asia, as this was quite common between the two regions. In addition, it is generally accepted that foreign-born religious scholars who settled in Aceh disseminated Islamic teachings and practices by marrying the daughters of distinguished individuals families, thereby quickly becoming members of Aceh's society.[53] Al-Firus al-Baghdadi must have followed this custom by marrying into a ruling family.

As soon as the *zāwiyah* was established, the family members dedicated their lives to developing the people's spiritual welfare. In regards to this, the family is assumed to have specialized in reproducing itself in each generation. One of its contributions to Aceh's religious life and history was the institutionalisation of the *zāwiyah,* which probably increased the speed and intensification of Islamization, and a Sūfi *ṭarīqah* (order). In addition, its leaders gradually assumed the position of *qāḍī* (judge) in the region. Given these assumptions, it might be argued that these were 'twin processes' of the family's existence. Moreover, Acehnese society was possibly encouraged to become closely linked to international Islam, as seen in the other Southeast Asian lands. There is a high probability that this relation caused the Islamic structure of Aceh to integrate into the global Islamic community.[54]

A *zāwiyah* has the sole function of serving as a centre of Higher Islamic Education. Mustafa ar-Rumi, a *murīd* (student) and *khalīfah* (successor) of Abdurrauf as-Singkilī, gave *ijāzah* (scholarly permission) to teach the Shattariyya *ṭarīqah*'s practices to a member of the family. This subsequently allowed the order to be established in the DTA. As Mustafa ar-Rumi had a Turkish father, this connection has evoked the present writer's interest.

The leaders' spiritual exercise and intellectual outlook, both of which were focused on following the Shattariyya order and establishing a library, gradually distinguished them from Aceh's other religious scholars. Hence the *zāwiyah* seemed to provide a unique example of the intellectual transmission of Islamic values into the indigenous society by creating a literate tradition. Based on this, the role of this *zāwiyah* in Acehnese history should be emphasised. As for the family's origins, it is assumed that its members played the role, as defined by Geertz, of a *cultural broker.*

The institution's chosen site raises a question about its relationship with Bandar Aceh's palace circles. It is not known whether its leaders made themselves independent of these circles or became affiliated with them and benefitted from their protection. The sultans almost always served as patrons for the *'ulamā'* not only for being pious Muslims, but also for political advantages. Starting from the reign of Queen Nur Alam Naqiyatuddin (1675-1678), the establishment of Sagou XXII Mukim as an administrative body like the other two Sagous gave the sultanate a new direction.[55] The impact that this administrative change had on the DTA's existence is also interesting. As mentioned earlier, its successive leaders also served as judges in the region. From this, it is assumed that there must have been some cooperation between the two bodies.

On the other hand, though, the reaction of the *dayah* leaders to the Dutch invasion of Aceh must be studied separately and in detail, for it may give some indication as to how the significant tendency for social disorder during this period thrust the *zāwiyah*'s leaders into a leadership role.

The genealogy

This part details the genealogy of the al-Firus al-Baghdadi family from its arrival in Aceh in 1627 till recent times. The people mentioned here have served, in succession, as the leader of the DTA *zāwiyah*. It should also be stressed that locating information about the family members in any documentary works was not possible until very recently for several reasons: the absence of any works written by family members or others and the destructive impact of the Dutch invasion, which caused many sources to be lost and/or destroyed. It is estimated that the DTA library once held some 10.000 books; today, it contains only 1000 books.[56] Among them could have been some works that included biographies of the Dayah's leaders. As a result, it has not been possible to list the birth and death dates of some of the *zāwiyah's* leaders.

Al-Firus al-Baghdadi

Al-Firus al-Baghdadi came to Aceh with six other people, three of whom were his brothers, in 1627.[57] He and his brothers settled in Tanoh Abee village, which is 50 kms outside of Banda Aceh. He might be regarded as the harbinger of the religious institution's glorious future, for he established a *dayah* that played a significant role in many aspects of Acehnese society till recently. He married an Acehnese lady and sired eight children, three of whom (viz., Nayan, Molek, and Hana Purba) also became religious scholars. After he passed away, his son Nayan assumed responsibility for the DTA.[58]

Shaikh Nayan al-Firus al-Baghdadi

Nayan received his early education from his father in the *dayah*, after which he studied under Syiah Davud b. Ismail b. Mustafa ar-Rumi[59] (a.k.a Teungku Chik Di Leupue) at Dayah Leupue di Kampung Mulia, Bandar Aceh, one of the distinguished *dayahs* of that period. He also received lessons from Shaikh Burhaneddin Ulakan (d. 1704), the *khalīfah* of Mustafa ar-Rumi.[60] Since this shaikh was a representative of the Shattariyya *ṭarīqah*,[61] it is highly possible that the long-term relationship between the *ṭarīqah* and the DTA leader began during this time. This was confirmed during the present writer's 2005 interview with Muhammad Dahlan, who stressed that the *zāwiyah* had been one of the headquarters for the Naqshbandiyyah and Shattariyya *ṭarīqahs*.

After his education at this *dayah*, Nayan al-Firus received his *ijāzah* and returned to Seulimum to run the DTA. In addition to teaching at the *zāwiyah*, he also became the *qāḍī* in Sagou XXII Mukim and thus inaugurated the tradition of the *zāwiyah* leader being both a religious leader and a leader in the local administration. Shaikh Nayan personally educated his successor.[62]

Shaikh Abdulhafiz al-Baghdadi

Under Shaikh Nayan, the *zāwiyah* made significant progress in educating the people about *fiqh*, Sufism, ethics, theology, *tafsīr*, and Ḥadīth. But it did not limit its curriculum to the Islamic sciences, for history, logic, mathematics, and philosophy were also included. These subjects might be taken as evidence that even from its first days, the *zāwiyah* sought to spread both Islamic and scientific knowledge. After this complete education, qualified students were able to assume positions in both educational and administrative bodies.

His marriage resulted in four children, one of whom was Abdulhafiz. This son, whose education he personally monitored, succeeded his father and continued the *zāwiyah*'s function as an educational centre. After Abdulhafiz moved the *zāwiyah* to Tuwi Ketapunang, near the Aceh River, the original structure became educational centre for women. Like his father, Shaikh Abdulhafiz led the *dayah* and became a *qāḍī*.[63] Even though it is not known whether any educational centre had existed before this, it should still be regarded as an important step in the *zāwiyah*'s development.

Shaikh Abdurrahim Hafız al-Baghdadi

As was the case in each period, Hafız al-Baghdadi also introduced some new elements into the *dayah*. For example, he rendered a great service by obtaining books from various Ottoman cities that were then placed in the library founded by his grandfather. Besides enriching the library, this contribution also helped to meet the demands for written materials. It is assumed that this new literature allowed students to access study materials and improve their skills in Arabic calligraphy. This may have been planned in order to improve calligraphy both as an artistic work and as a teaching method. Like his father, Hafız al-Baghdadi also assumed the position of *qāḍī* in the region. Of his five children, Muhammad Salih was the one who led the *dayah* after his father died.[64] It should be argued that due to the above-mentioned transfer of Islamic literature, there was a close relationship between the Ottoman empire and Aceh. In addition to being an art form, calligraphy is also understood to have been accorded a degree of importance and subsequently developed.

Shaikh Muhammad Salih al-Baghdadi (d. 1855)

Not much information is available on this figure; however, there is no doubt that the familial link was continued. As the previous leaders had done, he assumed the positions of both DTA leader and *qāḍī*. Of his five daughters and nine sons, only one son became a religious scholar. His term was relatively short, and he passed away in 1855.[65]

Shaikh Abdulwahab al-Baghdadi (d. 1894)

Given his features, Abdulwahab looked like his grandfather Shaikh al-Firus al Baghdādī. As his biography shows, however, he apparently achieved more than his grandfather did. While residing in Makkah and Madīnah to further his Islamic education, he developed his skill at calligraphy and brought his works back to Aceh, thereby doing much to enrich the library. It is said that during his period the library held nearly 10,000 books and the *zāwiyah* became a leading centre for Islamic studies. In his capacity as the *zāwiyah*'s and as an appointed *qāḍī*, he did what he could to help Tunku Panglima Polen Sri Muda Perkasa Banda Muda in implementing Islamic law in *Sagou XXII*.[66]

The Chik Tanoh Abee's main importance was seen in the prominent role he assumed in the anti-Dutch struggle, the most difficult period for the sultanate. The Dutch navy, intent upon occupying Aceh, appeared in front of Bandar Aceh's port after a long struggle that had begun in the early nineteenth century. This invasion was seen as significant not only for Aceh but, and more importantly, for the entire colonial period. The Dutch, who invaded, colonized, and ruled Java for several centuries, wanted to seize Aceh and make it another colony. To realize this goal, its navy attacked Aceh on 26 March 1873[67] and seized control of the sultan's palace (the Kraton) and its circles. The Acehnese army dispersed after the sultan died. At this critical moment, the *zāwiyah* assumed leadership. After seizing the city centre, the Dutch advanced to Seulimum and took control of this area in 1879.

The nobility (*uleebalang*) was largely ineffective as regards assuming leadership in order to continue the struggle. Therefore the warriors' leader, Panglima Polem Muhammad Saman Di Tiro, and several nobles visited Abdulwahab, the Teungku Chik Tanoh Abee, to ask for his suggestions and support.[68] This is assumed to be a turning point in the struggle. The mere fact that they approached him shows just how important the *zāwiyah* had become in Acehnese society. Abdulwahab, who had given priority to acquiring a pure heart before obtaining material things, pointed out the society's social and political disintegration and disturbances and reminded the people, especially the nobility, that all of them, without exception, should give back whatever they had unfairly seized from the common people. In other words, they were to undertake a moral war of self-purification to cleanse their hearts from their non-Islamic attitudes and actions before conducting a concrete and material war (*jihād*) against the Dutch invaders.[69] This approach should be understood not as a simple threat, but as a reminder to the Acehnese Muslims of the Islamic understanding that they had lost and therefore needed to embrace purity.

The leaders of various *dayahs* agreed ally themselves with the *uleebalangs* and the common people. Abdulwahab, who was about to leave for hajj, cancelled his trip in order to launch the struggle; other Muslims in Aceh took his approach as a model.[70] The region's other leaders decided to establish a military base in Sagou XXII. Like other religious scholars, Abdulwahab took an active part in this war, as did some of his sons and daughters. His contribution could be regarded, according to a mystic way of action, as a miracle. The last leader of the *zāwiyah* and his relatives mentioned this during the present writer's interviews.

Abdulwahab passed away in 1894, leaving behind thirty-three children by his four wives. Only one of his sons, Muhammad Said, had the capacity to lead the *dayah*.[71]

Shaikh Muhammad Said al-Baghdadi

Muhammad Said managed the *zāwiyah* during a most difficult period; the Dutch were still active in the region. In addition to leading the *jihād* to protect the realms, he also taught in the *zāwiyah*. Unfortunately, the Dutch army eventually raided this institution and caught and imprisoned Said in Kedah's jail (*bengis*). He remained there for roughly two years and three months, after which he died—still a prisoner. The Acehnese, who had great respect for this man, forbade the Dutch to conduct the funeral rites; rather, they carried his coffin on their shoulders while walking the 50 kms to Seulimum in order to bury him on the site of Tanoh Abee. He had three sons and two daughters.[72]

Shaikh Muhammad Ali al-Baghdadi (1861-1969)

Muhammad Ali assumed his father's position. Although the existing socio-political circumstances are assumed to have prevented him from attaining more prominence, his strong character and challenging struggle against the Dutch earned him a distinguished place in the *zāwiyah*'s history. Due to his mastery of the Jawi language, he was called as "expert of Jawi". After the Dutch took control of the palace, Muhammad Ali guessed (correctly, as it turned out) that they would soon attack Seulimum because the *zāwiyah* had by now become a significant headquarters for such institutions as the Dayah Lambirah, Dayah Rumpet, Dayah Indrapuri, and Dayah Lam Diran. He thus decided to move about 10,000 of the library's books to a safer place.[73] After concealing some of them in village houses around the *zāwiyah*, he accompanied the sultan's military groups who were carrying on their struggle in Keumala. During his voyage he placed some of the books in a cave located in Tereubeh village, in Janntho, Aceh Besar.

On 12 December 1900, the Dutch caught him and subsequently imprisoned him in Banda Aceh and imprisoned, just as they had done to his father and his brother Teungku Yahya in Kedah. Later on he was exiled, first to Betawi (Surabaya) and then to Manado. As he had foreseen, the Dutch did eventually attack and burn down the *zāwiyah*, just as they had done to the Beiturrahman mosque before. After five years of exile he was sent back to Aceh on 17 October 1905. Upon his return he began to reestablish the library by collecting the concealed books. But the humidity and some animals had already destroyed many of them. In the end he could only collect around 2,000 books. Muhammad Ali passed away in 1969, aged 108 years.[74]

Here it should be mentioned that burning down the *zāwiyah* was symbolically a very important event in the eyes of the Dutch, for they must have understood both its function and its role. There were also similarities between it and the Baiturrahman mosque, which they burned down during their first invasion.

Muhammad Dahlan al-Firus al-Baghdadi (1943-2006)

Muhammad Dahlan, a ninth-generation member of the family, continued the *dayah*'s educational services. He also worked zealously to protect the library, which had suffered such enormous losses during the Dutch war (26 March 1873-20 January 1903). He subsequently prepared a catalogue of the collection's approximately 1,000 books: *Katalog Manuskrip Perpustakaan Dayah Tanoh Abee*.[75] During this time, many foreign researchers visited the library; their names and titles can be perused in the visitors' book. Dahlan welcomed international researchers and helped them complete their studies.

Of his ten children, only three boys and two girls have survived. Before his death on 18 November 2006 in his home in Seulimum after some operations in Banda Aceh, he had stated during an interview that he had not yet decided upon his successor. Nevertheless, he did make it clear that he wanted the library to be protected so that it would benefit future generations.[76]

After his death, the family decided to pass place this responsibility upon Abdulhafiz, his eldest son.

Conclusion

The foreign-born Muslim scholars who came to Aceh helped to spread Islam from the Islamic heartland to the Malay Archipelago. The existence of al-Firus al-Baghdadi and his descendants has been accepted as a proof of this assertion.

Given the nine generations of uninterrupted leadership supplied by this family, the *zāwiyah* presents a long-lived dynasty of religious scholars in the Malay world. The centre's existence concretely proves the institutionalization of Islamic education in Aceh. Since this family originally came from Baghdad, a leading centre of Islamic knowledge and civilization that had been under the political and social control of various Turkic states for long periods of time, the present writer argues that scholars from that region likely participated in transmitting the Middle East's knowledge to Aceh. Since a detailed documentation about how much and in which way the al-Baghdadi represented this tradition in Aceh has yet to be uncovered, more research should be conducted.

To further conclude, the main aspects regarding the *zāwiyah*'s importance are as follows: (1) its presence proves that an institutional Islamic educational centre has been well-established in Aceh for a long time; (2) its leaders transmitted Islamic knowledge to the local people. In addition, calligraphy as an art form could be followed and taught as an academic subject; (3) an international link existed between Aceh and the larger Islamic world; (4) its leaders, who combined Sufism and the implementation of orthodox Sunnī Islamic jurisprudence, formed an elite Sūfī class and served as *qāḍīs* in the region; and (5) the *zāwiyah*'s leader, upon the request of an alliance among other distinguished *dayah* leaders and the nobles, was asked to lead the anti-Dutch struggle. The fact that members of the *'ulamā'* and the nobility sought his advice on how to defeat this enemy underlined the importance of his position in society.

It is hoped that this preliminary paper might open an avenue of further inquiry about the history of the *zāwiyah* Tanoh Abee. Further research is needed to determine how and in which aspects it was dominant during the course of history.

Notes

1. Nia Deliana contributed to this paper by translating it and the comments from Bahasa Indonesia into English.
2. Dr Mehmet Özay is a Senior Lecturer at the Faculty of Islamic Civilization and Thought, the University Technology Malaysia.
3. Hereafter "DTA" and "*zāwiyah*".
4. Hereafter "SEA."
5. Hereafter "ADS."
6. Gilber Khoo, and Dorothy Lo, *Asian Transformation: A History of Southeast, South and East Asia* (Singapore: 1977), p. 3.
7. Roy F. Ellen, "Practical Islam in Southeast Asia" (ed.), H.B. Hooker, *Islam in Southeast Asia*, p. 72.
8. Peter Riddell, *Islam and the Malay-Indonesian World: Transmission and Responses* (London: Hurst & Company, 2001), p. 103, 139.
9. Mohd Taib Osman (ed.), *Islamic Civilization in the Malay World* (Kuala Lumpur: Dewan Bahasa dan Pustaka, 1997), p. xxvii; Ira M. Lapidus, *A History of Islamic Societies*, 7th ed. (Cambridge: Cambridge University Press, 1995), p. 474; D.G.E. Hall, *A History of South-East Asia*, 3rd ed. (London: The Macmillan Press Ltd., 1976), p. 219.
10. A.H. Johns, "Islam in the Malay World: An Exploratory Survey with Some Reference to Quranic Exegesis," ed. Raphael Israeli and Anthony H. Johns, *Islam in Asia*, vol II: *Southeast and East Asia* (Jerusalem: The Magnes Press, The Hebrew University, 1984), p. 121.
11. Snouck Hurgronje, *The Acehnese*, tr. A.W.S. O'Sullivan, vol. I

(Leiden: E.J. Brill, 1906), p. 18, 209.

12 See Martin van Bruneissen, "A Note on Source Materials for the Biographies of Southeast Asian Ulama."

13 Anthony Reid, *The Blood of the Pople: Revolution and the End of Traditional Rule in Northern Sumatra* (Kuala Lumpur: Oxford University Press, 1979), p. 5; See Ismail Jakub, *Teungku Chik Di Tiro (Muḥammad Saman) Palawan Besar Dalam Perang Aceh (1881-1891)* (Jakarta: Bulan Bintang, 1960).

14. J.A.E. Morley, "The Arabs and the Eastern Trade," *JMBRAS*, vol. XXII, 1949, p. 150; Raymond LeRoy Archer, *Muḥammadan Mysticism in Sumatra* (Montana: Kessinger Publishing, 1935), p. 90; S. Soebardi and C.P. Woodcroft Lee, "Islam in Indonesia," *The Crescent in the East: Islam in Asia Major,* ed. Raphael Israeli (London: Curzon Press, 1982), p. 180-181; M. Yunus Djamil, "Wadjah Rakjat Atjeh Dalam Lintasan Sedjarah," *Seminar Kebudajaan Dalam Rangka Pekan Kebudajaan Atjeh Ke-II* (The Second Atjeh Cultural Festival, 20 August-2 September 1972) Dan Dies Natalis Ke XI Universitas Sjiah Kuala, Panitia Pusat Pekan Kebudajaan Atjeh Ke-II, Banda Aceh, 1972, p. 5.

15. G.E. Marrison, "Persian Influences in Malay Life: 1280-1650," *JMBRAS*, vol. 28, Part I, No. 169, 1955, p. 52-53, 55.

16. Roy F. Ellen, "Practical Islam in Southeast Asia," ed. H.B. Hooker, *Islam in Southeast Asia*, p. 72.

17. R. Winstedt, "Muslim Theology, Jurisprudence and History," *JMBRAS*, vol. XXX. Part 3, 1961, p. 112.

18. Moshe Yegar, *Islam and Islamic Institutions in British Malaya* (Jerusalem: Magnes Press, 1979), p. 5.

19. Francis E. Peters, "The Early Empires: Umayyads, Abbasids, Fatimids," ed. Marjorie Kelley, *Islam: The Religious and Political Life of a World Community* (New York: Praeger, 1984), p. 89.

20. Affan Seljuq, "Relations between the Ottoman Empire and the Muslim Kingdoms in the Malay-Indonesian Archipelago," *Der Islam*, 57, 1980, p. 302-303; V.D. Divekar, ed., "Maritime Trading Settlements in the Arabian Sea Region up to 1500 AD," *The Indian Ocean in Focus' International Conference on Indian Ocean Studies*, Section III: The History of Commercial Exchange & Maritime

Transport (Perth: People Helping People, 1979), p. 10.

21. Nuruddin ar-Raniri, *Bustan'us Salatin*, comp. Jelani Harun, Chapter II and III (Kuala Lumpur: Dewan Bahasa dan Pustaka, 2004), p. 338; Azyumardi Azra, *The Transmission of Islamic Reformism to Indonesia: Networks of Middle Eastern and Malay-Indonesian 'Ulama' in the Seventeenth and Eighteenth Centuries* (Hawaii: Hawaii University Press, 1992), p. 119; W. Juynboll and P. Voorhoeve, "Atjeh," *The Encyclopaedia of Islam*, ed. H.A.R. Gibb and J.H. Kramers, vol. I, A-B (Leiden: E.J. Brill, 1979), p. 742; A.C. Milner, "Islam and the Muslim State, ed. M.B. Hooker, *Islam in South-East Asia*, 2nd edition (Leiden: E.J. Brill, 1988), p. 44.
22. Moshe Yegar, *Islam and Islamic Institutions in British Malaya*, p. 7.
23. Nuruddin ar-Raniri, *Bustan'us Salatin*, p. 339; Syed Muhammad Naquib al-Attas, *A General Theory of the Islamization of the Malay-Indonesian Archipelago* (Kuala Lumpur: Dewan Bahasa dan Pustaka, 1969), p. 5, 16.
24. Henry Yule; Henri Cordier, *The Book of Ser Marco Polo The Venetian: Concerning the Kingdoms and Marvels of the East*, vol. 2, 3rd edition (New Delhi: Munshiram Manoharlal, 1920), p. 284; A.H. Hill, "Hikayat Raja-Raja Pasai," *JMBRAS*, vol. 33, Part 2, No. 190, June 1960, p. 32; R.O. Winstedt, ed., *The Malay Annals or Sejarah Melayu* (London: School of Oriental Studies, 1938), p. 71.
25. Azyumardi Azra, "Education, Law, Mysticism: Constructing Social Realities," *Islamic Civilization in the Malay World* (Istanbul: Ircica, 1997), p. 156; Ali Hasjmy, "Banda Aceh Darussalam Pusat Kegiatan Ilmu dan Kebudayaan," *Seminar Sejarah Masut dan Berkembangnya Islam di Aceh dan Nusantara*, Di Aceh Timur, 25-30 September, 1980, p. 3.
26. Taufik Abdullah, "Political Images and Cultural Encounter: The Dutch in the Indonesian Archipelago," *Studia Islamika: Indonesian Journal for Islamic Studies*, vol I., No. 3, 1994, p. 7; M.J. Pintado, ed., *Portuguese Documents on Malacca*, vol. 1: 1509-1511 (Kuala Lumpur: National Archives of Malaysia, year), p. 341, 407; Azyumardi Azra, *The Transmission of Islamic Reformism to Indonesia: Networks of Middle Eastern and Malay-Indonesian*

'Ulama' in the Seventeenth and Eighteenth Centuries, 1992, p. 100.

27. M.J. Pintado, ed., *Portuguese Documents on Malacca*, vol. 1: 1509-1511, p. 365; S. Soebardi and Woodcroft Lee C.P., "Islam in Indonesia," p. 182.
28. Anthony Reid, "Islamization and Christianization in Southeast Asia: The Critical Phase, 1550-1650, ed. Anthony Reid, *Southeast Asia in the Early Modern Era: Trade, Power and Belief* (Ithaca: Cornell University Press, 1993), p. 164.
29. Azyumardi Azra, "Education, Law, Mysticism: Constructing Social Realities," p. 156.
30. S. Soebardi; C.P. Woodcroft Lee, "Islam in Indonesia", p. 182.
31. Peter G. Riddell, "Aceh in the Sixteenth and Seventeenth Centuries: Serambi Mekkah and Identity," ed. Anthony Reid, *Verandah of Violence: The Background to the Aceh Problem* (Singapore: Singapore University Press, 2006), p. 45.
32. Peter Riddell, *Islam and the Malay-Indonesian World: Transmission and Responses*, p. 104, 110, 116, 123; D.A. Rinkes, *Nine Saints of Java*, trans. H.M. Froger, (Kuala Lumpur: Malaysian Sociological Research Institute, 1996), p. xxxi.
33. Syed Muhammad Naquib el-Attas, *A Commentary on the Hujjat Al-Siddiq of Nur al-Din Al-Raniri* (Kuala Lumpur: Ministry of Culture, 1986), p. 8; Abdul Hadi W.M. and L.K Ara, *Hamzah Fansuri: Penyair Sūfī Aceh* (Jakarta: Lotkala, 1984), p. 26; A.H. Johns, "Islam in the Malay World: An Exploratory Survey with Some Reference to Quranic Exegesis," p. 122.
34. Oman Fathurahman, "The Cultural Emergency Relief Action: The Rebuilding Manuscript Library in Dayah Tanoh Abee," Aceh, http://naskahkuno.blogspot.com/2006/09/cultural-emergency-relief-action.html.
35. Abdul Hadi W.M. and L. K Ara, *Hamzah Fansuri: Penyair Sūfī Aceh*, p. 7; Peter G. Riddell, "Aceh in the Sixteenth and Seventeenth Centuries: Serambi Mekkah and Identity," p. 44.
36. William Marsden, *The History of Sumatra* (Kuala Lumpur: Oxford University Press, 1966), p. 436 (reprint of the 3rd ed.); A.H. Johns, "Malay Sufism," *JMBRAS*, vol. XXX, Part 2, No. 178, August 1957,

p. 10; Anthony Reid, *Southeast Asia in the Age of Commerce 1450-1680,* vol. I: *The Lands below the Winds* (New Hawen, London: Yale University Press, 1988), p. 232; William Marsden, *The History of Sumatra*, p. 436; Arun Das Gupta, *Acheh in Indonesian Trade and Politics: 1600-1641* (New York: Cornell University, 1962), p. 57; A.H. Johns, "Islam in the Malay World: An Exploratory Survey with Some Reference to Quranic Exegesis," p. 121.

37. From my interview with Muḥammad Dahlan in 2005.
38. Arun Das Gupta, *Acheh in Indonesian Trade and Politics: 1600-1641*, p. 75; Ito Takeshi, *The World of the Adat Aceh: A Historical Study of the Sultanate of Aceh*, PhD Dissertation, Australian National University p. 49.
39. B. Schrieke, *Indonesian Sociological Studies*, Part I (Bandung: W. Van Hoeve Ltd—The Hague, 1955), p. 44; Horace St. John, *The Indian Archipelago: Its History and Present State*, vol. I (London: Longman, 1853), p. 91; H.M. Zainuddin, *Tarich Atjeh dan Nusantara*, 1st edition (Medan: Pustaka Iskandar Muda, 1961), p. 275; Denys Lombard, *Kerajaan Aceh Zaman Sultan Iskandar Muda (1607-1636)*, trans. Winarsih Arifin, KPG (Kepustakaan Populer Gramedia) Forum, 2nd edition (Jakarta: Kepustakan Populer Gramedia, 2007), p. 148.
40. Arun Komar Das Gupta, "Iskandar Muda and the Europeans," ed. Ali Hasjmy, *Sejarah Masuk Dan Berkembangnay Islam di Indonesia*, 3rd edition (Ptalmaarif, 1993), p. 45; Barbara Watson Andaya, Y. Leonard Andaya, *A History of Malaysia* (London: Macmillan Press, 1986), p. 61.
41. James Minahan, *Nations without States A Historical Dictionary of Contemporary National Movements* (Connecticut: Greenwood Press, 1996), p. 5; Ito Takeshi, *The World of the Adat Aceh: A Historical Study of the Sultanate of Aceh*, p. 97.
42. Azyumardi Azra, "Education, Law, Mysticism: Constructing Social Realities," p. 156; Ali Hasjmy, "Banda Aceh Darussalam Pusat Kegiatan Ilmu dan Kebudayaan," p. 7.
43. Peter Riddell, *Islam and the Malay-Indonesian World: Transmission and Responses*, p. 103.

44. A.H. Johns, "Islam in the Malay World: An Exploratory Survey with Some Reference to Quranic Exegesis," p. 121; S. Soebardi and C.P. Woodcroft Lee, *Islam in Indonesia*, p. 182.
45. Syed Muhammad Naquib al-Attas, *A General Theory of the Islamization of the Malay-Indonesian Archipelago*, p. 7, 8.
46. Syed Muhammad Naquib al-Attas, *A Commentary on the Hujjat Al-Siddiq of Nur al-Din Al-Raniri*, p. 7.
47. Teuku Iskandar, *Hikayat Aceh*, trans. Abu Bakar (Aceh: Departemen Pendidikan Dan Kebudayaan Direktorat Jenderal Kebudayaan Museum Negeri Aceh), 1986, p. 49-50; Ali Hasjmy, "Banda Aceh Darussalam Pusat Kegiatan Ilmu dan Kebudayaan," p. 9.
48. Peter Riddell, *Islam and the Malay-Indonesian World: Transmission and Responses*, p. 103-104.
49. Ibid., p. 111-132.
50. Ahmed Daudy, *Syeikh Nuruddin Ar-Raniry: Sejarah Hidup, Karya dan Pemikiran* (Banda Aceh: Diterbitkan Oleh Pusat Penelitian Dan Pengkajian Kebudayaan Islam (P3KI), IAIN Ar-Raniry, 2006), p. 37.
51. Oman Fathurahman, "The Cultural Emergency Relief Action: The Rebuilding Manuscript Library in Dayah Tanoh Abee," Aceh, http://naskahkuno.blogspot.com/2006/09/cultural-emergency-relief-action.html. (Note: Even though Baghdad was ruled by the Shiah Safavids from 1623-1638, from 1638 until 1916 it was an Ottoman province.
52. Ali Hāsjmy, ed., *Ulama Aceh* (Aceh: Mujahid Pejuang Kemerdekaan dan Pembangun Tamadun Bangsa, 1997), p. 3, 4.
53. Nakamura Mitsuo, "Introduction," *Islam & Civil Society in Southeast Asia* (Singapore: Institute of Southeast Asian Studies, 2001), p. 8.
54. Roy F. Ellen, "Practical Islam in Southeast Asia," ed., H.B. Hooker, *Islam in Southeast Asia*, p. 73, 76.
55. Ito Takeshi, *The World of the Adat Aceh: A Historical Study of the Sultanate of Aceh*, p. 69-70.
56. Different sources on the number of the books in the DTA library of DTA mention around 1000, 2000, and 3500 books. I prefer the first figure, based upon my interview with Mr Muḥammad Dahlan in

2005 and his observations on the library.

57. Ali Hāsjmy, *Ulama Aceh*, p. 3.
58. Ibid., p. 4.
59. The religious scholar's full name is Shaikh Davud b. Ismail b. Mustafa Rumi. He is also known by the title Teungku Chik di Leupue (Leupue is a district in Banda Aceh, the capital city of Aceh Province), Baba Davud, and Mustafa Rumi. It is believed that his ancestor came from Ottoman lands and that he became a leading student and a *khalīfah* of the well-known religious scholar Abdurrauf as-Singkilî (Syiah Kuala). It is presumed that Baba Davud lived in Banda Aceh sometime during 1650-1750).

    As for his importance in Aceh's history, he was a co-founder of the *Dayah Manyang Leupue* (along with Syah Kuala) and became a scholar in this institution. His *Risalah Masailal Muhtadi li Ikhwanil Muhtadi* has been taught at Islamic institutions in Aceh and around the Malay world. It is still taught in Aceh's religious schools. See Ali Hāsjmy, *Bunga Rampai Revolusi dari Tanah Aceh* [Jakarta: Bulan Bintang, 1978], p. 81). The word Rūm/Rumi refers to the Roma and Byzantine empires in Arab and Persian references. After it became the leading Islamic country in the second half of the 15th century, the Ottoman Empire was also called 'Rum.' This empire's political and cultural power was influential throughout the Malay-Indonesian archipelagos and in other regions of the Islamic world. Malay-Indonesian Islamic communities called the Ottoman Empire 'Raja Rum,' after it conquered Constantinople. See Azyumardi Azra, *The Transmission of Islamic Reformism to Indonesia: Networks of Middle Eastern and Malay-Indonesian 'Ulama' In The Seventeenth and Eighteenth Centuries*, p. 103.
60. Ali Hāsjmy, *Ulama Aceh*, p. 4.
61. The first Shattariyya *khalīfah* in the Indonesian Archipelago was Abdurrauf as-Singkilî. Later, some ulama also went to Arabia to study the Qur'an. This *ṭarīqah* gradually expanded in the archipelago. Thus, some branches of this school can be found in both Sumatra and Java. This expansion also shows that it could hold its own with the other *ṭarīqah*s. See Bruneissen, "Tarikatların

Güneydoğu Asya'daki Kökleri ve Gelişimi," p. 76; İsmail Hakkı Göksoy, "Endonezya'da Tasavvufi Hareketler ve Bazı Özellikleri," *Tasavvuf*, vol. 4, No. 11 (Istanbul: Temmuz-Aralık, 2003), p. 82-84.

62. Hâsjmy, *Ulama Aceh*, p. 5.
63. Ibid., p. 5.
64. Hâsjmy, *Ulama Aceh*, p. 6.
65. Ibid., p. 6, 7.
66. Hâsjmy, *Ulama Aceh*, p. 7.
67. Paul Van't Veer, *Perang Aceh: Kisah Kegagalan Snouck Hurgronje* (Jakarta: Grafiti Pers, 1985), p. 34; Hasan Di Tiro, "The Legal Status of Acheh-Sumatra Under International Law," www.asfnl.org.
68. Ismail Jakub, *Teungku Chik Di Tiro (Muḥammad Saman) Pahlawan Besar Dalam Perang Aceh (1881-1891)* (Jakarta: Bulan Bintang, 1960), p. 39
69. Ismail Jakub, *Teungku Chik Di Tiro (Muḥammad Saman) Palawan Besar Dalam Perang Aceh (1881-1891)*, p. 40; Anthony Reid, "Colonal Transformation: A Bitter Legacy," ed. Anthony Reid, *Verandah of Violence: The Background to the Aceh Problem* (Singapore: Singapore University Press, 2006), p. 100; Ismail Jakub, *Teungku Chik Di Tiro (Muḥammad Saman) Pahlawan Besar Dalam Perang Aceh (1881-1891)*, p. 39-40, 71; M. Hasbi Amiruddin, *The Response of the Ulama Dayah to the Modernization of Islamic Law in Aceh* (Bangi: Penerbit Universiti Kebangsaan Malaysia, 2005), p. 39.
70. Ismail Jakub, *Teungku Chik Di Tiro (Muḥammad Saman) Pahlawan Besar Dalam Perang Aceh (1881-1891)*, p. 71.
71. Hāsjmy, *Ulama Aceh*, p. 8-9.
72. Ibid., p. 9, 12.
73. Ibid., p. 10.
74. Ibid., p. 11-12.
75. Tgk. M. Dahlan al-Fairusy, and Dra Zunaimar, *Katalog Manuskrip Perpustakaan Dayah Tanoh Abee* (Banda Aceh: Pusat Dokumentasi dan Informasi Aceh, 1993).
76. Oman Fathurahman, "The Cultural Emergency Relief Action: The Rebuilding Manuscript Library in Dayah Tanoh Abee," Aceh, http://naskahkuno.blogspot.com/2006/09/cultural-emergency-relief-action.html.

4

Legal developments in the Ottoman state (1299-1926)

Ahmed Akgündüz[1]

Abstract

This article outlines the course of legal development throughout the Ottoman period. In a sense, the main topic will be introduced here. I have divided the Ottoman empire's history into two distinct periods: legal developments until the *Tanẓīmāt* reforms (699-1255/1299-1839) and legal developments in the post-*Tanẓīmāt* period (1255-1345/1839-1926). According to Sunnī Islamic law, the *ulū al-amr* have the following legislative powers: they can codify current Sharī'ah decrees like the *Majallah*; prefer and codify the various rulings made by the religious scholars, such as some of the preferences contained within in Ottoman Family Law legislation dated 1917; authorise the state to pass laws to maintain social order when faced with certain permissible issues; or ascribe limited legislative powers in some legal fields, such as determining the penalties for *ta'zīr* crimes (those which are not specifically mentioned in the Qur'an).

The Ottoman empire used all of these techniques, and thus we have an unlimited number of legal records and codes that deal with such matters. The legal rulings contained in books on *fiqh* began to be collected in the form of codes, instructions, and regulations through legal arrangements in order to meet the needs of the day. The *Majallah*, which was studied under the heading of *mu'āmalāt*, arranged the decrees related to loans, property, and procedures into a code of 1,851 articles. The land law, which consisted of *fatwā*s and *irādah*s (edicts promulgated by the sultan) regarding land, are the most typical examples of this.

Introduction

Before the *Tanẓīmāt* period, Islamic law dominated the Ottoman legal system. While this is true in general terms, it is important to make a distinction between private and public law. The Ottomans adopted Islamic private law in full, and its provisions were studied in great detail in the four basic sources: the Qur'an, the Sunnah, *ijmā'* (consensus), and *qiyās* (analogy). The resulting rules were compiled, and the elaboration of private law based upon the existing rules continued. The sultans only interfered with the *qāḍīs'* (judges) judgements in matters related to private law if they considered the rulings to be unjust. This was quite normal, as they considered themselves to be the Sharī'ah's protectors. For this reason, Islamic private law continued to be enforced in the Ottoman empire in all matters related to the law of persons, real rights, family, inheritance, obligations, and commercial law.

This was not the case with public law, however, for it gradually became impossible to govern an empire that continued to expand by enforcing only a few rules pertaining to public law. As a result, various administrative systems in the newly conquered lands were adopted during the reigns of the first four sultans. The subsequent Islamic states also complied with these principles and adopted those administrative systems that were compatible with their specific circumstances. For example, the *Majallah* (the Ottoman Penal Code, dated 1858) preferred and codified the rulings of the Ḥanafī legal school as regards Ottoman family law (dated 1917). It was authorised to legislate, for the well-being of society, on certain permissible issues, among them securing the first wife's permission to take another wife and determining the penalties for crimes committed against the state and for those not specifically mentioned in the Qur'an, as we observe in the Ottoman penal code (dated 1858). Its rulings were also followed in making all of the judicial, administrative, financial, and military arrangements needed to execute such public services as detailed in the regulations, especially after the *Tanẓīmāt* era, and in regard to the newly introduced laws related to public land and the *timar* (land granted by Ottoman Sultans) system.

The Ottomans viewed the caliph or sultan (*Imām-i Mashrû'* = Lawful Leader) as Allah's vicegerent on Earth in the sense that he is answerable to Him and has to obey the decrees of the Qur'an and Sunnah. If and when he does not do so, he is no longer entitled to his subjects' obedience. In addition, he is supposed to consult capable and competent statesmen in matters of administering the state. As his authority restricted by the divine decree and the laws derived therefrom, he cannot act as he pleases.

Islam is not comprised solely of religious doctrines; rather, it is a collection of codices and possesses its own legal system. Unfortunately, Europeans and many Muslims who studied in Europe remain unaware of this significant difference. This is an unjustified notion, as a serious reading of the Qur'an will reveal. The Sharī'ah communicated by Prophet Muḥammad (ṣ) cannot be changed or leave matters in doubt. As his statement that "This world is the field of the Hereafter" shows, the worldly sultanate was not neglected. The efforts of the *mujtahid*s (expounders of Islamic laws) are known. We therefore ask those who claim that Islam needs to be reformed by being "brought up to date": If Islam consists merely of the principles of faith, would there remain any hope and sign for its survival?

In the Ottoman empire, Islam consists of two elements: religion and state. Since the Sharī'ah (*Shar'-i Sharīf*) cannot separate these two, it comprises both devotions and acts. Thus the sultan is not only the state's absolute ruler, but also its commander-in-chief and prime imām. As the government is charged with executing the Sharīʿah's decrees as well as imposing and collecting taxes, it is also responsible for observing the devotions.

The Sharīʿah is composed of, in order of importance, the Qur'an, the Sunnah (in the form of books of jurisprudence [*fiqh*]), and *fatāwā* (viz., legal judgements issued by those imāms and *mujtahids* who specialized in jurisprudence). As a matter fact, the Qur'an is the Sharīʿah's foundation. Nevertheless, just as our judges seldom refer to the Constitution's decrees, so do our *qāḍīs* seldom refer to the Qur'an and its interpretations, for the decrees are dispersed throughout the Qur'an and the Sunnah. The Ottoman empire's essential laws are the jurisprudential texts that compile the *fatwās* and Sharīʿah decrees issued by notable *mujtahids*, the first of whom were the Companions, whose agreement is known as *ijmāʿ* (general concurrence and agreement among the legalists). The Qur'an, the Sunnah, and *ijmāʿ* form the essence and foundation of the legal decrees as well as the basis for other codes. The fourth source, *qiyās*, can only be used by those whose intellects have been illumined by the above-mentioned three sources and who obey the decrees thereof.

As a matter of fact, those great *mujtahids* who arranged the Islamic codes resembled the legalists of the Roman empire. Unlike our contemporary lawmakers, *mujtahids* possessed both a spiritual influence and such far-reaching mundane power and influence that even the *qāḍīs* had to obey their judgements. The case of a *qāḍī's* knowledge being comparable to that of a *mujtahid*, however, was an exception for the latter's power and influence was not granted by the ruler but originated from the justified fame they had earned among their peers. In essence, the ruler had no choice but to accept and endorse their judgements without challenge, negotiation, or consultation.

The first jurisprudential work adopted as the empire's official legal code was Ibrahim of Aleppo's (d. 1549) *Multaqā al-Abḥur* during 1648 and 1687. Translated into Turkish upon the order of Muhammad IV and retitled *Mawqûfât*, this Ḥanafī work consists of decrees dealing with *'aqā'id* (the fundamental articles of faith), laws, penalty, family, *ḥajr* (putting a legally incompetent person under restraint), *ḥajz* (confiscation), and international relations. Throughout the empire, which followed the Ḥanafī legal school, each *mujtahid* obeys the judgement made by a jurisprudent (*faqīh*) greater than himself. Accordingly, any jurisprudential books codified and written after this date only interpreted and expounded upon the said work and the *fatwās* upon which the legal system was based.

Traditional and customary rules completed the empire's legal edifice. In spite of this, however, a *qāḍī* could issue a judgement based upon such rules only if the jurisprudential texts specifically stated that these two sets of rules could be consulted.

A sultan could also make laws; however, the real laws were derived from the decrees made in the legal texts, which were derived from the *mujtahids*' interpretation of the Qur'an and the Sunnah. Thus any proposed code, edict, or imperial rescript not endorsed by the Shaikh ul-Islam, a judge, or a *muftī* could be implemented. On the other hand, if the sultan were a learned man who had obtained a diploma from the *muftī*, his regulations, edicts, and decrees would be enforced even in the absence of a *fatwā* to do so. Although he could force a *fatwā* to agree with his will, such a ruling could not violate the Sharī'ah's decrees. According to Europeans, Ottoman codices comprised the sultan's arbitrary decrees. Again, according to current opinions in Europe, the Muhammadan Canonical Law (*al-Sharī'ah al-Muḥammadiyyah*) fully authorized the sultan to act as he pleased and to make whatever laws he wished. As a matter of fact, this allegation is considered a great slander as regards the Sharīʿah and a major sin.

The Sharīʿah determined the sultan's attributes and power. He issued very few decrees concerning the empire's social, economic, and administrative order, which could only be amended according to the time and prevailing conditions. Accordingly, the legislative authority granted to him was restricted. Therefore, Süleyman the Lawmaker formulated a legal code in 1519 and 1566 that dealt with handling administrative and military matters; it remained in force until 1846 and afterwards was corrected and amended by new regulations.[2]

Legal developments until the *Tanẓīmāt* reforms

General information

Before the proclamation in 1839 of the Imperial Decree of Reform (*Khatt-i Sharīf* of Gülhane), the Ottoman legal system covered many fields. First, there were principles of private law or rules of civil law taken completely from Ḥanafī *fiqh*. The Seljuk ruler ʿAlāʾ al-Dīn stressed to Osman I, founder of the Ottoman empire, in a special decree the necessity of abiding by these principles. This decree also conferred upon him legal authority and power and acknowledged his independence. According to this decree, the existing judges were to continue as the enforcers of administrative law in order to ensure that the Sharīʿah would remain the law of the land. Thus, all rulings related to personal and family law, inheritance, contracts, real estate, and *fiqh* were observed and enforced. In penal law, the *ʿuqūbāt* (crimes and punishments) were applied in cases of *ḥudūd* (the class of punishments that are fixed for certain crimes) and *jināyāt* (criminal code). As for *taʿzīr* (reproof) crimes and penalties, however, authority was invested in the *ulū al-amr* (state authorities and judges).[3]

The Ottoman empire began to implement Islam's legal decrees from the very first years of its foundation. As a matter of fact, the first state officials appointed by 'Uthmān Beg were *qāḍīs* and *subashis* (chief of police) vested with the authority to execute the *qāḍīs*' judgements.[4] In addition to Islamic law, the state's official legal system was influenced, to a certain degree, by the empire's unique features. This influence has been interpreted in several ways. According to some, the empire applied Islamic law only in certain branches of private law and largely in a symbolic fashion, while following customary law (viz., the sultan's will) in other fields. According to others, however, Islamic law was replaced by customary law especially in the field of public law, for the legal texts contained no suitable decrees that could be applied.[5]

But neither of these opinions reflect the truth, for their adherents have been unable to support their claims through archival documents. The Ottomans did not follow a different path than other Muslims did when it came to implementing Islamic law. It is clear judgements were implemented, based upon the Ḥanafī legal school viewpoint. Leaving aside the application of any opinion against Islamic law, they even bound the implementation of non-Ḥanafī rulings to very strict formal conditions. Nevertheless, wherever Islamic law bestowed a limited legislative power upon the authorities and officials *(ulū al-amr)*, certain legislative formalities were followed and thus determined the laws, which were also known as customary law. These two groups looked after the "affairs of the servants of Allah upon the basis of Sharī'ah and Laws" and settled all legal disputes by referring to the "Holy Sharī'ah and the Blessed Decrees of Laws."[6] Since we will analyze the details of this subject in the section on public law, here we will only make brief references to certain historical developments.

In our view, the most noteworthy features of Islamic law during this period are the following:

a) The method of teaching Islamic law and settling legal disputes on that basis, which had been the practice of earlier Turkish Muslim states, continued to be applied. Again, the *qāḍī's* major legal references were the books on *fiqh*. Chosen from madrasah graduates, these officials were well versed in *fiqh*. Moreover, the state appointed eminent *qāḍī*s to the office of *qāḍī 'askar*. As a result of this long-standing policy, the traditional method of studying Islamic jurisprudential texts, annotations, and footnotes continued. Molla Khusraw's (d. 885/1480) *Al-Ghurar* and *Al-Durar* (which interpreted the former) were used at the court as manuals. On the other hand, Ibrahim al-Ḥalebi's *Multaqā al-Abḥur* and Shaykh al-Islām Abdurrahman (Dāmād) Effendi's *Majma' al-Anhur* (an exegesis of the former) are examples of such works.[7] As a matter of fact, the *Multaqā al-Abḥur* became the empire's official legal code in 1648 and 1697 by imperial decrees.[8]

b) Due to the sufficient number of systematic books on Islamic jurisprudence, Ottoman jurists focused on codifying books of *fatāwā* compiled in response to questions submitted. Although such works had existed in the past, their number increased greatly as they now assumed the function of a Supreme Court. Accordingly, every officially appointed jurist who issued *fatāwā* or executed important judicial offices compiled his rulings. The resulting books, which followed the system of *fiqh* books, consisted of legal decrees on issues for which no *fiqh* had been developed and generally functioned as a catechism. Most of them provide the legal texts that serve as the legal bases for *fatāwā*. Some journals, such as the *Fatāwā* of Abu al-Su'ūd Effendi and Abdurrahim (Menteşezade) Effendi, remain the most significant references for contemporary Islamic law.[9]

c) Another noteworthy feature of that period is that the *Divan-i Humayun* (the Imperial Council) and the *Padishah*, who functioned as the *ulū al-amr,* implemented important legal arrangements in certain areas under the name of *Qānūnnāme* (legal code) with the legislative power vested in them by Islamic law. Actually, some weak views of Islamic law that fell under the authority of a particular authorised party (i.e., the *walī al-amr* [caliph, president, etc.]) and thus restricted certain Sharīʿah decrees and implementation were preferred and applied if they were considered necessary for the public good. In effect, this turned a weak view into a strong view based upon the authorised party's preference. Given that such legal decrees may change over time points to this type of decree. Moreover, when the ruler issued an order on a matter that was not overtly against the Sharīʿah, it was adopted as a principle to be obeyed just like a law. The *Majallah* explained this principle in the following terms:

- 1801. The jurisdiction and powers of the judge are limited by time and place and certain matters of exception.
- If an order is issued by the sovereign authority, those actions relating to a particular matter shall not be heard in the public interest; the judge may not try such action. Action, the judge may be authorized to hear certain matters only in a particular court and no other. The judge may try only those cases he is authorized to hear and judge,
- An order is issued by sovereign authority to the effect that in a certain matter the opinion of a certain jurist is most in the interest of the people, and most suited to the needs of the moment, and that action should be taken in accordance therewith. The judge may not act in such a matter in accordance with the opinion of a jurist that is in conflict with that of the jurist in question. If he does so, the judgement will not be executory.[10]

Ottoman legislators who took the aforementioned legal principles as their basis actually legislated more than 1000 codes to deal with property issues, prescription, *ta'zīr* penalties, and other matters. The codifications undertaken by Muhammad the Conqueror, Süleyman the Lawmaker, and Ahmad III were among the general and most well-known examples. We will refer to these codifications, which were actually complementary parts of Islamic law, from time to time.[11]

d) Before the *Tanẓīmāt* reforms, other legislation movements emerged due to the empire's close relationship with Europe's legal and economic life. Nevertheless, the actual beginning of the codification movements in today's sense was the promulgation of the *Tanẓīmāt* movement.

Although some researchers hold that the legal progressions display a customary law (*'urfī ḥuqūq*) that was completely distinct from Islamic law, this was not the case. We will provide supporting evidence for this statement in the section on public law.[12]

The branches of law arranged by legal codes (Qānūnnāmes)

Indicating those branches of law arranged by legal codes involves indicating the degree of legislative authority granted by Islam to the rulers, as understood within the Ottoman empire, and what would happen if the Ottoman legal system became secular. As it would take too much space to expound upon the legal decrees, contents, and Sharī'ah basis of the legal codes, here we will only look at the two most comprehensive examples to clarify the nature of the Ottoman legal system. It is possible to classify all Ottoman laws into two main exemplary categories: (1) essential Ottoman law, which covers various decrees pertaining to different branches of law. We will base our analysis upon Sultan Süleyman the Lawmaker's law, since it is the most comprehensive and regular, and (2) Sultan Mehmed the Conqueror's Law for Organization, which organize the questions of constitutional and administrative law.

Sultan Süleyman's consisted of three chapters: penalties, property and financial law, and various private matters. The first chapter arranged the *ta'zīr* (reproof) penalties pertaining to criminal law, or rather punishments consisting of fines and beating with a stick conveyed to rulers in four sections. Seven types of crimes and *ḥadd* penalties (principles pertaining to all crimes committed against an individual and their penalties) were not included in this law, for they had been arranged according to the Sharī'ah rules codified in the jurisprudential literature. In other words, only one-fifth of criminal law was dealt with; the jurisprudential literature took care of the remaining four-fifths.

The second chapter arranged some decrees regarding property and financial law. The basis of this chapter was the state property (land subject to *kharāj* [tribute]) and excise taxes collected in return for the *kharāj* tax (land tax paid by non-Muslim subjects). One topic, known as *bāj*, covered the details of the chapter on '*āshir*' (tithe collector) in the jurisprudential literature. As a consequence, this chapter arranged property law (land law) issues, the origin and essence of which are based on the Sharī'ah, and some topics on financial law. But issues such as *yaya* (infantry), *musallam* (recruits engaged in military service in lieu of tax payments), and the like pertain to military law, which was not a very important among the branches of law.

The third chapter arranged some private topics concerning military and administrative law. Thus this general law, which formed a basis for 90 percent of the Ottoman legal codes, codifies one-fifth of criminal and military law, solely state land under property law, and some matters related to administrative law.

Our second example, the Law for Organization, arranged only some issues concerning administrative law and, by exception, constitutional law. On the basis of these brief explanations, the following question ought to be posed: Were Ottoman legal codices composed only of criminal law, finance law, property law, administrative law, and military law? Of course not. Then what was the real legal system? It is possible to answer to this question by undertaking a brief scrutiny of the Sharīʿah courts' records, which were examples of applied law.

Nevertheless, it can be stated that these codices were composed of military law, administrative law, certain fields of financial law, and such principles of criminal law with respect to crimes and punishments that were not contrary to Islam,[13] for Islam bestowed the necessary authority upon the religious scholars and the rulers.

The Ottoman legal system according to the Sharīʿah courts' records

The decrees of the Ottoman courts, known as the Sharīʿah courts' records (*al-Sijillāt al-Sharʿiyyah*) are the most important source for providing an accurate view of the Ottoman legal system. Analysing these records will allow us to see clearly the sources of Ottoman law; to what extent the Ottomans applied the Sharīʿah the restricted legislative powers entrusted to the sultans and state officials; and the practical fields of consuetudinary laws, which were not mentioned in the Qur'an or the Sunnah and thus were left to the limited legislative power of those state officials of the time (viz., issues arranged by the legal codes). Adopting any opinion on Ottoman law without studying these records would be both prejudicial and unscientific. Accordingly, we will now study closely how these records arranged the various branches of law.

Personal law

This category was considered a branch of private law. Ottoman law recognized both natural and legal persons, and the Sharī'ah decrees regarding competence, disappearance, personal rights, and similar issues were applied precisely. The essential reference in this topic are the Sharī'ah rules found in the jurisprudential texts.

Those exemplary records on family law reveal how the Muslims' family structure, becoming engaged and married, and similar institutions were formed in conformity with the Sharī'ah and that women also had the right to obtain a divorce (namely, this was not a male-only right, as many people believe). Issues related to children, guardianship, maintenance allowance, and similar issues, however, were judged in accordance with Islamic leal texts.

The majority of those records dealing with inheritance law are composed of inheritance contracts (*tahāruj*), the state's right of inheritance, heritage divisions, and exemplary wills. In all of these, the principles of *'ilm al-farā'iḍ* (dividing an inheritance) were strictly observed. The only exception is that of transferring the disposal right for the public estate, which was left to the legal codes. Judgements handed down in cases related to commodities, loans, and trade followed precisely the decrees of transactions (*mu'āmalāt*) found in the Islamic legal texts. The sole exception was the disposal right for public estates, which was arranged via legal codes.

These examples prove that the Sharī'ah rules as regards the state's private law were applied and that the *dhimmīs* (non-Muslim subjects) were judged (at their own discretion) by the Sharī'ah's decrees on issues that did not involve civil status (*al-aḥwāl al-shakhṣiyyah*) and devotion (*'ibādah*).

Criminal law

Since discussions about Ottoman law focus on civil law, it will be useful to study this subject from the perspective of the Sharī'ah courts' records. In essence, those records show that in the case of criminal law, the Ottomans applied the Sharī'ah's decrees. Nevertheless, this issue should be evaluated within the framework of its own features. Islamic law classifies crimes and penalties into three main groups, as follows: (1) Those mentioned specifically in the Qur'an and/or the Ḥadīth literature (*ḥadd*), such as slandering a virtuous woman (*ḥadd al-qadf*), robbery *(ḥadd al-sirqah),* banditry (*qat' al-ṭarīq),* adultery *(ḥadd al-zinā),* drinking alcoholic beverages *(ḥadd al-shurb),* and insurgence *(ḥadd al-baghy, hirābah).* The records show that the Ottomans applied the mandated punishments; (2) Crimes committed against individuals. Again, the records show that the Ottomans applied the relevant retaliation (*al-qiṣāṣ*), blood money (*al-diyah*), and other mandated penalties. Even 'Umar Hilmi Effendi's *Mi'yār al-'Adālah* (Criteria of Justice) was adopted as a semi-official penal code toward the end of the empire; and (3) Other crimes and punishments, such as *jazā' al-ta'zīr, jazā' al-siyāsah al-Shar'iyyah* or *jazā' al-siyāsah,* the degrees and methods of application of which were transferred to senior empire officials. These crimes and penalties, as well as the relevant decrees, were mentioned in the first sections of the general legal codes devised by Sultan Mehmed the Conqueror, Bayezid II, Selim the Excellent, and Süleyman the Lawmaker. The records use the term "punishment of reproof following the code" for such penalties.

These same court records reveal that the Ottomans applied the Sharī'ah's regulations with reference to the law of trial procedure evidence, whereas in *rasm al-qismah* and similar exceptional issues they adhered to the traditions, customs, and socioeconomic conditions of the time. The most outstanding example of this is the issue of deeds. Since this issue is very explicit, we will not look at the details here. On the other hand, judgements related to execution and bankruptcy were arranged according to the Sharīʿah's principles, and the many problems associated with the laws of finance were also resolved in conformity with the essentials of Sharīʿah law. Administrative and constitutional law, composed of imperial edicts (*firmans*), codes of law (*yasaqnamahs*), *adālatnamahs* (sultanic rescript), and rescripts, was also arranged within the framework of the limited legislative power entrusted to the empire's officials.

These records are the most important evidence of what we have presented so far. Recent research into them conducted by historians, jurists, and theologians prove the above-mentioned facts exactly. We now conclude this issue by citing Fethi Gedikli's doctoral thesis, "*Muḍārabah* Partnership in the Ottoman *Sharʿiyyah* Records in the XVI and XVII Centuries: The Example of Galata," which shows that the decrees contained within these records were in complete accordance with the Sharīʿah's rules as found in the books of Islamic jurisprudence.[14]

Ottoman law as a whole

The analysis presented above leads to the following conclusions. First, Ottoman law was restricted to administrative law, various subjects related to constitutional law (a very rare occurrence), property law (with respect to state land), military law, financial law, specific crimes and their punishments (*taʿzīr*) mentioned in the Qur'an and Ḥadīth literature,and decrees related to some exceptional issues of private law. Decrees adhered to the codified Sharīʿah principles, for those matters upon which the rulers could rule would be decided according to such secondary sources as the public good, custom, and traditions. Since any legal system could not consist only of the above-mentioned subjects, no one can claim that those issues were arranged in a way that ignored the Sharīʿah. Moreover, looking at these legal codes, which make up only about 15 percent of the Ottoman legal system, and not examining their contents prevents us from calling a legal system secular or anything else. Second, studying these records prove that the Ottoman empire regarded the Sharīʿah decrees as the basis for personal law, family law, inheritance law, *jus obligationum*, commodity law, and financial law; for all branches of private law, including international private law; for procedural public law; for 80 percent of penal law; the majority of financial law; and the general principles of *jus gentium*, administrative law, and constitutional law. All of these, when taken together, make up about 85 percent of all legislation.[15]

Legal developments after the *Tanẓīmāt* reforms

We will concentrate here on certain information that indicates the course of these developments. A completely new page was opened in the history of Ottoman law with the *Gülhane Khatt-i Humayunu* (imperial edict), which was promulgated at Gülkhane Park on 26 *Shaʿbān* 1255/1839. The westernization movement, which started with Sultan Selim III and continued with Sultan Mahmud II, began to yield fruit with the *Tanẓīmāt Firman* (imperial decree) promulgated under Sultan Abdulmejid. It stated, in part: "Some new codes must be introduced so that the Ottoman empire can be governed in the best way. These codes will be legislated particularly in the fields of the security of lives, property and chastity, tax law and the army." These laws would be prepared "in perfect pursuance to ... Sharīʿah Law and the Decrees of Holy Qur'an."[16] Nevertheless, there was some duality in Ottoman law after 1839, for the supreme authorities (*ulū al-amr*) exceeded the limits of their authority from time to time and discriminated between legal regulations as codes with a religious and national basis and those codes with a European basis. As we will discuss such discrimination later, here we will merely indicate the outstanding features of this period:

a) The Sharīʿah decrees in the *fiqh* books began to be codified, according to the requirements of the time, in the form of codes, instructions, and regulations through legal arrangements. The *Majallah*, which was studied in books on jurisprudence under *muʿāmalāt*, arranged decrees regarding loans, property, and procedures into a code of 1,851 articles. Another category was the land law, which consisted of *fatwā*s and *irādah*s (the sultan's edicts) regarding land. These two categories are the most typical examples of this.[17]
b) The trend of codification continued and even expanded as the reasons for such works increased. These movements gained momentum due to the development and increase of both domestic and international economic relationships, the resulting emergence of new legal institutions, growing companies in Europe (e.g., insurance and brokerage companies), the severe requirement for certain contractual conditions of which the Ḥanafī school did not approve (e.g., the *pey akcha [ʿurbūn]* earnest money) the government's desire to regulate real estate, the requirement for registering a title deed and similar formal conditions, and the falling number of wise Muslim jurists who could find Sharīʿah solutions to newly emerging legal issues. The limits of the legislative power which the *ulū al-amr* could wield in commercial law, real estate law, and the law of procedures were excessive. Some codes, like the law of criminal procedures, were adapted from Europe word for word.[18]

In our opinion, the codes introduced after the *Tanẓīmāt* were of two types with respect to quality:

The first group consisted of codes of legal provisions that were directly related to the quintessence of the law and required systematic changes, such as whether one could sell a piece of real estate in the possession of a minor or regulations connected with menstruation (*'iddah*). Jurists endeavoured to follow Islamic legal principles while codifying the aforesaid type of decrees. They did not interfere with the *ḥadd* penalties and *qiṣāṣ* (retaliation), but only arranged the *ta'zīr* penalties that were left to the rulers' discretion. Nevertheless, some violations took place in that field as well.

The second group consisted of formal laws in which the changes made did not necessitate any changes in the system. The Law of Criminal Procedures (dated 1296/1879) and the Trade Law could be considered examples of this group. Legal arrangements were also carried out in such fields as insurance and interest, about which either no decree had been issued or the practice had been forbidden. Many of these types of laws were borrowed from the West after the *Tanẓīmāt* had been proclaimed.[19]

c) Turs began to move beyond their centuries-long adherence to the Ḥanafī *maḍhab* after the *Tanẓīmāt* reforms, particularly during the period which would ultimately end in Turkey becoming a republic. Those jurists who studied different legal codes, especially European civil law, worked on formulating similar domestic codes that were to be introduced and enforced in Ottoman society and preparing them in such a way that they would conform with the time's perception and requirements. They analysed the views of the other *madhhabs* and then began to refer to the *fiqh* books of all Sunnī legal schools; however, very little non-Ḥanafī jurisprudence actually appeared in the *Majallah*. The first and most significant example of this new legislation was the decree designed to regulate family law (1917). The committees of *al-aḥwāl al-shakhṣiyyah (Family Law)* and *Wājibāt (requirements)*, which were established after the Republican Age began, adopted that method as their basis of their own work. Furthermore, those committees went even further and sought to integrate European laws into the principles of Islamic law.[20] The laws introduced by the *Majlis al-Mab'ūsān* (Parliament), which became the legislator of Ottoman Law along with the constitutional monarchy promulgated after *Tanẓīmāt* reforms, were disputed because they did not, in the opinion of some, always conform with the Sharī'ah.

The history of Islamic law in the Ottoman empire can be divided into three periods. The first period, which lasted from the empire's founding until the *Tanẓīmāt* reforms (1839), was characterized by reliance upon *fiqh* books and legal texts (*qānūns* and *fatwās*). The texts of the laws enforced during this period are recorded in the *Divan-i Humayun* (the record of the state). In 1247/1831, these texts were printed and announced in the *Taqwīm-i Waqāyi'* (an official paper giving in full all laws and decrees. There second period, from the *Tanẓīmāt* reforms to 1324/1906, saw the reinstitution of the constitutional system of government. The third, and final, period can be said to be those laws promulgated after that event and up to the end of the First World War.[21]

Ottoman Civil Law: the *Majallah*

We will give more detailed information about the *Majallah* in the fourth book (on Private Law); here, we provide general information relating to the history of Islamic law.

The full name of the Ottoman Civil Code (hereinafter *Majallah*) was the *Majallah al-Aḥkām al-'Adliyyah.* In Europe, it was known as the *Qawānīn al-Mulkiyyah li al-Dawlah al-'Aliyyah* (The Civil Code of the Ottoman Empire). The *Majallah* was a codification of those Sharī'ah decrees concerning loans, effects, and the law of procedure that had existed in books on *fiqh* based on the ruler's restricted power, which was expressed as legislating Sharīʿah decrees. The actual term is defined as a book comprising diverse issues. Since it is out of the question that the *Majallah* would include the opinions of anyone other than those involved in Islamic law, non-Ḥanafī views were included only when dealing with some exceptional issues. Due to the reasons we will indicate below, those Sharīʿah decrees in the *Multaqā*, which had served as a law book for centuries, was developed into a law book comprised of 1,851 articles and in close reference to other books on *fiqh* and *fatāwā* The resulting law book was called the *Majallah*.

It was produced mainly to meet the needs of the newly established civil courts (*Mahkama-i Nizāmiyyah*) and to increase the competency of its judges. As was the case with all post-*Tanẓīmāt* arrangements, there was pressure from the West. Since *Tanẓīmāt Firman* (Edict of Reforms) had been promulgated in consultation with the West, its demands were always a driving force as well. The *Majallah* gives an additional reason for its preparation: over time the Ḥanafī School had developed several views on some matters. While these had been adopted and applied for several centuries by the various Turkish kingdoms, it was now time to single out and apply the strongest view.

Judgements arising from *ijtihād* may change along with changing customs and traditions in order to ensure the public good and for similar circumstances. This principle is stated in the *Majallah* "The amendment of some legal decrees cannot be denied with the changing times."[22] Furthermore, the social, legal, and economic changes before and after the *Tanẓīmāt* actually necessitated the preparation of a civil law. The *Majallah* attempted to respond to these newly emerging requirements within the framework of Islamic law by abandoning, whenever possible, the Ḥanafī School's dominant opinion and referring to the views of the other legal schools in the *Majallah's* amendments.

These above-mentioned reasons show that legislation movements in the West and in the preparation of *Majallah* underwent similar developments in the social, economic, and legal fields. There was, in fact, no similarity with respect to the other reasons. Unlike the West, the *Majallah* was not the result of any developments in the science of law or of any new movements in philosophy or law. Rather several reasons, which we mentioned above and which were not related to the quintessence of the issue, led to the codification of the existent Sharīʿah decrees. This point is worth mentioning.

Deficient as it might have been, the *Majallah* truly merited its status of the empire's civil law, for it contained those Sharīʿah decrees concerning the procedures related in *fiqh* books that were codified through the ruler's use of his restricted legislative authority. This legislative power was only a formal power, and the ruler's power was reflected only in some disputed matters. Furthermore, all Sharīʿah decrees bound the empire's Muslims due to its being ratified by the ruler from the position of jurisdiction, which was indicated in its Protocol. While the *Majallah* did lack chapters on such matters as family and inheritance law, which prevented it from becoming an absolute civil code, it actually originated from the fact that Islamic law granted privileges to minorities regarding civil status. The fact that the *Majallah* consisted of procedural decrees was the result of that era's existing realities and the structure of the Ottoman judicial institution.

The *Majallah* followed the system found in the *fiqh* books. In other words, and contrary to the allegations of some, it was not casuistic. Perhaps this is because they went into details on some issues in connection with the tradition of codification, at that time a mixed method that could be called *abstract/casuistic* Its expressions are accurate and fluent, in perfect Turkish. The objection that a civil code cannot be composed of just 1,851 articles—aside from those on family and inheritance—is unjustified, for the *Majallah* consisted of decrees dealing not only with effects and loans, but also with procedure. If some 400 articles deal with procedure, 200 with commerce, and 100 with general principles, there are still 1,100 articles left over. In fact, the Turkish Civil Code and the Law of Obligations have more than 900 articles on goods and loans. We hold that a difference of 200 articles does not necessarily require any methodical differentiation.

The Protocol mentions that the *Majallah's* sources were books dealing with Ḥanafī *fiqh* their explications and footnotes, and books of *fatāwā*, in brief, Islamic law. As a matter of fact, the *Mir'āh al-Majallah* was written to prove that very fact and to show the sources of the *Majallah's* articles. Claims that *Majallah* was prepared under the influence of the Napoleonic Code or Roman law are false.

The *Majallah* consisted of a prologue and sixteen books. The first 100 articles cover general law principles under the category *al-Qawā'id al-Fiqhiyyah* (The General Rules of Islamic Jurisprudence). It was designed to shed light on Islamic law's general spirit and serve as an exclusive guide for judges. Since these rules ensured the easy comprehension of individual legal issues, they also constituted the sources and rationale of legal decrees. They are also consistent with natural law and the principles at which modern law had arrived after many disputes and phases of progression. These said rules might be classified as rules of legal interpretation, procedure, prescription, obligation, participation, administrative disposals, wrongs, and the like. Most of the remaining sixteen books of pertained to loans, goods, and the law of procedure. The chapter concerning incorporations was quite significant.

At that time the French encouraged the Ottoman empire adopt French civil law, a proposal that Grand Vizier Ali Pasha cautiously submitted to the sultan in 1284/1867. The sultan, however, had already instructed the grand vizier to have the *Code Civile* translated from Arabic to Turkish. Our view here is supported by the efforts of the then-charge d'affaires of France in Istanbul. In fact, Jawdat Pasha mentions in his *Ma'rūḍāt* the role of French ambassador De Bourre, who stated plainly that various Ottoman civil servants had become tools of French policy. Consequently, the French ambassador convinced Ali Pasha to pursue France's agenda. But his efforts proved to be of no avail, for in a dispute among the Council of Ministers, the motion for adopting French civil law was rejected due to the objections made by Ahmed Jawdat Pasha,[23] Fuad Pasha and Shirwani-zādah Rushdu Pasha and despite the insistent demands of Ali Pasha and Qabuli Pasha. The sultan eventually decreed that the *Majallah* be prepared.

The Association of the *Majallah* (*Majalla Jam'iyyeti*) was formed to devise this new civil law code. Under the chairmanship of Ahmed Jawdat Pasha, Minister of *Dīwān-i Aḥkām-i 'Adliyyah* (Civil Court), this body prepared the first 100 articles and the first book, *Kitāb al-Buyū'*. These were submitted to the scrutiny of jurists, particularly the Shaykh al-Islām. After the necessary corrections had been made, it was submitted to the Office of the Grand Vizier with a Protocol (dated 1285/1869) and took effect following the imperial decree issued that same year. Fifteen other books were added later on. The final book, *Kitāb al-Qaḍā'*, was dated 1293/1876.

During this code's eight-year (1868-1876) preparation, those civil servants who were opposed to it and French ambassador De

Bourre, did their best to undermine it. As result of these efforts, Jawdat Pasha was dismissed as Minister of *Dīwān-i Aḥkām-i 'Adliyyah* in 1287/1869 and, after the fourth book was completed, from the association as well. However, those civil servants who maintained that his presence was essential to carrying out this task had him reappointed and promoted him to even higher positions. The eminent jurists of the time were consulted, especially Jawdat Pasha, in the preparation of *Majallah.*

Since the *Majallah* comprised significant reforms with respect to the legal system and its contents and had been written with very sound legal reasoning, it was adopted and applied in present-day Turkey, Egypt, the Hejaz, Iraq, Syria, Jordan, Lebanon, Cyprus, Palestine, and Israel. In fact, it remained in force until 1928 in Albania and Bosnia-Herzegovina, and until 1984 in Kuwait. Research has revealed that some of its decrees remain in force in Israeli law even today.[24]

We should mention here that in the Ottoman empire, the relationship between the four Sunnī *madhhabs* was ranked accordingly. The Sharī'ah court *qāḍīs* ruled according to their own school and would naturally consult a *muftī* from his own school. If the case was referred to a higher court or a *majlis,* however, it came into a multi-school body.[25]

Conclusion

Islamic law is based upon the broadest and most comprehensive systems of legislation in the world. It was applied, through various schools of thought, from one end of the Muslim world to the other and had a great impact on many nations and cultures, mainly by way of Andalucia, Sicily, Turkestan, Bukhara, and the Balkans. In our owns time, it is considered one of the sources of international law. The Turks, who even while they were nomads had formulated important legal principles and institutions, became Islamic law's latest supporters after their conversion to Islam.

The judicial organization or the Sharī'ah court system arose during the empire's early period. Offices such as the Shaykh al-Islām, *qāḍī 'askar*, and *qāḍī* formed the main part of the Ottoman judicial body. Several developments affecting the Ottoman judiciary occurred under Mahmud II, during the *Tanẓīmāt* period (1839-1876), and in the following period. These developments brought about changes in the status and function of the key Ottoman judicial officials, namely, the *shaykh ul-Islam*, *Qadhaskar*, and *qāḍī*.

Based upon on evaluation of over 10,000 Sharī'ah records, I have argued that any assessment of Ottoman law that does not use these records is inadequate. The Ottomans applied the Sharī'ah, which gives restricted legislative power to the sultans and the statesmen (*ulū al-amr*). The field of customary law, which is not specifically mentioned in the Qur'an or the Sunnah, was left to the ruler's limited legislative power. The Sharī'ah rules in the *fiqh* books were considered fundamental references.

Ottoman court records were preserved better than they were in other pre-modern Muslim lands because the empire took care to preserve them in its laws, decrees, and some local orders. The first law dealing with the preservation of court records, a legal decree enacted by Sultan Bāyezid I, contained rules about writing and preserving documents and registration procedures. Under Mehmed II (1451-1481), we can see the same rules in the Ottoman legal code. After him, the authorities enacted new and independent legal guidelines on how to register these records. Known as *Qanunnāme-i Rusūm* (Legal Code for Court Fees). After the *Tanẓīmāt* movement, new arrangements were made for writing and preserving these records.

The various codifications of Islamic law started again with *Majallah*, which arranged the laws of property, loans, and procedures: the *Majallah al-Aḥkām al-'Adliyyah* an official Ottoman codification of Ḥanafī law undertaken by a special committee, the *Majalla Jam'iyeti,* headed by Ahmed Jawdat Pasha. It represents the last stage in the development of Ḥanafī doctrine. The committee's report is worth reading. The most important commentary upon it was Khoja Emin Efendi Zadeh Ali Haydar's four-volume Turkish-language *Durar al-Ḥukkām Sharḥ Majallah al-Aḥkām,* which was published in Constantinople (1330/1914). The best and most scholarly work of its kind, it is still used as a text in the Istanbul Law School and by lawyers and judges.

Notes

1. Prof Dr Ahmed Akgündüz is a professor of Islamic Law at the Islamic University of Rotterdam.
2. PA, YEE, no. 14-1540, *Devlet-i Aliyye'deki Islahât-ı Kanuniye* (Legal Reforms in the Ottoman State), pp. 5ff, 26-27.
3. Abu al-Ula Mardin, "Development of the Sharia under the Ottoman Empire," Majid Khadduri and Herbert J. Liebesny, *Origin and Development of Islamic Law, Law in the Middle East* (Clark: The Lawbook Exchange, Ltd., 2008), pp. 279-280.
4. Osman Nuri Ergin, *Majalla-i Umur-i Baladiyyah* (Istanbul: 1922), vol. I, pp. 265ff; cf. Abu al-Ula Mardin, "Development of the Sharia under the Ottoman Empire," pp. 279-284.
5. Ömer Lütfi Barkan, *XV ve XVI. Asırlarda Osmanlı İmparatorluğunda Ziraī Ekonominin Hukukī ve Malī Esastarı* (Legal and Financial Principles of Agricultural Economy in the Ottoman State in the XV and XVI Centuries) (Istanbul: Introduction, 1943), pp. iv-xxv.
6. *Tawqi'i Abdurrahman Pasha Qānūnnāmesi* (Codes of Tawkii Abdurrahman Pasha) MTM, vol. I, pp. 498-500; cf. Barkan, *Qānūnlar*, pp. ixff; Ergin, *Majalla-i Umur*, vol. l, pp. 273ff.; Kafesoğlu,

Türk Millī Kültürü, pp. 346 ff; *İlmiye Salnāmesi*, (Istanbul: Mashikhat-i Islamiye, 1334/1916), pp. 316ff.

7. The Committee, *'İlmiye Salnāmesi*, pp. 308ff.
8. PA, *Ottoman Archives*, YEE-14-1540, p. 14.
9. The Committee, *İlmiye Salnāmesi*, pp. 314ff; Barkan, *Qānūnlar*, pp. xxxivff; Muṣṭafā Aḥmad Zarqā, *al-Fiqh al-Islamī fī Thawbih al-Jadīd*, vol. l (Damascus: Dār al-Kutub, 1964), pp. 201-202.
10. The Committee, *Majalla-i Aḥkām-i 'Adliyyah* (The Ottoman Courts Manual [Ḥanafī]), Article: 1801.
11. Akgündüz, *Osmalı Qanunnameleri ve Hukuki Tahlilleri,* vol. 1-9 (Istanbul: OSAV, 1989-1992); Muḥammad Amīn b. 'Umar b. al-'Ābidīn, *Radd al-Muḥtār 'alā al-Durr al-Mukhtār*, vols. 1-6, (Cairo: Maktabah al-Ḥalabī,1967), vol. I, pp. 55, vol. 3, pp. 395-396; Zarqā, *al-Fiqh al-Islāmī,* 1/202ff; Barkan *Qānūnlar*, pp. ixff; PA, *Tapu Tahrīr Defterleri* (Title-Deed Office Registry Books); Serkiz Karakoç, *Külliyāt-i Qavānīn* (A Collection of Legal Codes). (Ankara: TTK Library), File 1; MTM, vol. l, pp. 49ff.
12. Cf: Herbert J. Liebesny, *The Law of the Near and Middle East: Readings, Cases, & Materials* (Albany: New York State University Press, 1975), pp. 46-63; Halil Cin and Ahmed Akgündüz, *Türk Hukuk Tarihi,* vol. I (Konya: Selçuk University, 1989), pp. 148-150.
13. Topkapı Palace Museum Library, no. R. 1935, doc. 10/B-14/a.
14. Nu'man Effendi Dabbaghzadah, *Jāmi' al-Sak* (Istanbul: Dersaadah, 1214), pp. 288-291, 298-310, 312, 335; Ahmed Akgündüz, *Shar'iyyah Sijilleri*, vol. 1 (Private Law), vol. 2 (Public Law) (Istanbul: Türk Dünyası, 1989); Fethi Gedikli, *XVI. ve XVII. Asır Osmanlı Şer'iyye Sicillerinde Mudārebe Ortaklığı: Galata Örneği*, PhD dissertation (Istanbul: Istanbul University, 1996).
15. Ibn al-Qayyim al-Jawziyyah, *I'lām al-Muwaqqi'īn 'an Rabb al-'Ālamīn,* v. 1 (Beirut: Dār al-Kutub al-'Ilmiyyah, 1996), pp. 372-378; PA, YEE, no. 14-1540, p. 12ff; Cin-Akgündüz, *Türk Hukuk Tarihi,* vol. 1 (Konya: Selçuk University, 1989) pp. 140, 157.
16. *Gülkhane Khatt-i Humayūnu* (Imperial Edict of Gülhane), *Dustūr* I. Tartīb, vol. 1, pp. 4-7; Halil Cin, *İslām ve Osmanlı Hukukunda*

Evlenme (Marriage in Islamic and Ottoman Codes) (Ankara: Ankara University, 1974), pp. 285ff.

17. Ahmed Akgündüz, *Mukayeseli Islam ve Osmalı Hukuku Kullīyāti* (Diyarbakir: Dicle University 1986), pp. 364ff; Zarqā, *al-Fiqh al-Islāmī*, vol. 1, pp. 208-212; Serkiz Karakoç, *Tahşiyeli Qavānīn*, vols. 1-2 (Istanbul: Cihān Matba' asi, 1911), I/Aff; Osman Öztürk, *Majalla* (Istanbul: 1973), pp. 10-123.
18. Akgündüz and Cin, *Türk Hukuk Tarihi*, vol. 1, pp. 150-152; Cf. Liebesny, *The Law of the Near and Middle East*, pp. 46-63.
19. Musṭafā Aḥmad al-Zarqā, *al-Fiqh al-Islāmī fi Thawbih al-Jadīd* (Damascus: Dār al-Qalam, 1998), vol. 1, pp. 212-219; Cin, *Evlenme*, pp. 289ff; Öztürk, *Majalla*, pp. 10ff.
20. Mecelle Esbāb-ı Mūcibe Mazbatası (Report on the Raison d'Etre of Majalla), Akgündüz, *Külliyāt*, pp. 375ff; Hukuk-u Aile Kararnamesi Mazbatası (Report on Decree of Family Law), Akgündüz, *Külliyāt*, pp. 313ff; Ukūd ve Vācibāt Komisyonları īalışma Esasları (Working Principles of Commissions of Uqud and Wājibat), *Jarida-i Adliye* (Judicial Gazette), 2nd Series, Issues 12-21, Supplementary Sheets, pp. 3ff; Issue 16, Supplementary Sheet, Vācibat Komisyonu Zabıtları (Minutes of Wājibat Commission); al-Zarqā, *al-Fiqh al-Islāmī fi Thawbih al-Jadīd*, vol. 1, pp. 219ff.
21. Abu al-Ula Mardin, "Development of the Sharia under the Ottoman Empire," p. 290.
22. The Committee, *Majalla-i Aḥkām-i 'Adliyyah,* The Article: 39.
23. Ahmed Jawdat Pasha (1822-1895), a famous Ottoman statesman, historian, sociologist, and legist, played an important role in preparing the *Mecelle*, the civil code of the Ottoman Empire, in the late 19th century. This was the first codification of Islamic law with European standards. Cevdet Pasha, who oversaw its formulation, is also well known for his book on Ottoman history: *Cevdet Paşa Tarihi* (*History of Cevdet Pasha*). Ahmed Cevdet Pasha's grave is located in the cemetery of Istanbul's Fātih Mosque.
24. Ahmed Jawdat Pasha, *Ma'rūḍāt* (Petitions) (Istanbul: Enderun, 1980), p. 200; Ali Fuad Türkgeldi, *Rijal-i Muhimma-i Siyasiyyah* (High Officials of Politics) (Istanbul: TTK, 1928), p. 127; Z. Fahri

Fındıkoğlu, *Hukuk Sosyolojisi* (Istanbul: Istanbul University, 1958), p. 244; Abu al-Ula Mardin, *Medenī Hukuk Cephesinden Ahmed Jawdat Pasha* (Istanbul: Istanbul University, 1946), pp. 64-65, 66-88; Baron de Testa, *Recucil des Traites de la Porte Ottomane*, vol. VII (Paris: 1892), p. 469; Ahmed Jawdat Pasha, *Tadhakir* (Ankara: TTK, 1967), vol. 4, pp. 95f.; *Ma'rūḍāt* (Petitions), p. 201; for Protocol see: PA, İrade-Dosya Uşūlü, no. 65/7; Akgündüz, *Külliyāt*, pp. 372ff.

25. Cf. Knut S. Vikør, *Between God and the Sultan: A History of Islamic Law* (Oxford: Oxford University Press, 2005), pp. 219-220.

5

Evolution of the Muslim judicial system

Saim Kayadibi[1]

Abstract

In the Islamic legal tradition, the judiciary has always played an important role in a state's relationship with its citizens. The *qāḍī* (jurist) and the *maḥkamah* (court) are well-known concepts. Their essential requirements, however, by means of which judicial development and practical considerations are essentially made, are less obviously identified. By undertaking detailed research on their roles in Muslim states, I show how social, cultural, political, and historical elements have shaped both of their roles in secular and non-secular environments.

In the modern period, most Muslim-majority countries steadily adopted western legal systems and institutions due to the economic and political influence of their colonial masters. Out of this borrowing emerged a dual court system consisting of Sharī'ah courts as well as western-style secular and national courts.

This paper analyzes the evolution of the judiciary and its institutions within Muslim states, including the function of dual court systems, with regard to the influence of social, cultural, and political elements.

Introduction

Human beings have always had the social character of dealing with others, for they cannot live on their own, as evidenced by the creation of Eve as Adam's life partner. Although people are completely independent of others they cannot live alone, for it is part of human nature to interact with each other. The ensuing interdependency results in social, political, and economic relationships that may cause some conflict that require the application of judicial sanctions. Given that one party's personal, cultural, economic, and even religious rights may infringe upon those of the other party, isolating the resulting disputes is sometimes not an easy matter. This is especially true when one party may have more power than the other(s), a situation that may engender injustice. In this case, the sensitivity of jurisdiction and its power to implement sanctions become difficult matters.

Assuring all members of society that they have a right to receive justice would create a mutual and calm society. For this reason, the Sharī'ah (Islamic law) claims to establish complete justice in society and the Qur'an supports the claim that each person is religiously obligated to establish justice and a just society: "We sent aforetime our messengers with clear signs and sent down with them the Book and the Balance (of Right and Wrong), that people may stand forth in justice."[2] Due to this objective the judiciary's development is highly distinctive, despite the various internal and external factors that cause fluctuations both within it and its components. What are the strengths and weaknesses that bring about these fluctuations? Obviously, time always moves forward and expectations change. Despite all of these changes and developments, however, human beings remain the same. How do we analyze the judiciary's evolution? Can the Sharī'ah maxim that "it is an accepted fact that the *aḥkām* (terms of law) vary with the changes in the times"[3] be applied to the judiciary system?

In certain matters, especially those related to traditional Islamic values, talking about evolution, reform, or even change cause so much social and cultural rejection that it is extremely difficult to convey one's real intention without any type of bias. Undoubtedly time brings about continuous change, which changes everything that is subject to change.[4] The fundamental religious duties and the concept of God, however, are exempt from this rule. But irrespective of this fact one must deal with development and transformation, for evolution is an unavoidable phenomenon as regards both practical and theoretical instruments as well as social, economic, political, and judicial institutions.

What is the fundamental basis of change in the Muslim world's court systems? Is the main reason to establish a just society in line with "O you who believe, stand out firmly for justice as witnesses to Allah, even as against yourselves, your parents, or your kin, and whether it be (against) rich or poor, for Allah can best protect both. Follow not the lusts (of your hearts), lest you swerve. If you distort or decline to do justice, verily Allah is well-acquainted with all that you do,"[5] or there are other reasons, such as political, militarily, or imperialistic demands and social welfare? Although *qaḍā'* (to give judgement) is one of God's rights and should be the highest authority in jurisdiction, the ruler can limit the authority of the *qāḍī* (jurist), change his office, or appoint him to carry out political and administrative duties.

Evolution of the judiciary

Both Muslim and non-Muslim scholars have made enormous contributions to understanding Islam's judicial institution (system).[6] The basic terms of the judiciary, which has existed from the onset of the Islamic revelation, are emphasized in the Qur'an. Among them are the terms derived from the roots حكم and قضي, which characterize the Muslim understanding of "judging" as well as the Prophet's (ṣ) significant role as a judge. Even before his prophethood, he had served as a judge in the Black Stone (*ḥajar al-aswad*) controversy[7] and other cases due to his reputation for honesty.[8] Although these words do not often occur in the Qur'an, the verb *ḥakama* and its derivatives,[9] as well as the noun *qaḍā'*, occur there quite frequently to emphasize the sovereign ordinance of God and His Prophet and in relation to the Day of Judgement.[10] Surely, neither Makkah nor Madīnah had any judicial institutions, because such institutions can arise only within a state. Nevertheless, the Prophet settled disputes among his people and, as soon as he established the first Islamic state, devised a constitution that consisted of fifty-two clauses.[11]

In the early and medieval Islamic eras, the authority belonging to legislation was appropriated by the principles and competent Sharī'ah scholars (*'ulamā'*). As these scholars possessed the sole authority given by the Sharī'ah, all political authorities who wanted to be considered legitimate could not ignore it. Moreover the *'ulamā'*, who had the power to control the state's agenda, made up the judiciary.[12] Protecting the state and the *ummah* (Muslim community) was the caliph's responsibility, whereas elaborating and interpreting the law was that of the *'ulamā'*,[13] who were held to be the Prophet's deputies after his death as well as the custodians[14] and inheritors of the Sharī'ah. This understanding relies on the prophetic tradition that "the scholars are the inheritors of the Prophets."[15]

Through the ordinance of the Qur'an, as the *ipsissima verba* of God, judicial activities began and were upheld by the Prophet's (ṣ) teachings. As the community's greatest judge and leader, he soon established a just society in Madīnah and appointed many competent judges. The most famous of these was Mu'ādh b. Jabal, who was sent to Yemen. As the community's leader, the Prophet, in his capacity as God's messenger (*Rasūl Allāh*),[16] performed the central role in establishing a model for the ideal judge.[17]

Nevertheless, the state's leadership remains under a governor appointed by the head of state, for judicial responsibility relied on judges sent by the Prophet (ṣ).[18] Consequently, it should be noted that the administration of the state and the judiciary were separated right from the beginning.

In practice, the *'ulamā'* have played a significant role in the history of Islamic law. Although these scholars were not brought together into a formalized institution until the Ottoman era, they shouldered several responsibilities related to jurisdiction and governmental administration, such as *qāḍī* (judge), *muḥtasib* (supervisor of morals and the marketplace), *mu'allim* or *mukattib* (schoolteacher) and *mudarris al-fiqh* (lecturer in legal science), and *mustashār* (political advisor) to the caliph or sultan[19] in religious matters. More importantly, these officials were entrusted with such additional functions due to their administrative reputations in the eyes of people. In addition to their judicial duties, they were entrusted with such non-judicial roles as *nā'ib* (delegate) of the caliph, *amīr* (governor of a province), *'ārīf* (tribal administrator), *'āmil* (tax collector), *'imārah* (governorship), *qā'id* (military commander), *imām* (prayer leader), *bayt al-māl* (supervision of the treasury) and *kharāj* (land tax), *ṣāḥib al-shurṭah* (chief of police), *ṣāḥib al-ḥaras* (chief of the caliph's personal guard), *qāṣṣ* (preacher, story teller), and *kātib* (vizier).[20]

The period of the Rightly Guided Caliphs (632-661) was one of the important periods for developing the institute of the judiciary: 'Umar b. al-Khaṭṭāb established an independent institution for the judiciary and let it become an independent body. Following the Prophet's (ṣ) appointment of muftis, the first four caliphs were the first authorities to appoint muftis and *ḥakams* (arbitrators) to meet the government's judicial needs by delegating its judicial authority to them as *qāḍī*s (judges) in the new empire's major garrison towns. It is reportedly said, however, that Mu'āwiyah was the first caliph to appoint *qāḍīs* in the newly formed garrison towns. The appearance of the *qāḍī*'s office is directly connected to the Umayyad dynasty's establishment of garrison towns in al-Kūfah, al-Baṣrah, and al-Fusṭāṭ in response to difficult cases.[21] The Sharī'ah was regarded as independent from any political and social controls; the Islamic judiciary also maintained its independence, despite some political interference. Even the caliph, the head of the Islamic world, understood that he was accountable to it and must obey and try to protect it. This belief, which gave the *'ulamā'* a special role right from the very early days of the Islamic states, helped them to remain self-governing and free from the caliphs' arbitrary power in religious matters.[22] They also served as the state's general representatives and defenders.[23] Nevertheless, political changes often altered a *qāḍī*'s power as, for instance, when the authorities removed them or ignored their decisions[24] because they were seen as threats to their own power.

The office of judgeship (*qaḍā'*) carries heavy responsibilities, and God will judge how these responsibilities were borne. In juridical terms, a just person must have a strong personality supported by a thorough and intricate knowledge of Islamic law. Ibn Qudamah writes that the *qaḍı* should also be a *mujtahid* (one qualified to make religious rulings), not just a *muftī*, for such a religious scholar is obliged to implement the rules.[25] Due to this heavy spiritual responsibility, some pious and devoted jurists did their best to avoid holding it, among them Abū Ḥanīfah (699-765 CE), Ibn Fārūq, Sa'd b. Mas'ūd, 'Abd al-'Azīz al-Darawardī (186 AH), Salmah b. 'Ikrimah, Ibn Wahb (d. 737 CE), Abū Qulābah (d. 726 CE), Muṣ'ab b. 'Imrān (d. 774), and 'Alī b. Khayrān.[26] This appointment was not rejected simply to oppose the ruler; more interestingly, it was rejected because the appointees were afraid to shoulder a responsibility that was so heavy in God's sight.

Distribution of the *qāḍī's* jurisdiction

The *qāḍī*'s jurisdiction did not yet extend to the surrounding countryside or towns inhabited by non-Muslims (e.g., Christians, Zoroastrians, Jews, and others); rather, it was confined to the garrison towns and to resolving disagreements among Arab tribesmen and their relatives and customers in the third quarter of the first Islamic century.[27]

Under the Umayyads (661-750), the *qāḍīs* served as Mu'āwiyah's provincial governor after he proclaimed himself *khalīfah Allah* (God's caliph). In addition to resolving disputes, the earliest *qāḍīs* served as governors, tax collectors, military commanders, prayer leaders, and supervisors of the public treasury and land tax. They also engaged in trade and commerce to meet their daily needs, for they used to refuse payment for their judicial services.[28] A *qāḍī* was expected to remain independent, as opposed to a *muftī*, who functioned as a legal counsellor and court expert,[29] an author-jurist, and a professor. But these latter roles were seldom mutually exclusive, for a jurist could assume one or more of them if he wished to do so.[30]

Despite the religious character of the *qāḍī*'s office evidenced in 'Umar b. al-Khaṭṭāb's letter appointing Abū Mūsā al-Ash'arī (d. 44 AH) *qāḍī* of al-Kūfah, both this post as well as the judgeship became professional offices due to the Arab empire's rapid expansion and the growing unsuitability and complexity of the state's judicial apparatus. Yet the *qāḍī*'s role appeared to be limited to resolving legal disputes and administering the emerging judicial apparatus in the last decades of the first Islamic century. Eventually the judiciary became politicized because of increasing political tension. Beginning with Sulaymān b. 'Abd al-Mālik (r. 715-717), judges were appointed directly by the caliphs reigning in Damascus, who employed important and influential religious figures[31] as *qāḍīs* to propagate their ideology and maintain the system's reputation.[32]

The emergence of the *'ulamā'* in the early 'Abbāsid period (750-1250) was distinctive. They were influential on both the society and the rulers. Accordingly the *'ulamā'* had influence on the caliphs' decisions upon judicial administration.[33] Al-Mahdī (r. 775-785) was the first caliph to establish a system through which people could present their petitions and complaints. Known as *maẓālim*[34] (courts of complaint), they consisted of a *qāḍī*, guards, jurists, scribes, and notaries. The caliph or one of his governors could involve himself directly with the court and could serve as a court of appeal against the *qāḍī*'s decision. He was also responsible for allocating and confiscating the *iqṭā'* (land grant). Although a strict judicial procedure applied in the *qāḍī* court—it was, after all, a single-judge court—the rules and the procedures of a *maẓālim* court was not very strict and complicated.[35] Another difference was that a *maẓālim* court could use force, if necessary, to make litigants and witnesses appear before it. In due course, this court system was integrated into the system of government and eventually became part of the bureaucracy.[36]

A question arises here as to whether the *qāḍī*'s decision could be appealed. Despite different opinions on appellate review, no piece of evidence supports the right to an appeal. In addition, it did not occur during the Prophet's lifetime or under the Rightly Guided Caliphs. 'Umar's (634-644) rulings in two identical cases of inheritance, known as the *ḥimārīyatayn,* is a potential example of appellate review, however. Kamali concluded that the *qāḍī*'s decision cannot be reviewed even by the one who originally made it.[37] Meanwhile, it has to be clarified that if the court's decision was based on clear evidence from Qur'an, as the *ipsissima verba* of God, the Sunnah, and *ijmā'* (scholarly consensus), then Islamic law validates appellate review.[38]

Abū Yūsuf (d. 798) was appointed as the first *qāḍī al-quḍāh* (chief *qāḍī*), the caliph's deputy in all matters related to jurisdiction, by Hārūn al-Rashīd (r.786-809) to centralize the judicial administration.[39] The 'Abbāsids used *qāḍī*s to propagate their religious ideology and enhance their regime's recognition, and thus the latter played a significant role in guiding the caliphs on how to administer matters of state. For example, Abū Yūsuf wrote his well-known *Kitāb al-Kharāj* to advise Hārūn al-Rashīd on matters of public finance, land rules, taxation, and criminal justice.[40]

The status of the *qāḍī al-quḍāh* changed when Mu'taḍid (r.892-902) appointed his vizier, instead of this official, as second-in-command to the caliph, despite the fact that these two offices appeared at about the same time. Accordingly, the *qāḍī al-quḍāh*'s appointment now had to be approved by the vizier because of the latter's superiority in terms of protocol and social standing.[41] The *qāḍī*'s and *qāḍī al-quḍāh's* loyalty to the caliph and willingness to implement his policies in the district where he served was one of the main reasons for his nomination. The nomination process caused the government to centralize the legal system and helped it tighten its control over the judiciary. Such appointments were not only the result of the 'Abbāsids' wishes, however, for the local *'ulamā'* had to agree to them as well. Thus, the caliph would not appoint a *qāḍī* who was unacceptable to them.[42]

The rulers' interference in the affairs of the judiciary is undeniable. In fact, on some occasions they forced the *'ulamā'* and the *qāḍī*s to implement their own theological views on judgements, as in the case of al-Ma'mūn's *miḥnah* (ordeal) of 218/833. Such a power conflict among the rulers against the scholars was a way to limit expression and to politicize religious matters. Al-Ma'mūn's imposition of his Mu'tazilī understanding of Islam lasted for fifteen years, until the reign of al-Mutawakkil (r.847-861).[43]

Given this reality of occasional political cooperation among the *'ulamā'* and the *qāḍī*s, al-Māwardī is considered a lifesaver. He wrote his important work on Islamic political theory, *al-Aḥkām al-Sulṭānīyah* (The Ordinances of Government), in response to the caliph's orders to tackle the situations of the time. In order to maintain stability during times of conflict among political realities and the Sharīʿah, the caliphs needed the commitment of both religious and political leaders.[44] In his capacity as a *qāḍī* (he was not a politician), al-Māwardī developed and systematized the opinions of his predecessors and, after adapting the materials to the realities of his time, enabled their implementation.[45] A number of chapters deal with jurisdictions; for example, chapters 6 and 7 focus on the office of *qāḍī* and tribunals for appeals. Since all power was centralized in the caliph, the *qāḍī* was actually no more than his deputy who had no real personal authority of action. The unity of jurisdiction structured by the influence of the Islamic governing system, after the Persian and Roman models, subjected the *qāḍī* to the control of a council (*shūrā*). While there is no classification of a court of instance, appeal, and cassation as in modern times, a *qāḍī* court could have different classification.[46]

The judiciary, which is based on a certain *madhhab* (school of legal thought), is changeable according to the ruler's ideological bias. No concrete evidence implies that the ʿAbbāsid-era *quḍāh* made their judgements based only upon the rulings of one *madhhab*. For instance, al-Subkī and other scholars highlight that these judges were Shāfiʿīs;[47] alternatively, Ibn Tagrī Birdī claims that the judges in Egypt were Ḥanafīs.[48] Al-Kindī's investigation indicates that the judgeship was led by different schools of thought: out of Egypt's twenty-seven *qāḍī*s, for example, twelve were Shāfiʿīs, six were Mālikīs, and four were Ḥanafīs. Despite this diverse legal environment, however, after the Fāṭimīds came into power only one *madhhab* was followed, namely, that of the Ismāʿīlī Shīʿah.[49] Under Ṣalāḥ al-Dīn al-Ayyūbī power passed to the Shāfiʿīs, who allowed no scholars of the other schools of thought to become judges; rather, they could serve only as deputies with partial jurisdiction. This situation ended under Sultan Baybars (r.1260-1277), who appointed a *qāḍī al-quḍāh* from the Shāfi'ī school, Tāj al-Dīn 'Abd al-Wahhāb b. al-A'azz, and deputies from each of the other Sunnī schools of thought. When the results of this policy proved unsatisfactory, he followed Jamāl al-Dīn Aydughdā's advice and appointed an independent *qāḍī al-quḍāh* from each Sunnī school of thought.[50] This model lasted for centuries, and the office of *qāḍī al-quḍāh* was held by Ḥanafī, Shāfi'ī, Ḥanbalī, and Mālikī *'ulamā'*.[51]

Despite the 'Abbāsids' auto-control of the judiciary in the Middle East, rulers in other parts of the Muslim world managed to remain independent of the central government's control. For example, 'Abd al-Raḥmān (r.756-788) of Andalucia declared his independence from the 'Abbāsids by appointing a military judge (*qaḍī al-jamā'ah*); the Fāṭimīds (990-1171) appointed *qāḍī al-quḍāh* in Cairo who exercised his authority in the name of the Hidden Imām (in shī'ah belief). From 969 to 1517, there were only two *qāḍī al-quḍāh* in the entire Muslim world: Cairo and Baghdad. The Mamlūks (1250-1517) also followed a policy of *madhhab* diversity by appointing a *qāḍī al-quḍāh* for each Sunnī school of thought. Eventually, Cairo's *qāḍī al-quḍāh* bestowed his authority on other *qāḍī al-quḍāh* in the empire's major provinces.[52]

Dynasties in Moghul India (1526-1858), Safavid Iran (1501-1722), and the Ottomans (1526-1858) followed similar policies. Unlike the hierarchical structure led by the military judges (*qāḍī 'askar* named differently from *qaḍī al-jama'ah)* and the Shaykh al-Islām or state *muftī*, Selim I (r.1512-1520) and Süleyman I (r.1520-1560) appointed the *quḍāh* to the various provinces (*mawlawiyāt*) and, under them, local *qāḍīs* whose jurisdiction was limited to one district (*qaḍā*) or subdistrict (*nāḥiyah*). This policy was designed to control the judiciary by establishing a better organization (tighter control) over the territories. The *qāḍī*'s office as well as the judiciary, therefore, played a significant role in conveying the caliph's or the sultan's decrees to the districts[53] in their capacity as his representatives.[54]

The Ottomans made a major contribution to the jurists' field of action by formulating *qānūn* and *qānūnnāmes*. This undertaking enabled them to develop secular criminal law, procedures, and justice and ease them into the customary and religious law imposed by the rulers to control the administration of justice.[55] Changing the court systems and secularizing the judiciary is not a new paradigm in the Islamic world; rather, it is a long-standing journey that started mainly in the Ottoman empire in 1451 and concluded only in 1926 with adoption of the Swiss Civil Code.[56] The *sijill* (court documents) studies enlighten the court system and its process in Muslim states, especially during the Ottoman period. These records themselves may be considered as evidence to show how the *qāḍī*s used legal reasoning to reach legal judgements. Although these documents are basically a reflection of the society being investigated, they may still be a source of enlightenment as regards the process of legal practices in that society, which is related to the multi-cultural reflection.[57]

Islamic perspectives of the judiciary

Muslims hold that the laws of justice, and therefore the judiciary, are among God's main concerns when it comes to embedding equity and justice among the people. For every nation and society, at least one righteous person has been sent[58] to guide them to the straight path so that on the Day of Judgement they cannot claim unawareness of the truth and, therefore, of having been judged unfairly. As Muslims consider God's law to be the sole source of judgement, as reflected in Anderson's statement that "the competence of the Sharī'ah Courts was as wide as the scope of the law they administered, for in orthodox theory there was no other law and no other Courts,"[59] the law and the court must be administered by God's rules.

The Islamic judicial system and its basis in the Islamic judiciary, both of which are structured on the Qur'an and the Prophet's (ṣ) Sunnah, seek to settle disputes: "… and that you should judge between them by what Allah has revealed. Do not follow their vain desires and be cautious of them, lest they seduce you away from part of what Allah has revealed to you. But if they turn back, then know that Allah desires to afflict them on account of some of their faults. And most surely, many of the people are transgressors."[60] The Qur'an orders the Prophet (ṣ) to enjoin justice: "If you judge, judge between them with equity. Surely Allah loves those who judge equitably."[61] Any litigation between the parties involved was ended by the judge's verdict, which had to be in accord with God's injunctions, although their personal judgements (*ijtihād*) were also involved. Prophet Muḥammad (ṣ), as well as all of the previous messengers, was considered to be a judge. This group of people held the same responsibility and thus played a major role in their societies: "O David, surely We have made you a ruler in the land. So judge between people with justice and do not follow desire, lest it should lead you astray from the path of Allah. (As for) those who go astray from the path of Allah, they shall surely have a severe punishment because they forgot the Day of Reckoning."[62]

According to the narration of 'Amr b. al-'Āṣ, the Prophet (ṣ) encouraged his Companions to pass judgements: "If a judge gives a judgement using his best judgement and is correct, then he receives a double reward (from God); if he spends his effort to devise the best judgement but at the end was mistaken, then he still receives a single reward."[63]

According to Muslim belief, the judiciary is an obligatory duty (*farḍ 'ayn*) placed upon the Muslim nation. If some individuals consent to fulfil this duty, this collective duty is dropped. This differs from other such duties, such as the whole Muslim nation being called upon to be just with others: "O you who believe, be maintainers of justice, as witnesses to Allah."[64] The concept of justice, therefore, makes Muslims consider it as something important to every part of their lives, an attitude that is in stark contrast to Greek civilization. According to Edward, Greek civilization reflects the popular conception of tragedies and the philosophical ideas underlying the works of Plato and Aristotle.[65]

Subsequently, as is the case for all nations, a judicial system must be established so that the ruler can enforce justice among the citizens. As enjoining justice cannot be carried out in the absence of such a system, it is therefore a requirement for a nation's prosperity and development, as well as for a society's security, to protect the rights of the oppressed, control the oppressor, enjoin what is right, and forbid what is wrong. But even more importantly, this is a vital requirement for maintaining the society's normal functioning. If this duty is not fulfilled, the society will veer toward chaos and turmoil, thereby allowing immoral behaviour to occur, endangering the five fundamental necessities asserted by Islam (viz., religion, life, property, intellect, and lineage), and preventing the development of the environment and civilization, not to mention spiritual and mental development. In other words, justice is just as necessary to maintaining all of a society's requirements as is water to ensuring the continuation of human life.

A single-judge court

The *qāḍī* court system, as indicated earlier, is a single-judge court; however, *qāḍī*s were allowed to consult with other erudite jurists or muftis to arrive at a just solution. This court system also includes several assistants to carry out its administrative duties: a scribe (*kātib* or *amīn*), a chamberlain (*jilwāz*), and a witness investigator (*ṣāḥib al-masā'il* or *muzakkī*). The scribe must be knowledgeable in the law, pious and just, and skilled in the art of writing. He was responsible for recording all claims, counterclaiming and depositing the litigants, drafting legal documents, scheduling cases, and similar matters. The chamberlain, who was expected to be present in the court, was expected to be near the litigants and was entrusted with ensuring discipline at the court and meting out its punishments. The witness' honesty and personality were assessed by the witness investigator, and all records of the qualified witnesses were kept by him.

The *qāḍī*'s staffs were seated where he could easily see them. All of the records reserved by him were filed away in a bookcase, which was located in his *dīwān* (archive). *Mahḍar*s (court protocol) and *sijill*s (judicial verdicts) were the *dīwān*'s two primary components. This *dīwān* contains the record of the witness investigator, details of other information related to the judiciary (e.g., the names and payment details of endowment supervisors); a register of widows, guardians of orphans, divorcees, and bequests; copies of correspondence between *qāḍī*s; and the written records of contracts, pledges, gifts, and acknowledgements.[66] In addition to their judicial role, *qāḍī*s also had general supervisory administrative roles based on a hierarchical division: *shaykh al-Islām*, *qāḍī' 'askar*, *qāḍīs,* and *nā'ibs*, *mullahs*, *'ulamā'*, and muftis.[67]

When litigation arises, the scribe first receives and collects the petitions in order to present them to the *qāḍī* for scheduling. The *qāḍī* can hold court when necessary; however, if the court sessions were fewer than seven, cases were usually heard on Monday, Thursday, and Saturday.[68] The plaintiff (*mudda'ī*)[69] and the defendant (*mudda'ā 'alayhi*)[70] had to be summoned to the court and be present during the hearing. If the defendant could not be present, the *qāḍī* was supposed to ask him/her to submit a written statement of his/her situation.[71] According to the Shāfi'ī, Māliki, and Ḥanbalī jurists, the judgement was pronounced against the defendant if the plaintiff presented valid evidence.[72] In the court, according to the rules of procedure, this evidence had to be based on the fundamental principle of *al-bayyinah 'alā al-mudda'ī* (producing evidence relies on the plaintiff). The role of the litigant as plaintiff or defendant could change during the hearing.[73] For example, if an action proved the defendant's defence, then the plaintiff's action would be dismissed. If the case was not proved, the first plaintiff would be called upon to swear an oath denying his/her guilt. If he/she did so, the first plaintiff's actions would return back to him/her; if the plaintiff refused to swear an oath, the defendant's defense would be considered proved.[74]

Establishing a statement's truth involves testimony (*shahādah*), an oath (*yamīn*), an acknowledgment (*iqrār*), circumstantial evidence (*qarīnah*), and a letter of the *qāḍī* (*kitāb al- qāḍī*). In normal circumstances, the Qur'an[75] and the Sunnah require two witnesses so as to emphasize the clarity of the testimony and that the witness must see the affair as clearly as he/she "sees the sun."[76] There are two types of witness: eyewitness testimony (*mu'āyanah*), defined as an event witnessed by a person while it was happening and seen with his/her own eyes, and hearsay testimony (*shahadah bi al-khabar*), defined as an event witnessed by someone who could not be present in the court. The witness' personality and honesty are also considered when determining the truth of his/her testimony. Although all Muslims are qualified to testify, the "sinner" (*fāsiq*) who has been convicted (or even accused) of slander cannot testify.[77]

The oath functions as a method of proof when evidence is not presented. Taken by the person who rejects the allegation, it is thus based on the principle of "the oath for one who denies the claim" (*al-yamīn 'alā man ankara*).[78] Acknowledgement and confession have the same value of evidence accepted by a *qāḍī*. A personal confession, which is regarded as a kind of proof,[79] must be made in the presence of a *qāḍī*; no witnesses are necessary for its validation. In the Egyptian Code of Procedure of 1897, a written confession has the same value as a verbal confession.[80] Although all Sunnī school of thought views circumstantial evidence as valid, its acceptability depends upon the type of case.[81] A *qāḍī*'s written communication with another *qāḍī* (*khitāb*) can also be presented as evidence in the *qāḍī*'s court. Another type of letter, known as a *kitāb*, is a composed letter that indicates a specific claim, one that differs from the one mentioned in the *khitāb*.[82] Correspondence designed to convey testimony from one *qāḍī* to another (*kitāb al-qāḍī ilā al-qāḍī*) is considered as the conveyance of evidence (*shahādah naql*).[83]

The *qāḍī* is both bound and guided by procedural law. Since his principal mission is to arbitrate legal cases to establish legal facts that will serve as a basis of his ruling (*ḥukm*), he is not compelled to issue a judgement unless the plaintiff asks him to do so.[84] His judgement was expected to be based on the truth, abide by the jurists' consensus (*ijmā*ʿ), and be restricted to cases upon which consensus had not yet materialized. A *qāḍī* who is qualified to conduct *ijtihād* (independent reasoning) should not limit his judgements on others' opinions; he should exercise his *ijtihād* within the boundaries of his own school. Despite these juristic boundaries, however, some prominent jurists did cross those boundaries in order to reach a fair judgement.[85] An error can happen in jurisdiction, just as it can happen in an accusation. If a *qāḍī* commits an unintentional error (*khaṭa' al-qāḍī*), it does not cause much of a problem; however, if his error was intentional he should be dismissed and punished.[86]

The *qāḍī* system and application of the Sharīʿah within this institutional framework has undergone some change from the nineteenth century to the present time. The most significant characteristics of this change were centred around the following points: "the abolition of *siyāsah* or discretionary criminal justice—in the interest of the state and public order—and the promotion of respect for the rule of law; bureaucratization of the *sharī'ah* courts; codification of the *sharī'ah*; the emergence, in most countries, of a dual judiciary composed of (a) secular, national courts that apply Western-style legal codes; and (b) *sharī'ah* courts that apply Islamic legal doctrine in fields such as family relations and inheritance; the gradual integration of the *sharī'ah* court system into the national court systems."[87] Although the majority of Muslim countries adopted western legal codes because of the West's economic and political influence, the *qāḍī* court system was not immediately influenced because the independent states had some room for political manoeuvre. First, they tried to implement western laws by creating institutions that would function simultaneously alongside the *qāḍī* courts;[88] and later on they tried to establish a complete western style court system. Although the traditional roles of the *qāḍī* and *qāḍī* court system were seriously changed by the impact of westernization, Muslim society still pays great attention to Islamic law and its components.[89]

The rapid increase in the West's industrial strength enabled it to achieve supremacy over the East, and, consequently, the Muslim world's long political and economic superiority over the West weakened. The affinity of Muslim intellectuals for western products, lifestyles, education systems, as well as their use of all kinds of western products without trying to understand how and why they were being developed, revealed that their dominance was drawing to an end. For instance, in many Muslim countries, particularly the Ottoman empire and Egypt, the indigenous intellectual elite began to obtain a western education and European traders circulated throughout the empire with full official permission to find new commercial opportunities and markets for their products. These opportunities eventually brought troops to the Muslim countries, and finally western ideas spread throughout the empire as well. The various independence movements also ignited society-wide changes and reforms.[90] All of these helped the western countries spread their ideas throughout the world, along with the idea that change is unavoidable in every aspect of life: social, economic, judicial, and political.

The modernization of the Ottoman legal system took place in three important steps: the establishment of Meclis-i Vala'i Aḥkām-i 'Adliye (the Supreme Council of Justice) in 1838, the Gülhane Decree of 1839, and the *mecalis* (provincial councils) that opened membership to Christians (1840). These three steps also limited, to a degree, the sultan's power as well as that of high state officials and prevented them from using arbitrary and *siyāsah* justice to centralize and modernize the empire.[91] This achievement was followed by the establishment of new special courts and councils. The *nizamiye* courts, established in 1864, replaced the provincial councils set up in 1840. Although the *qāḍī* courts were subjected to a process of bureaucratization, the freshly established secular courts did not replace them. In fact, they continued to provide services until 1886, when the Ministry of Justice finally limited their jurisdiction to matters related to family law and personal status, inheritance, homicide as well as wounding, and to claims involving retaliation and blood money. Although the *nizamiye* courts heard other cases, the parties involved could still submit their case to the Sharī'ah courts if they agreed to do so.[92] The *Mecelle*, the Ottoman civil code of Ḥanafī law, was applied by each type of court in 1870; in 1917 its last three chapters, which deal with procedure, evidence, and sentencing, were revoked and replaced by a new law. Shortly thereafter the *qāḍī* court system as a whole was abolished and a completely new secular system was introduced after the Republic of Turkey was founded in 1923.

The new republic's legal structure has not yet been completed, in the sense of its legal components being fully established. Even the *Mecelle* had never been completed as a civil code. The suitability of the Swiss Civil Code (SCC) for a multi-cultural society was, however, another issue. The empire's enormous legal heritage needed to be reinterpreted and evaluated so that it would be in accord with the SCC; the SCC faced the same issue. The lawyers and judges who were trained in the new knowledge of the SCC differed from those who were trained in the SCC's country of origin,[93] and the judges of the *nizamiye* courts were unskilled in Sharīʿah law.[94] Although a dual system no longer existed, problems remained because of the unsettled court system. The reasoning and interpretation of both Islamic law and the newly adopted secular law created different outcomes when applied to family and inheritance cases. Cases needed to be resolved in a manner that was welcomed by the state and its citizens. Whatever the state did to develop the judiciary so that legislation could be democratized or secularized, problems still existed because the citizens remained wary of accepting the new court's judgements on religious matters.

The impact of Europeans and legal duality

Over time, this duality increased in Muslims states, for although the new system was, the majority of Muslim states allowed their citizens to take certain cases to the Sharī'ah courts, such as those dealing with family matters, inheritance, and guardianship (*wilāyah*). Moreover, the role of Sharīʿah courts differ from country to country; some Muslim countries actually do not allow them to hear any cases, even though the overwhelming majority of their citizens are Muslim.

Legal reforms in the Ottoman empire created a dual legal system: all cases dealing with family matters and inheritance were sent to the Sharīʿah courts, and all other cases were sent to the statutory courts. Under the colonial rulers, the jurisdiction of the *qāḍī* courts was not only limited to family law, inheritance, contracts, and personal property, but was also subjected to the colonial powers' control and supervision: France (in Algeria and Tunisia), Holland (in Indonesia), and Italy (in Libya). In India and Nigeria, however, the British colonialists employed a different method: local laws were recognized if they did not contradict "natural justice, good conscience, and equity." Thus, no dual court system ever arose there.

In Bengal, the situation was different: the British and the Mughals agreed that the Sharīʿah legal system (basically Ḥanafī law) would remain supreme. But even Bengal's judiciary was reformed, for the newly established criminal and civil courts employed British judges with an assistant: *maulvi*s (experts on Islamic law) for Muslims and *pundit*s (scholars versed in Hindu law) from local law offices for Hindus. In India, Bangladesh, and Pakistan, the national regular courts, as opposed to the specialized Sharīʿah courts, mainly implemented Ḥanafī law. In Nigeria, Mālikī law was implemented in most fields and procedures, an arrangement that continued even after the country became independent in 1960.[95]

Growing European activities in Egypt, not to mention the strong effect of their political and economic orientations, began to change Egyptian judicial structures. The increasing importance of the cotton trade for Europeans caused them to expand their activities in Egypt, where cotton was grown, and try to take advantage of every chance offered as regards trade and investment. Judicial reforms dramatically increased during the early years of the nineteenth century. Muhammad Ali Pasha and his successors focused on these legal changes by introducing *qānūn* and establishing new ministers, councils and courts, and high courts for civil matters (*majlis al-aḥkām*).[96] Legal activities were undertaken to fully protect the rights of Europeans by allowing their consulates to supervise them. The increasing number of Egyptian-European disputes engendered the idea of what became known as the "mixed courts" system. The notable work of Nubar Pasha,[97] whom Khedive Ismā'īl appointed minister of foreign affairs, accelerated judicial reforms that favoured the Europeans.

In 1867 the judicial reform negotiations began to launch the mixed courts system, which was approved by an internationally agreed establishment.[98] The codification of law, namely, the *Mecelle,* was applied in *nizamiye* courts extended its scope, together with mixed court system, in different Middle East countries:[99] Egypt embraced the *nizamiye* court system completely, although Ismail Pasha's judicial and administrative independence prevented the *Mecelle* from being applied. Napoleon's invasion of Egypt changed the judicial authority: mixed courts were established in 1875 and the *nizamiye* courts were replaced by native courts in 1883.[100] These courts, both sources of significant judicial authority between 1875 and 1949, dealt with many issues related foreign people in terms of political, social, and economic involvement.[101]

The success of the mixed court system aroused the western powers' appetite to go even further: They wanted to establish secular courts to oversee all matters related to civil and criminal issues.[102] Abdel Razzaq Ahmed al-Sanhouri Pasha, appointed director of the committee set up to establish a new civil code before the mixed courts were closed down, did his best to include the heritage of Islamic law. For example, in Article 1 (2) of the 1949 Egyptian civil code he inserted the following statement: "In the absence of an applicable legislative provision, the Judge shall decide according to custom, and, in the absence of custom, according to the principles of the Islamic Sharī'ah. In the absence of these principles, the Judge shall have recourse to natural justice and the rules of equity." A new socialist agenda engendered its own laws after 1952, when King Farouk abdicated and went into exile.[103] Social factors, which were mainly based on the Islamic heritage, also influenced the formulation of Egypt's 1971 constitution. The judicial changes showed just how large a role political, social, and economic influences could play in the judiciary as well as the administration.

Giving extra privileges to westerners through the mixed court system irked Ottoman bureaucrats and, due to the heavy burden of the capitulation treaties, encouraged them to demolish it. Altering a legal system, however, should not be considered without taking into consideration the state's internal and external factors. In the case of the Ottoman empire, its multicultural and multiethnic social structure and economic independence were *de facto*. At the same time, it tried to accommodate and adjust the European powers' economic encroachment, which caused some internal problems. The processes of secularizing and changing the mixed court system were prevented by the capitulatory system, which were designed to continue European privileges within the empire. When the empire unilaterally abrogated the capitulation treaties in 1914, France, Great Britain, and the United States refused to accept this decision because it went against their interests. Within the empire, non-Muslims were tried under international law rather than Ottoman law.[104] This burdensome capitulatory system[105] had to be abrogated or else the newly established Republic of Turkey would remain under the western powers' social, economic, and political domination.

The colonial powers' interference in the empire's judiciary system created, to a certain extent, a conflict between the two court systems. For example, a conflict between Sudan's grand *qāḍī* and the legal secretary spilled over to the Sharīʿah courts and native courts.[106]

In addition to that, the United Kingdom, Germany, and other western countries allowed Muslims to apply the Sharīʻah in family and financial cases; however, not only did the Muslims in western countries do this, but the governments themselves began to apply and even establish more Islamic banking and finance institutions, especially in France, Germany, the United States, the United Kingdom, and Switzerland.[107] This newly developing banking system, which needs to obtain the approval of those responsible for ensuring Sharīʻah compliance for every financial transaction, created a dual legal system in the West as a court instrument.

A society's cultural factors also shape the country's legal system. In this sense Qatar is unique, for its legal system is based on indigenous tribal law, Sharīʻah law, and modern law (rooted in the British legal system since 1916). Its growing oil income encouraged the government to modernize the country's legal, educational, and governmental systems. This attempt resulted in a dual judicial system: Sharīʻah law is applied in Sharīʻah courts, and western civil law is applied in *ʻadliyyah* (courts), the rules of which were adopted from the Romano-Germanic legal system.[108]

Religious needs, which have always been a vital factor in any society, eventually demand new institutions from the state. The West's increasing Muslim population, either indigenous or immigrant, persuades western leaders to accommodate institutions that will allow the Muslims to observe their religious duties. Recently, Britain officially allowed Sharīʻah tribunals to hand down legally binding rulings on matters related to marriage, divorce, and inheritance. Christians and Jews have long had their own court systems in Britain. Jack Straw, Britain's justice minister, even stated: "There is nothing whatever in English law that prevents people abiding by *sharīʼah* principles if they wish to, provided they do not come into conflict with English law."[109] Lord Nicholas Philips, Britain's chief judge, has also made a highly noteworthy statement: "There is no reason why principles of *sharī'ah* Law, or any other religious code should not be the basis for mediation or other forms of alternative dispute resolution."[110]

Unavoidable continuous change

Since the advance of European powers in the middle of nineteenth century and their physical and ideological spread throughout the world, especially in the Ottoman empire, the framework of the Sharī'ah and secular law has been fairly defined: any matters related to family rights and obligations, as well as certain penal and inheritance laws, were to be adjudicated according to the school of Islamic law prevailing in the *qaḍī*'s court. Criminal actions, however, were generally referred to the police (*shurṭah*) courts, and all commercial disputes and taxation matters were taken to the relevant tribunals.[111]

In the Middle East, legal reforms assumed an evolutionary rather than a revolutionary character in an attempt to maintain the two separate legal systems. The already established legal systems, however, only attempted to change or evolve. In Egypt of the 1880s and Qatar of the 1970s, any cases could be considered in the Sharī'ah courts, and even the staff members working in the new courts cooperated with them. The government was directly involved in such undertakings, as it sought to harmonize both court systems until the late nineteenth century. After that, such collaboration was abandoned.[112]

A persuading factor for the government to change or evolve the legal system was the lack of social opposition. While national courts were being established in 1883, the promulgation of European law faced few demonstrations.[113]

Egyptian courts served as the test cases for this evolution. Some procedural changes, among them the necessity of eyewitness testimony, were altered in 1931.[114] When the Sharī'ah courts were abolished, their duties were transferred to the national courts. In addition, many changes in the Egyptian courts and legal system soon appeared. For example, Egypt enacted new civil codes in 1949. The *Mecelle* (*Majallah*) remained prevalent in Lebanon and even moreso in Syria,[115] and Jordan's Law of Family Rights replaced Ottoman law (1951). In Saudi Arabia, Yemen, and Oman, the traditional religious law remains in effect, to a certain extent, because these countries are still strictly conservative. In fact, Saudi Arabia has declared the Sharīʿah the fundamental law of the state.[116] Nevertheless, change was legislated by Turkey's family law court in 1951. Syria, which enacted its Code of Personal Status in 1953, was eventually followed by Tunisia (1957), Morocco (1958), Iraq (1959), and Sudan (1967). Egypt and Tunisia abolished their Sharīʿah courts in 1956 and 1957, respectively.[117] Tunisia's judiciary seems to be a patchwork of both Mālikī and Ḥanafī Sharīʿah courts, Mosaic law, and the (Christian) French civil code applied by its national courts. In order to please its French and Christian populations, the Sharīʿah was modified and the government settled intra-Muslim conflicts.[118]

Despite the fact that Sharīʿah courts and Islamic laws still prevail in some Muslim states, others (e.g., Turkey and Albania) have implemented completely secular systems. In Saudi Arabia, the Gulf states, and Iran, the Sharīʿah is the sole law of land, which means that each law must be in accord with its principles. In Indonesia, nationwide Sharīʿah courts work side-by-side with civil courts (*pengadilan negeri*).[119] This is also the case in Malaysia[120] and Zanzibar.[121] After Sudan gained its independence in 1956, the influence of British law remained highly palpable. Although the country's legal system was based on local custom derived from Islamic law, the structural organization of its court system basically relies upon the British model.[122] The legal systems of India, Pakistan, and Bangladesh were all formed by their respective experiences with British colonialism; hence, Sharīʿah justice functions more like the national court system than special Sharīʿah courts.[123]

In order to protect the constitution of modern states, the Supreme Constitutional Court was established and "entrusted with the exclusive power to adjudicate the validity of legislative provisions with regard to their compliance or irreconcilable variance with the Constitution."[124] Hence, it ensures that the laws comply with the constitution—a kind of a constitutional assurance. This independent judiciary and highest judicial power vis-à-vis the state was launched in Egypt (1979), where it replaced the constitutional court of 1969,[125] and in Turkey (1962), with the ordinance of the provisions of its 1961 constitution.[126]

Indonesia, Lebanon, Malaysia, Qatar, and several other majority-Muslim states have a dual court system. Malaysia's system is highly interesting, as it takes into consideration the entire society. Its law is basically applied according to the following hierarchical standing: beginning with the federal court, it descends to the court of appeal, which is subdivided into the high courts in Malaysia and the high courts in Sabah and Sarawak. Under the former subdivision of the high court in Malaysia are the Sharīʿah courts (which are not applied to non-Muslims), then the session courts, magistrates' courts, small claims courts, and *penghulu* courts. In the case of Sabah and Sarawak, the hierarchy is similar. Beginning with the high court, which is parallel to the high court in Malaysia, it descends into the native courts and Sharīʿah courts, session courts, magistrates' courts, and small claims courts. Prior to 1 January 1987, the final court of appeal in Malaysia was the privy council. The country's highest court, the Federal Court, was abolished on the same date in 1987.[127] It had consisted of the chief justice, the president of the court of appeal, the chief judge of Malaysia, the chief judge of Sabah and Sarawak, and six federal court judges.[128]

From time to time, Islamic law's involvement in the judiciary has been limited to family and personal matters. For example, Oman's judiciary began to go beyond the Sharīʿah courts during the 1970s, although its basic law relies totally upon it. Although the Sharīʿah court system has been amended by the Basic Law, secular courts were introduced to deal with penal and commercial matters.[129] Due to the political influence on the judiciary, Pakistan's recent attempts to Islamize its court system has not gone beyond political concerns, for example, introducing the Federal Sharīʿah Court (FSC) and the Sharīʿah appellate bench in the Supreme Court and appointing many *ad hoc* judges to the high courts and the Supreme Court while transferring some high court judges to the FSC. Despite this dilemma, however, Pakistan achieved judicial independence in 1985[130] and has done its best to remain a democracy despite the various ongoing political frustrations.

Conclusion

In this paper, I have tried to investigate the fundamental basis of change in the Sharīʿah court systems of several Muslim states; how the system started and developed in light of some political or military factors that sought to interfere, as well as imperialistic demands, social welfare, and the requirements of modernity; and how some rulers sought to impose their ideas or hegemony by using the judiciary's authority and the ensuing effects upon the administration of the judiciary system.

The case studied in this essay revealed that the judiciary, as an institutional framework, as well as the application of the Sharīʿah have changed over time, especially during the twentieth century, when western economic and political influence caused the majority of Muslim countries to adopt western legal codes. The rapid increase in industrial power enabled the West to assert its supremacy over the East, especially in Muslim lands, due to the West's need for the latter's natural resources. This encouraged the colonial powers to involve themselves in the Muslim world's judicial activities by introducing the mixed court system in order to protect their own interests. After a while, however, this system created disputes as regards their political agenda as well as within Muslim society at large.

This essay has shown that the judiciary reached its modern form by passing through many stages. The simple appointment of a judge for legal matters at the time of the Prophet (pbuh) was developed under the Companions, the Rightly Guided Caliphs, and especially under ʿUmar b. al-Khaṭṭāb, who established an independent judiciary and appointed muftis, *ḥakam*s, and judges to different cities and garrison towns while allocating a private building (court) for legal matters. This setup helped the rulers to interfere in legal matters, as seen in Muʿāwiyah's appointments of *qaḍīs* to newly formed garrison towns, among them al-Kūfah, al-Baṣrah, and al-Fusṭāṭ. This situation differed greatly from the pre-Umayyad period, a time when the judiciary was free of any political and social control, a time when the caliph himself was accountable to the Sharīʿah and had to obey the ruling of the court. This privilege enabled the *ʿulamāʾ*, jurists, and muftis to deal independently with all legal cases, because they did not have to worry about the caliph's use of arbitrary force and power in legal and religious matters.

As the Islamic state expanded, the jurists' role changed due to the extra responsibilities they acquired. For example, although *qāḍīs* were professionals whose field of activity was limited to resolving legal disputes and administering the emerging judicial matters at the time of ʿUmar, beginning with Muʿāwiyah they were also expected to function in such non-judicial capacities as governors, tax collectors, military commanders, prayer leaders (*imāms*), and supervisors of the public treasury and the land tax. In addition, they often engaged in trade and commerce to meet their own daily needs due to their customary refusal to accept any financial remuneration for their judicial-related services.

In order to control the society, the rulers interfered in the judiciary and thus ensured that the resulting political tension would politicize it. Beginning with Sulaymān b. ʿAbd al-Mālik (r.715-717), judges were appointed directly by the caliphs, who employed important and influential religious figures as *qāḍīs* to propagate their ideology and maintain the system's reputation. On some occasions the rulers would even force the *ʿulamāʾ* and *qāḍīs* to implement their personal theological views, the primary example being the *miḥnah* established by al-Maʾmūn in 218/833.

Every era brought some changes to the judiciary, both positive and negative. For instance, upon coming to power the ʿAbbāsids implemented a judiciary based upon a diversity of legal schools. The Fātimīds of Egypt converted this into a single *madhhab* system (the Ismāʿīlī Shīʿah); Sultan Baybars (r.1260-1277) implemented the chief *qāḍī* system; and later on this system was headed by an official appointed from the Ḥanafī, Shafiʿī, Ḥanbalī, and Mālikī schools of thought. The changes and developments made throughout the ʿAbbāsid period were upheld by the Mughals (1526-1858), the Safavids (1501-1722), and the Ottomans (1526-1858). The latter's establishment of the *qānūn* and *qānūnnāmes* helped develop secular law within the judiciary. The society's cultural factor was also incorporated into the state's legal system. Introducing the Meclis-i Valaʾi Aḥkām-i ʿAdliye (the Supreme Council of Justice) in 1838, the Gülhane Decree (1839), the *mecalis* (provincial councils) that opened membership to Christians, were profound changes. These were followed by the *nizamiye* courts (1864) and the *Mecelle* (Ottoman civil code of Ḥanafī Law), which was applied in both the Sharīʿah and the *nizamiye* courts in 1870 and in 1917, respectively. The eventual termination of the *qāḍī* court system helped the Middle East, especially the Ottoman empire, modernize and secularize its legal systems.

Notes

1. Associate Prof Dr Saim Kayadibi, associated with the Faculty of Economics and Management Sciences, Department of Economics, International Islamic University Malaysia, Kuala Lumpur. Email: saim@iium.edu.my / skayadibi@yahoo.com
2. Qur'an: 57:25.
3. This legal maxim first appears in Abū Sa'īd Muḥammad al-Khādimī, (d.116/1755), *Manāfi' al-Daqā'iq fī Sharḥ Majāmi' al-Ḥaqā'iq* (Istanbul: 1305 AH), 328. Also see *Majallah al-Ahkāḥm,* clause 39. For a discussion of this maxim, see Ibn Qayyim al-Jawziyyah, "I'lām al-Muwaqqi'īn", 3:14-70; Ibn 'Ābidīn Muḥammad Amīn (d.1252/1836), *Nashr al-'Urf fī Binā' ba'ḍ al-Aḥkām 'alā al-'Urf* (Beirut), 114-146; and Ibn 'Ābidīn, *Ḥāshiyah Nasamāt al-Asḥār* (Cairo: Muṣṭafā Bābī al-Ḥalabī), 1:69.
4. Saim Kayadibi, "*Ijtihād* and Modernist Perspectives towards Islamic Law and Thought," *Journal of Islamic Law Studies* 11 (2008): 114.
5. Qur'an: 4:135.
6. Aḥmad Abū Bakr al-Khaṣṣāf (874 CE), *Islamic Legal and Judicial System* (New Delhi: Adam Publishers, 2005); al-Khaṣṣāf, *Sharḥ Adab al-Qāḍī li al-Imām Abī Bakr Aḥmad b. 'Umar al-Khaṣṣāf* (Beirut: Dār al-Kutub al-'Ilmiyyah, 1994); Fahreddin Atar, *Islam Adliye Teşkilatı*, 4th ed. (Ankara: Ministry of Religious Affairs of Turkey, 1999); Muhammad Khalid Masud, Rudolph Peters, David S. Powers, eds., "Qadis and Their Courts: An Historical Survey" in *Dispensing Justice in Islam: Qadis and Their Judgments* (Leiden and Boston: Brill, 2006), 1-6.
7. Abū Ja'far Muḥammad b. Jarīr al-Ṭabarī (838-923), *Ta'rīkh al-Umama wa al-Mulūk* (Cairo: 1939), 2:41. Abū al-Fidā' Ismā'īl b. Abī Ḥafṣ b. Kathīr (701-774), *al-Bidāyah wa al-Nihāyah* (Cairo: 1932), 2:299; Abū Muḥammad 'Abd al-Mālik b. Hishām (d. 833 CE), *al-Sīrah al-Nabawiyyah*, ed. Muṣṭafā Ibrāhīm (Egypt: 1936), 1:209; Muḥammad b. Manī' al-Baghdādī b. Sa'd (784-845 CE), *Ṭabaqāt al-Kubrā* (Leiden: 1917), 1: 1, 94.
8. Ibn Sa'd, *Ṭabaqāt al-Kubrā*, 1: 1, 102:

كان يتحاكم الى رسول الله صلى الله عليه وسلم في الجاهلية قبل الاسلام ثم اختص في الاسلام

9. Qur'an 4:65, 105; 5:42, 48-49; and 24:48, 51.
10. Masud, Peters, and Powers, "Qadis and Their Courts," 7.
11. Salih Tuğ, *İslam Ülkelerinde Anayasa Hareketleri* (Istanbul: İrfan Yayınevi, 1969), 31-43.
12. Jorgen S. Nielsen, "Sultan al-Ẓāhir Baybars and the Appointment of Four Chief Qāḍīs, 663/1265" *Studia Islamica* 60 (1984): 167.
13. B.A. Roberson, "The Emergence of the Modern Judiciary in the Middle East: Negotiating the Mixed Courts of Egypt," in *Islam and Public Law*, ed. Chibli Mallat (London: Graham & Trotman, 1993), 107.
14. Bernard Lewis, "Politics and War" in *The Legacy of Islam*, ed. Joseph Schacht, 2d ed. (Oxford: Clarendon Press, 1974), 172.
15. Imām Ahmed b. Ḥanbel, *El-Müsned*, trans. Rıfat Oral (Konya: 2003), 1:262, ḥadīth no. 13:210.
16. Qur'an 48:29
17. Masud, Peters, and, "Qadis and Their Courts," 7.
18. Atar, *Islam Adliye Teşkilatı*, 49.
19. For more about caliphs and sultans, see H. Yanagihashi, "The Judicial Functions of the Sulṭān in Civil Cases According to the Mālikīs up to the Sixth/Twelfth Century," *Islamic Law and Society* 3, no. 1 (1996): 41-74.
20. Irit Bligh Abramski, "The Judiciary (Qadis) as a Governmental-Administrative Tool in Early Islam," Journal of the Economic and Social History of the Orient 35, no. 1 (1992): 40-71.
21. Masud, Peters, and Powers, "Qadis and Their Courts," 8.
22. Irit Bligh Abramski, "The Judiciary (Qadis)," 40-71.
23. H.A.R. Gibb and Harold Bowen, *Islamic Society and the West*, vol. 2 of *Islamic Society in the Eighteenth Century* (London: Oxford University Press, 1957), 2:81.
24. D. Bonderman, "Modernization and Changing Perceptions of Islamic Law," *Harvard Law Review* 81, no. 6 (1968): 1176.
25. Robert Gleave, "The Qadi and the Mufti in Akhbari Shi'i Jurisprudence," in *The Law Applied: Contextualizing the Islamic Shari'a: A Volume in Honor of Frank E. Vogel*, ed. Peri Bearman, Wolfhart Heinrichs, and Bernard G. Weiss (London: I.B. Tauris, 2008), 236.

26. N.J. Coulson, "Doctrine and Practice in Islamic Law: One Aspect of the Problem," *Bulletin of the School of Oriental and African Studies* 18, no. 2 (1956): 211-219.
27. Masud, Peters, and Powers, "Qadis and Their Courts," 8.
28. Ibid., 9.
29. W.B. Hallaq, "Model Shura Works and the Dialectic of Doctrine and Practice," *Islamic Law and Society* 2, no. 2 (1995): 123.
30. Wael B. Hallaq, *Authority, Continuity and Change in Islamic Law* (United Kingdom: Cambridge University Press, 2001), 167.
31. The jurist al-Sha'bi (d. 721), who tutored the sons of 'Abd al-Mālik, was appointed for a diplomatic mission to the Byzantines and served as *qāḍī* of al-Kūfah during the caliphate of 'Umar b. 'Abd al-'Azīz (r. 717-720); al-Ḥasan al-Baṣrī (d. 728) served as a secretary for the government of both 'Abd al-Mālik and 'Umar b. 'Abd al-'Azīz (r. 719-723) and as *qāḍī* of al-Baṣrah during the latter's reign; Ibn Shihāb al-Zuhrī (d. 741-742), appointed as a judge by Yazīd II and tutor for the sons of Hishām, also circulated pro-Umayyad traditions. See Irit Bligh Abramski, "The Judiciary (Qadis)," 61-66.
32. Masud, Peters, and Powers, "Qadis and Their Courts," 10.
33. Muhammad Qasim Zaman, "The Caliphs, the 'Ulamā', and the Law: Defining the Role and Function of the Caliph in the Early 'Abbāsid Period," *Islamic Law and Society* 4, no. 1 (1997): 1-36.
34. This term signifies unjust and oppressive actions. The singular form is *maẓlimah*: Arabic *dār al-maẓālim*. Courts that served as tribunals of administrative law where the public directly appealed to the ruler or his deputies against the abuse of or failure to exercise power by other authorities, as well as against decisions made by judges, quoted from John L. Esposito, *The Oxford Dictionary of Islam* (New York: Oxford University Press, 2003), 198.
35. For detailed research on the *maẓālim* courts, see Aḥmad Sa'īd al-Mūminī, "Qaḍā' al-Maẓālim: al-Qaḍā' al-Idārī al-Islāmī," *Jam'iyyah 'Ummāl al-Maṭābi' al-Ta'āwuniyyah* (Amman: 1991); 'Abd al-Ḥamīd al-Rifā'ī, *al-Qaḍā' al-Idārī bayn al-Sharī'ah wa al-Qānūn* (Beirut: Dār al-Fikr al-Mu'āṣir, 1989).
36. Jorgen S. Nielsen, "Maẓālim," *The Encyclopedia of Islam*, new ed.

(Leiden: E.J. Brill, 1991); quoted from Masud, Peters, and Powers, "Qadis and Their Courts," 11-12.

37. Muhammad Hashim Kamali, "Appellate Review and Judicial Independence in Islamic Law," in *Islam and Public Law*, 50-52.
38. Ibid., 52.
39. Irit Bligh Abramski, "The Judiciary (Qadis)," 56-57.
40. Ibid, 62-65.
41. Ibid, 69.
42. Nurit Tsafrir, "The Beginnings of the Ḥanafī School in Iṣfahān," *Islamic Law and Society* 5, no. 1 (1998): 10.
43. Muhd Qasim Zaman, "The Caliphs, the 'Ulamā', and the Law," 25. For more details of the *miḥnah*, see W.M. Patton, *Ahmad ibn Hanbal and the Mihna* (Leiden: 1897); N. Hurvitz, "Miḥna as Self-Defense," *Studia Islamica* 92 (2001): 93-111; W. Madelung, "The Origins of the Controversy Concerning the Creation of the Koran," in *Orientalia hispanica sive studia F.M. Pareja octogenario dicata*, ed. J.M. Barral (Leiden: E.J. Brill, 1974), 1:504-525; J.A. Nawas, "The Miḥna of 218 AH/833 AD Revisited: An Empirical Study," *Journal of the American Oriental Society* 116, no. 4 (1996): 698-708; J. A. Nawas, "A Reexamination of Three Current Explanations for al-Ma'mun's Introduction of the Mihna," *International Journal of Middle East Studies* 26, no. 4 (1994): 615-629.
44. Ira M. Lapidus, *A History of Islamic Societies*, 2d ed. (Cambridge University Press: 2002), 148.
45. E.J. Jurji, "Islamic Law in Operation," *The American Journal of Semitic Languages and Literatures* 57, no. 1 (1940): 38-39.
46. Emile Tyan, *Histoire de l'organization judiciaire en pays d'Islam* (Paris: 1938), 140; quoted from Jurji, "Islamic Law in Operation," 44-45.
47. Al-Subkī, *al-Ṭabaqāt al-Shāfi'īyāh al-Kubrā*, 6 vols. (Cairo: 1324 AH), 5:134, quoted from Nielsen, "Sultan al-Zāhir Baybars," 168.
48. Ibn Taghrī Birdī, *al-Nujūm al-Zāhirah*, 13 vols. (Cairo: 1929-1956), 7:133.
49. Nielsen, "Sultan al-Zāhir Baybars,"168.
50. Ibid., 169-170.

51. Al-ʻUmarī, *al-Taʻrīf bi al-Muṣṭalaḥ al-Sharīf* (Cairo: 1312 AH), 75; al-Qalqashandī, 4:44, quoted from Nielsen, "Sultan al-Zāhir Baybars,"175.
52. Masud, Peters, and Powers, "Qadis and Their Courts," 15.
53. Ibid.
54. Chibli Mallat, "From Islamic to Middle Eastern Law: A Restatement of the Field (Part II)," *The American Journal of Comparative Law* 52, no. 1 (2004): 210; Saim Kayadibi, *Doctrine of Istihsan Juristic Preference in Islamic Law* (Konya: Tablet, 2007), 94.
55. G. Baer, "The Transition from Traditional to Western Criminal Law in Turkey and Egypt," *Studia Islamica* 45 (1977): 139.
56. Dora Glidewell Nadolski, "Ottoman and Secular Civil Law," *International Journal of Middle East Studies* 8, no. 4 (1977): 517-518.
57. D. Ze'evi, "The Use of Ottoman Sharīʻa Court Records as a Source for Middle Eastern Social History: A Reappraisal," *Islamic Law and Society* 5, no. 1 (1998): 38. For more about *sjill* studies, see W.B. Hallaq, "The 'qāḍīs dīwān (sijill)' before the Ottomans," *Bulletin of the School of Oriental and African Studies* 61, no. 3 (1998): 415-436.
58. "We never punish until We have sent a messenger," Qur'an 17:15.
59. J.N.D. Anderson, "Recent Developments in Sharīʻa Law II," *The Muslim World* 41, no. 1 (1951): 34.
60. Qur'an 5:49.
61. Qur'an 5:42.
62. Qur'an 38:26
63. ʻAbd al-Ḥayy b. ʻAbd al-Kabīr al-Kattānī (d. 1962), al-Tarātīb al-Idāriyyah (Rabat: 1346 AH), 1: 258; ʻAlī b. ʻUmar al-Dāraquṭnī "Sunan" (Delhi: Maṭbaʻah al-Anṣārī, 1310 AH), 511.
64. Qur'an 4:135.
65. Jurji, "Islamic Law in Operation," 32.
66. Wael B. Hallaq, *The Origins and Evolution of Islamic Law* (Cambridge, UK: Cambridge University Press, 2004), 93-94; quoted from Masud, Peters, and Powers, *Dispensing Justice in Islam*, 21-22.
67. Gibb and Bowen, "Islamic Society and the West," 1:121-138; for more about these terms and their practical usages in eighteenth-century Ottoman society, see ibid.

68. Abū al-Ḥasan ʻAlī b. Muḥammad b. Ḥabīb al-Māwardī (d. 1058), *al-Ḥāwī al-Kabīr*, 23 vols. (Beirut: Dār al-Fikr, 1994), 16:28, quoted from Masud, Peters, and Powers, ibid, 22.
69. The person who is making a claim is called plaintiff.
70. The person against whom the claim is made is called the defendant.
71. David S. Powers, "Four Cases Relating to Women and Divorce in al-Andalus and the Maghrib 1100-1500," in Masud, Peters, and Powers, *Dispensing Justice in Islam,* 406.
72. Wahbah Zuḥaylī, *al-Fiqh al-Islāmī wa Adillatuh*, 8 vols. (Damascus: Dār al-Fikr, 1996), 6:511.
73. Masud, Peters, and Powers, "Qadis and Their Courts," 23.
74. *The Mejelle,* trans. C.R. Tyser, D.G. Demetriades, and Ismail Haqqi Efendi (Kuala Lumpur: The Other Press, 2001), 279, maxim no. 1632.
75. Qur'an 2:282.
76. Zuḥaylī, *al-Fiqh al-Islāmī,* 6:556.
77. Masud, Peters, and Powers, "Qadis and Their Courts," 26.
78. *The Mejelle,* 13.
79. See the ḥadīth in Mālik b. Anas (d.711-795), *al-Muwaṭṭa'*, 1: 41.
80. J.N.D. Anderson, "Recent Developments," 42.
81. Zuḥaylī, *al-Fiqh al-Islāmī,* 6:782.
82. Masud, Peters, and Powers, "Qadis and Their Courts," 27
83. Layish Aharon, "Shahādat Naql in the Judicial Practice in Modern Libya," in Masud, Peters, and Powers, *Dispensing Justice in Islam,* 495-497.
84. Christian Müller, "Settling Litigation without Judgment: The Importance of a Ḥukm in Qāḍī Cases of Mamlūk Jerusalem," in ibid., 48.
85. Baber Johansen, "The Constitution and the Principles of Islamic Normativity against the Rules of Fiqh: A Judgment of the Supreme Constitutional Court of Egypt," in ibid., 172.
86. U. Rebstock, "A Qāḍī's Errors," *Islamic Law and Society* 6, no. 1 (1999): 1-37.
87. Masud, Peters, and Powers, "Qadis and Their Courts," 32-33.
88. Ibid., 33.

89. L. Rosen, "Equity and Discretion in a Modern Islamic Legal System," *Law & Society Review* 15, no. 2 (1980): 217-218.
90. Bonderman, "Modernization and Changing Perceptions," 1171.
91. Masud, Peters, Powers, "Qadis and Their Courts," 34.
92. Niyasi Berkes, *The Development of Secularism in Turkey* (New York: Routledge, 1998 [repr.]), 170.
93. Nadolski, "Ottoman and Secular Civil Law," 536.
94. J.N.D. Anderson, "Recent Developments," 34.
95. Masud, Peters, and Powers, "Qadis and Their Courts," 38-41.
96. E. Hill, "Al-Sanhuri and Islamic Law: The Place and Significance of Islamic Law in the Life and Work of 'Abd al-Razzaq Ahmad al-Sanhuri, Egyptian Jurist and Scholar, 1895-1971," *Arab Law Quarterly* 3, no. 1 (1988): 40.
97. Nubar Pasha was an Armenian Christian and a nephew of Baghus Bey, Muhammad Ali's old foreign minister. Educated in France and Switzerland, he had long experience with serving the ruler of Egypt; quoted from Roberson, "The Emergence of the Modern Judiciary in the Middle East," 121.
98. Ibid., 117-124; J.N.D. Anderson, "The Significance of Islamic Law in the World Today," *The American Journal of Comparative Law* 9, no. 2 (1960): 189.
99. J.N.D. Anderson, "Law Reform in the Middle East," *International Affairs* 32, no. 1 (1956): 44.
100. J.N.D. Anderson, "Recent Developments," 35.
101. M.S.W. Hoyle, "The Mixed Courts of Egypt: An Anniversary Assessment," *Arab Law Quarterly* 1, no. 1 (1985): 60.
102. Ahmad Hidayat Buang, *Studies in the Islamic Law of Contracts: The Prohibition of Gharar* (Kuala Lumpur: International Law Book Services, 2000), 16.
103. Hoyle, "The Mixed Courts of Egypt," 60-62. Al-Sanhuri made an undeniable contribution to codifying the law and establishing the new law, a mixture of Islamic and civil law. For more his life and work, see Hill, "Al-Sanhuri and Islamic Law," part I, 3(1): p. 33-64; and part II, 3(2): p. 182-218.
104. Nadolski, "Ottoman and Secular Civil Law," 517-525.

105. See more about the capitulatory system and the Treaty of Lausanne of 1923 in Bernard Lewis, *The Emergence of Modern Turkey* (London: Oxford University Press, 1961); L.E. Thayer, "The Capitulations of the Ottoman Empire and the Question of Their Abrogation as it Affects the United States," *The American Journal of International Law* 17, no. 2 (1923): 207-233; N. Bentwich, "The Abrogation of the Turkish Capitulations," *Journal of Comparative Legislation and International Law* 5, no. 4 (1923): 182-188; J.B. Angell, "The Turkish Capitulations," *The American Historical Review* 6, no. 2 (1901): 254-259; P.M. Brown, "The Lausanne Treaty," *The American Journal of International Law* 21, no. 3 (1927): 503-505; Kadir Misiroglu, *Lozan Barış mı Hezimet mi?* (Istanbul: Sebil Yayınevi, 1965); P.M. Brown, "The Lausanne Conference," *The American Journal of International Law* 17, no. 2 (1923): 290-296.
106. A.A. Ibrahim, "Tale of Two Sudanese Courts: Colonial Governmentality Revisited," *African Studies Review* 40, no. 1 (1997): 13-33.
107. Saim Kayadibi and Ahmad Hiyadat Buang, "Impact of Globalization on Higher Education from the Viewpoint of Islamic Law" (paper presented at the International Conference on Higher Education Research and Development, Dhurakij Pundit University, Bangkok, Thailand, 9-12 July 2009), 13.
108. A. Nizar Hamzeh, "Qatar: The Duality of the Legal System," *Middle Eastern Studies* 30, no. 1 (1994). 80-86.
109. Elaine Sciolino, "Britain Grapples with Role for Islamic Justice," *New York Times*, November 18, 2008.
110. Lord Phillips, "Equality before the Law" (speech of Lord Chief Justice, East London Muslim Centre, 3 July 2008), 9.
111. Bonderman, "Modernization and Changing Perceptions," 1176.
112. N.J. Brown, "Sharia and State in the Modern Muslim Middle East," *International Journal of Middle East Studies* 29, no. 3 (1997): 363-367.
113. Ibid., 369.
114. N. Safran, "The Abolition of the Shar'i Courts in Egypt," *The Muslim World* 48 (1958): 20-28 and 125-135.

115. J.N.D. Anderson, *Law Reform in the Middle East"*, 49.
116. Joseph Schacht, "Islamic Law in Contemporary States," *The American Journal of Comparative Law* 8, no. 2 (1959): 136; J.N.D. Anderson, "The Significance of Islamic Law," 196.
117. Bonderman, "Modernization and Changing Perceptions," 1176. For more about the enactments, see J.N.D. Anderson, "The Tunisian Law of Personal Status," *The International and Comparative Law Quarterly* 7, no. 2 (1958): 262; J.N.D. Anderson, "A Law of Personal Status for Iraq," *The International and Comparative Law Quarterly* 9, no. 4 (1960): 542; J.N.D. Anderson, "Reforms in Family Law in Morocco," *Journal of African Law* 2, no. 3 (1958): 146; J.N.D. Anderson, "The Syrian Law of Personal Status," *Bulletin of the School of Oriental and African Studies* 17, no. 1 (1955): 34; N.O. Akolawin, "Personal Law in the Sudan: Trends and Developments," *Journal of African Law* 17, no. 2 (1973): 150; and J.N.D. Anderson, "The Family Law of Turkish Cypriots," *Die Welt des Islams* 5. nos. 3/4 (1958): 165.
118. Bonderman, "Modernization and Changing Perceptions," 1184-1185.
119. John R. Bowen, "Fairness and Law in an Indonesian Court," Masud, Peters, and Powers, *Dispensing Justice in Islam*, 117.
120. Muhammad Hashim Kamali, *Islamic Law in Malaysia: Issues and Developments* (Selangor: Ilmiah Publishers, 2000), 46.
121. Erin Stiles, "When Is a Divorce a Divorce? Determining Intention in Zanzibar's Islamic Courts," *Ethnology* 42, no. 4 (2003): 274; Erin Stiles, "Broken Edda and Marital Mistakes: Two Recent Disputes from an Islamic Court in Zanzibar" in Masud, Peters, and Powers, *Dispensing Justice in Islam*, 95.
122. Chibli Mallat, "From Islamic to Middle Eastern Law," 278; C. Fluehr-Lobban and H.B. Hillawi," Circulars of the Sharīʿa Courts in the Sudan (*Manshūrāt El-Mahākim El-Sharīʿah fi Sūdān*) 1902-1979," *Journal of African Law* 27, no. 2 (1983): 80.
123. Masud, Peters, and Powers, "The Qadis and Their Courts," 42.
124. ʿAwad al-Morr, "The Supreme Constitutional Court of Egypt and the Protection of Human and Political Rights," in *Islam and Public Law*, 229.

125. T. Moustafa, "Law versus the State: The Judicialization of Politics in Egypt," *Law & Social Inquiry* 28, no. 4 (2003): 883-930.
126. R. Aybay, "Some Contemporary Constitutional Problems in Turkey," *Bulletin: British Society for Middle Eastern Studies* 4, no 1 (1977): 24.
127. Lee Mei Pheng, *General Principles of Malaysian Law* (Selangor, Malaysia: Penerbit Fajar Bakti Sdn. Bhd., 1990), 31-33.
128. Ibid., 67.
129. N.A. Siegfried, "Legislation and Legitimation in Oman: The Basic Law," *Islamic Law and Society* 7, no. 3 (2000): 377-378.
130. Martin Lau, "The Islamization of Laws in Pakistan: Impact on the Independence of the Judiciary," in *The Rule of Law in the Middle East and the Islamic World: Human Rights and the Judicial Process*, ed. Eugene Cotran and Mai Yamani (London: I.B. Tauris in association with the Centre of Islamic Studies and Middle Eastern Law, School of Oriental and African Studies, University of London, 2000), 150-163.

6

Fiqh education at Ottoman madrasahs: A case study of Süleymaniye madrasahs

Servet Bayındır[1]

Definition of *fiqh* and its subdivisions

The word *fiqh* derives from "فقه," which is defined as "to understand clearly and exactly, to conceive, to know and to comprehend."[2] As an independent branch of knowledge, the development process of *fiqh* has taken several stages. First, knowledge of the faith (*i'tiqād*), acts of worship (*'ibādāt*), and social interactions (*mu'āmalāt*) are derived from the Qur'an and Sunnah through *ijtihād* and are implemented in the Muslims' daily life. In order to differentiate this knowledge from the Qur'an and Sunnah, the concept of *fiqh* eventually emerged. Initially, any religious knowledge generated by the human intellect that was derived from the primary sources (knowledge of person's rights and obligations) was called *fiqh.* In that sense, this term can be traced back to the era of Abū Ḥanīfah (150/767). Broadly speaking, this term was used to cover all Islamic knowledge and continued in this capacity until the fifth Islamic century, when it was used to designate the *furū' al-dīn* (branches of the religion) including knowledge on *ilmihal* (*ibādāt* and *akhlāq*), *mu'āmalāt*, and *'uqūbāt* (penal codes). Consequently, *fiqh* became one of Islam's sciences.[3] Abū Ḥanīfah described it as "the knowledge of soul (person), its rights and obligations,"[4] whereas Shāfi'ī described it as "the knowledge of the divine legislators (Shari' rules), pertaining to conduct that have been derived from their specific evidences."[5] The *Majallah* defines *fiqh* as "the knowledge of the divine legislator, pertaining to conducts."[6] Today, it is widely accepted that fiqh is "the knowledge of the divine legislator, pertaining to conducts that have been derived from their specific evidences."[7] Western legal system only regulates relationships among human beings, whereas *fiqh* regulates the human being's relationship with God in addition to his relationship with other creatures.

Fiqh primarily consists of two divisions: *furū‘ al-fiqh* and *uṣūl al-fiqh*. Within these two categories, once can also find the history of *fiqh, qawā‘id, shurūṭ*, and *sijillāt, ‘ilm al-khilāf* and *jadal, ḥikmah al-tashrī‘, ḥiyal* and *mahārij, siyāsah shar‘iyyah, fiqh al-sīrah* and *maghāzī, fatāwah, ṭabaqāt al-fuqahā', masāil, alghāz, farāi'd, da‘wah and tablīgh, iṣṭilāḥāt, furūq, amwāl*, and *iqtiṣād*.[8]

The place of *fiqh* among the systematic sciences

Throughout Islamic history, the sciences have been classified according two fundamental approaches. The first approach prioritizes human intelligence (*‘aql*), whereas the other prioritizes revelation (*waḥy*). This approach, however, did consider the balance between *‘āql* and *waḥy*. Fārābī (339/950), who obtained and further developed Aristotle's knowledge classification scheme, represents the first approach together with Ibn Sīna (428/1036); Khawārizmī (387/997) and Ghazālī (504/1111) follow the second one.

In his *Taḥṣīl al-Sa‘ādah*, Fārābī classifies the sciences into two categories: *naẓarī* (theoretical) and *‘amalī* (practical). He does not mention *fiqh* in this classification.[9] In his *Iḥṣā' al-‘Ulūm*, he studies the sciences under five main subtitles (1) *‘Ilm al-Lisān* and its subdivisions, (2) *‘Ilm al-Manṭiq* and its subdivisions, (3) *‘Ilm al-Ta‘līm* and its subdivisions, (4) *Ṭabī‘iyyāt* and *Ilāhiyyāt*, and (5) *‘Ilm Madanī* and its subdivisions. Both *fiqh* and *kalām* fall under this subtitle.[10] Ibn Sīnā, who also classifies the sciences as *naẓarī* and *'amalī*, adds another category under the first group: narratives pertaining to *siḥr* (magic) as *'ilm ṭabī'ī*.[11]

In his *Miftāḥ al-'Ulūm*, Khawārizmī divides sciences into *'Ulūm Shar'iyyah* (Religious Sciences) and *Ulūm 'Ajamiyyah* (Foreign Sciences). *Fiqh*, *uṣūl al-fiqh*, and *kalām* fall under the first category, as do *lughah* (language), *shi'r* (poetry), and *'arūẓ* (science of poetry). The second category is further subdivided into *naẓarī* and *'amalī* sciences, following the framework of Fārābī and Ibn Sīnā.[12]

On the other hand, Ghazālī categorized sciences as *shar'ī* and *ghayr shar'ī* sciences. *Tafsīr*, *uṣūl al-fiqh*, *ḥadīth*, and *uṣūl al-ḥadīth* are classified as *shar'ī* sciences. The Qur'an, the Sunnah, and the Companions' ḥadīths are the main sources for these sciences. Likewise, Khawārizmī's classification, *lughah* and *naḥv* (syntax), are classified as *shar'ī* sciences category because they form the *muqaddamāt*, the tools required to study the *shar'ī* sciences. The *ghayr shar'ī* sciences are divided into praised sciences (e.g., accounting, medicine, and sciences that deal with worldly matters), permissible sciences (e.g., poetry and history), and condemned sciences (e.g., magic and casting spells).[13]

Hocazâde Muslihuddin Mustafa (893/1488) and his son Taşköprülüzâde Ahmed İsamuddin Efendi (968/1561) are the two prominent Ottoman classifiers of the sciences who examined the approaches to science and provided appraisals and valuable information on this field. Muslihuddin Mustafa classified sciences under three main categories: (1) *Taqrīrī* and non-*taqrīrī* sciences, as well as sciences that can be expressed literally and in written form. *Fiqh*, *tafsīr*, and ḥadīth fall under this category; (2) Sciences that can be expressed (*taqrīr*) but should not be written down (*taḥrīr*), and sciences that can be expressed literally but not written down. Speculations used in debates to fire back at one's opponents, interpretations, reasoning, twisting, and paronomasia fall under this category; and (3) Sciences that cannot be expressed, or interpreted (*ta'bīr*), or written down or described (*taṣwīr*). *'Ilm Ladunnī* (divine knowledge) falls under this category.[14] As Taşköprülüzâde states, Muslihuddin Mustafa referred to the sciences in second group, generally those related to *kalām* (theology) and *falsafah* (philosophy) as useless. According to Muslihuddin Mustafa, the *'ulamā'* should be concerned with the first group, as its sciences are useful.

In his famous *Shaqāiq*, Taşköprülüzâde divided the sciences into *ẓāhirī* and *bāṭinī* science. *Fiqh, uṣūl al-fiqh, tafsīr, ḥadīth, kalām, ṣarf, naḥū,* and *bidā'ī* are considered *ẓāhirī* sciences. *Mujtahid*s consider *fiqh* to be the most valuable science, since people in this field better serve the Islamic community by deriving judgements (*ḥukum*) from the Qur'an. What Taşköprülüzâde means by *bāṭinī* sciences is similar to Muslihuddin Mustafa's third group of sciences: sciences that cannot be expressed (*taqrīr*) or interpreted (*ta'bīr*).[15] According to both, Sufism (*taṣawwuf*) is part of this category.

The tradition of classifying the sciences pioneered by Khawārizmī and Ghazālī was widely accepted in the Ottoman academy. In order to maintain the classification system's core values, different titles were given to the categories; *shar'ī* and *ghayr shar'ī* sciences, *'aqlī* and *naqlī* sciences, religious and positive sciences, *ẓāhirī* and *bāṭinī* sciences, useful and useless sciences, and supreme and instrumental sciences.

The conceptual framework of existence, instruments for acquiring knowledge, subject, purpose, objective, belief, and approaches were the main determinants for the classification of sciences. Followers of Khawārizmī and Ghazālī's tradition viewed the *shar'ī* sciences as primary in their value system. Principally, these sciences take into consideration the relationship between

Allah and His servants. Since Allah is supreme, sciences that deal with one's relationship with Allah are also considered supreme and promise happiness in this word and the Hereafter. Therefore, they are referred as *maḥmūd* (praised) and useful. Since they are transmitted from one generation to the next, they are regarded as *naqlī*. *Fiqh* is the most reputable *shar'ī* science due to its competence and ability to tackle the issues confronting individuals and societies based on the rulings derived from the Qur'an and the Sunnah. Therefore, it was always regarded as the most respected science in Islamic education.

Furthermore, *fiqh* is not an extant or a detached science, because it is highly dependent upon *ṣarf*, *naḥv*, *bedāy'e*, *tafsīr*, *ḥadīth*, *kalām*, *fiqh al-sīrah*, and other *shar'ī* sciences, in addition to such *'aqlī* sciences as *manṭiq* (science of logic). It is an undeniable fact that no *ḥukum* (ruling) can be made in the absence of the knowledge and methods of these sciences. Therefore, throughout history *fiqh* has always been strongly related to them.

Places where *fiqh* was taught in history

The first place where religious sciences, including *fiqh*, were taught was in the house of a Makkan Companion named Arqam. Prior to hijrah, the Companions would gather and study the newly revealed Qur'anic verses and the Prophet's explanations of them in this house.[16] Perhaps such proceedings led to decisions being reached on issues pertaining to *i'tiqād*, *'ibādah*, and *mu'āmalāt*. Additionally, they were reviewing current developments and devising future strategies. These activities are, in a way, related to *fiqh* because they involve deriving conclusions from the Qur'an and the Sunnah concerning *i'tiqad*, *'ibādah*, and *mu'āmalāt*.

Similarly, the science of *fiqh* used to be taught in a mosque. This is considered an imitation of Prophet Muḥammad (ṣ), who first established a multipurpose mosque (Masjid Nabawī) after his migration to Madīnah (1/622). In addition to the personal rooms surrounding it, the Prophet allocated rooms for education and training services, called "Ṣuffah," and the students were referred to as "Aṣḥāb al-Ṣuffah". Many of the religious scholars and diplomats sent to surrounding tribes and countries were educated in this place. In general, they possessed high mental abilities yet were comprised largely of poor people whose expenditures were met by wealthy Muslims.[17] The education and training institution was established in Madīnah as a role model in order to pioneer many educational foundations to set up within and outside the *masjid* and many other educational *waqf* (fund) to be established.

In the early stages, mosques were places for performing the daily prayers (*'ibādāt*) as well as educational institutions in which various religious sciences would be taught. Especially in the mosques of Damascus and Cairo, sections (madrasah) taught the *fiqh* of all four Sunnī legal schools. These places were called "*zāwiyah.*" For example, eight *zāwiyahs* taught *fiqh* in Amawī Mosque (Damascus) and al-Jāmi' al-'Atīq (Cairo): three were for Ḥanafīs, two were for Shāfi'īs, one was for Mālikīs, and one was for Ḥanbalīs.

Indeed, the place in the mosque in which the lecturers would conduct their lessons and lectures was called a *majlis*, as that word was used for any educational activity or scientific discussion. The lecturers' teachings at the mosques were instructed by the legal authorities, who were also selected by the *waqaf* board or had special authorization to conduct such activities. In order to meet the students' housing needs, hostels were built around the mosques. Due to these classrooms, hostels, and other related structures, the Mosques would evolve into a *kulliyyah* or what some may call madrasah. Apart from the mosques, fiqh classes were also held in the *'ulamā's* houses, palaces, and bookstores.[18]

Various reasons and factors were given for educational activities in the Sunnī Muslim world ranging from mosques to madrasah; increase in the number of students, development of controversial sciences and their expansion, there was also a demand for educating the government staff, the establishment of Dār al-'Ilm institution which aimed to promote Shī'ah movement and the Sultans' desire to gain the support of *'ulamā'* who were the most favourable authorities in the view public.[19]

The emergence of madrasahs

The term *madrasah* is derived from the Arabic word درس, which indicates places where education and training activities are held and different kinds of scientific activities are conducted.

There are various theories as to when, where, and under what circumstances the first madrasah was established. The vast majority which hold that they appeared around Horasan and Turkistan toward the end of ninth century.[20] Yet, madrasahs were first established by Karahans (840-1212) in Turkistan, expanded by Ghaznalis (961-1187), and further organized by the Seljuk Turks (1040-1157).

The first Seljuk-era madrasah was established by Sultan Tuğrul Bey (993-1063) in 1046 in Nishabur. Niẓām al-Mulk (1063-1092), vizier to both Alparslan (1063-1072) and Melikshah (1072-1092), ordered the construction of a madrasah in Baghdad. Education at this madrasah, which was placed around the Tigris River (Dijle), started in 1066-1067. Subsequently Niẓām al-Mulk established madrasahs in Balkh, Nishabur, Harat, Isfahan, Baṣrah, Marw, Taberistan, and Mosul. Providing bursar and accommodation services, these madrasahs and schools were open to all and free.[21] Taftazanī (879/1474), who influenced the Ottoman scholars (*'ulamā'*) of the fourteenth and fifteenth centuries, lectured at Niẓāmiyyah Madrasahs.[22]

This trend, pioneered by the Seljuks, was followed by many sultans, viziers, governors, and queens who were influenced by these activities and established madrasahs and schools throughout the Islamic world. For instance, Caliph al-Mustanṣir (640/1242) established al-Mustanṣiriyyah Madrasah in 1234 to provide education on the four Sunnī legal schools. Nureddin Zengi followed suit by establishing madrasahs in Mosul and Damascus, as did the Umayyads in al-Andalus. During the Timurids' rule, especially that of Uluğ Bey (the grandson of Timur; 1046-1049), *fiqh* reached its peak in Samarqand. Ali Kuşçu (1410-1474), the famous lecturer of Sahn-i Seman Madrasahs established by Fatih, was educated in Samarqand.[23] A large number of madrasahs were also established by the Anatolian Seljuks and the Beylikler (districts governed by Begs). During this period, madrasahs were considered continuations of the Great Seljuks. Specialization in madrasahs took place during Anatolian Seljuks time. For example, Konya's Ince Minareli Medrese specialized in *ḥadīth*, the Sırçalı Medrese in *fiqh*, one of the Çifte Medrese in Kayseri in medicine, and Kırşehir and Kütahya madrasahs specialized in *hay'ah* (astronomy) and *nujūm* (stars).[24]

In the beginning, the Ottoman's madrasah system appeared as a continuation of the Anatolian Seljuk's and the Anatolian Beglik's madrasah system. The first madrasah of the Ottoman period, the Orhaniyye Medresesi, was established by Orhan Gazi (1281-1359) in 1330-1331 in Iznik after the conquest of the city; Davud-i Kayseri (751/1350) was appointed as its lecturer. Upon the conquest of Bursa (1326), Orhan Gazi established another madrasah and turned a church into a madrasah in 1335. Murat Hüdavendigar (1364-1389) ordered to erection of a large madrasah in Çekirge-Bursa, and Bayezid I (1389-1402) established madrasahs, *kulliyyah*, and bimarhane buildings in Bursa and Edirne; his son Çelebi Mehmed (1413-1421) did so in Bursa, and Murad II (1421-1451) followed this example in Bursa and Edirne. Apart from the sultans, leading figures among the governors (e.g., Lala Şahin Pasha and Çandarlı Hayrettin Pasha) followed this tradition by establishing madrasahs bearing their names.[25] The Ottoman madrasah system reached its peak with the conquest of Istanbul (1451) and the subsequent establishment of Sahn-i Seman Madrasahs in 1471 by Fatih Sultan Mehmet (1432-1481) and Süleymaniye Madrasahs in 1557 by Kanuni Sultan Süleyman (1520-1566). This system, which was given a framework during the Kanuni period, lasted until the beginning of the nineteenth century.[26]

After the *Tanẓīmāt* reforms of 1839, western-style schools were established in opposition to the madrasahs in order to train bureaucrats. Upon the declaration of Meşrutiyet II (constitutional monarchy), serious and dramatic changes took place in 1910 with the issuance of Medāris-i İlmiyye Nizamnamesi. The management of madrasahs, the lecturers' authority, the students' rights, and the curricula were all reformed. Based on the Nizamname, the study period of madrasah was increased to twelve years and offered new courses, such as mathematics, geometry, physics, chemistry, astronomy, cosmography, history, geography, and Persian.[27] Islâh-i Medāris Nizamnamesi was introduced in 1914 and Istanbul's madrasahs were united under the Dār'ul-Hilafet'il-Aliyye Medreseleri. With this nizamname, the madrasah system was modified so that it could offer three levels of four-year education: Tālī-i Qısm-i awwal, Tālī-i Qısm-i sāni, and ʻĀlī. In 1910, the Mekteb-i Nuwwāb, which had been established in 1854 to train *qāḍīs* (judges) and *nā'ibs* (acting judges) was renamed the Mekteb-i Kuzat. The Medresetu'l-Vāizin was established in 1912 in Istanbul for propagating Islam (*tablīgh*), and Medresetu'l-Eimme ve'l-Khutabā toward the end of 1913 to train imāms, preachers, and *mu'adhdhins*. In 1917, the Medresetu'l-Mutekhassisîn was established for those graduates of the three-level-madrasah education who wanted to further master their specialization.[28]

Consequently, madrasahs were affiliated to Ministry of National Education based on Article 430 of the Tawhid-i Tedrisāt Kānunu (unitarian nationalist education policies), passed on 03.03.1924. All educational institutions and learning centres within Turkey were attached to Ministry of National Education. Vasif Bey, education minister of the time, shut down the madrasah schools on 13.03.1924, an event that marked the end of the madrasah period in Ottoman history.[29]

The importance of the Süleymaniyyah madrasahs

Before we talk about the importance of Süleymaniyyah Madrasahs, we need to mention its brief history. After building Yavuz Sultan Selim Kulliyyah in 1522 in the name of his father and Şehzade Kulliyyah built in 1548 in the name of his son Mehmet,[30] Süleyman the Lawgiver ordered a *kulliyyah* for himself and entrusted the famous architect Sinan (1490-1588) with constructing and supervision it. Shaykh al-Islām Ebussuūd Efendi (1491-1574) laid the first stone on June 13, 1550. According to the plan, the mosque would be placed in the centre and surrounded by a medical school (*madrasah al-ṭibb*) and a *ṣibyān* (junior) madrasah, a first and second madrasah on the west, a third and fourth madrasah on the east, Dār al-Ḥadīth on thc southcast, and a caravanserai on the northern lower ground. The Dār al-Shifā', Tabkhâne, and Imâret were built on the northern upper ground. Construction on the *kulliyyah* started in 1550 and finished in 1556-1557. The third and fourth madrasahs were completed in 1552-1553, and the first and second madrasah 1558-1559.[31] Based on the available resources, it appears that of the six units dedicated to education and training, five of them related to religious social sciences (four traditional madrasah buildings, a Ḍār al-Ḥadīth, and a Ḍār al-Ta'līm) and one was related to the medicine (Ḍāru't-Ṭip).[32] Some researchers add a Ḍār al-Qurrā' to this list; however, no reliable information about this is available in the Ottoman inscriptions (*waqfiyyah*).[33] The first and second madrasah consisted of 23 rooms each, whereas the third and fourth ones each had 21 rooms.[34] We learn from the *waqfiyyah* that each madrasah, including the Ḍāru'l-Ḥadith, was made up of 21 personnel; 1 lecturer, 1 assistant lecturer, 15 students, and 4 officers. Each lecturer in each of the four madrasahs was paid 60 coins (Ottoman *Akçe*), each lecturer in the Ḍār al-Ḥadīth 50 coins, each assistant lecturer 5 coins, and each student 2 coins. On the other hand, the Ḍāru't-T'alîm featured a *ḥāfiẓ* (a person who had memorized the Qur'an), a *khalife* (his assistant), and 30 students of Qur'an. The *ḥāfiẓ* was given 8 coins and the *khalife* 3 coins; the students were not paid.[35] Based on this information, we can conclude that when all four madrasahs (except for the medicine madrasah and the Daru't-T'alim) ran at full capacity, the *kulliyyah* had 60 students and 10 academic staff members; 5 lecturers and 5 assistant lecturers.

The Süleymaniye madrasahs mark the highpoint of the hierarchical Ottoman madrasah system. Prior to the Lawgiver, Sultan Mehmed the Conqueror had laid down some regulations regarding the madrasahs and classified the madrasahs within the empire's borders. According to his classification, madrasahs are listed from bottom to top as follows: Hāshiye-i Tecrid Medreseleri, Miftah Medreseleri, Kırklı Medreseleri, Hāriç Elli Medreseleri, Dāhil Medreseleri (Tetimme), and Sahn-i Semân Medreseleri.

The Kırklı and Hāriç Elli madrasahs were comprised of madrasahs that had been established in pre-Ottoman times by the emperors of Anatolian Seljuks and Anatolian Beyliks, their families, viziers, governors of *sanjaks* (administration division), and the *umerā'* (e.g., high class government officers, chiefs, and commanders). The Dāhil madrasahs were built by the Ottoman sultans, their wives, and children (*şehzade*). Although the Mûsila-i

Sahn (Tetimme) Madrasah was initially considered on the same level as the Dāhil madrasahs, it was referred as Mûsila-i Sahn (prior to Sahn, transmitted to Sahn) rather than the Dāhil Madrasah. The madrasahs' ranking depended solely upon the lecturers' wages. When the Süleymaniye madrasahs began functioning, another grade was added to this ranking: the Süleymaniye madrasahs were at the top, as they had a 60-coin wage. As a result, a new classification system was established. This was, from the lowerst to the highest, as follows: Hâsiye-i Tecrid Medreseleri, Miftah Medreseleri, Kirkli Medreseleri, Hâric Elli Medresleri, Dâhil Medreseleri (Tetimme), Sahn-i Semân Medreseleri, Süleymaniye Medreseleri, and Süleymaniye Dār al-Ḥadīth.

Education at the Süleymaniye madrasahs was dispensed on five week days, one more than the traditional four week days of classes offered by the older madrasahs.[36] According to Gelibolulu Ali (1009/1600), any student who finished the first-level compulsory classes and who wanted to further his knowledge could enter the lowest ranked Hāşiye-i Tecrid Madrasah. If he passed his exams, he could then register for the Miftah Madrasah with his *temessuk* (a transcript of the courses and books he had studied). After graduation, he could then finish all of the madrasahs according the existing ranking.[37] Previously, the Sahn madrasahs had offered the highest academic degree, but this changed with the advent of Süleymaniye madrasahs, which produced students and lecturers who sought to reach high positions in the Ottoman bureaucracy. Therefore, these madrasahs were key to one's becoming a judge. Judges at the Sharī'ah courts of Istanbul, Makkah, Madīnah, Jerusalem, Damascus, Aleppo, Cairo, Edirne, and Bursa could earn up to 500 coins, as could a *kazasker* (military judge) or a chief religious officer in the empire.[38]

Teaching *fiqh* in the madrasahs

Several components are required to establish an education and training structure designed to meet the needs of society by providing students with quality education and training services. Some of these are lecturers (trainers), students (trainees), principals, physical (madrasah, school) and social environments, and educational programmes. Any institution of higher education and learning should inform the target group about the society's readily available accumulated knowledge and culture and help its members adapt to it; show them how to adjust to a changing world; and train and educate civil servants, artists, scientists, vocational professionals, and bureaucrats. In addition, it should spread the accumulated knowledge throughout society, strive to help the people absorb it, and reproduce science and knowledge by adding to the accumulated knowledge at hand.[39] Madrasahs influenced the scientific, educational, cultural, and social fabric from the empire's first days right up till the end of twentieth century. These institutions serve their purpose, especially during the empire's establishment and expansion periods, by assuming the leading role in educating and training the leaders, judges, doctors, and other professionals demanded by political, judicial, and social life.[40]

No system of education can remain uninfluenced by its society's philosophical, cultural, and social structure as regards training the role models. The cultural and philosophical grounds for the madrasah system can be traced back to the models of education and learning started by the Prophet. This unstructured system was transformed into one of systematic lectures conducted at mosques during Umayyad dynasty. Each scholar classified knowledge according to his own philosophical approach, generally based on *waḥy* (revelation), and produced his own lecture and training method. The madrasah programmes that appeared in the eleventh century were, in essence, the lecture programmes found in mosques and then adjusted to fit the conditions of the time. But this adaptation required certain philosophical and social preferences and filtrations that were caused by choice. Madrasahs were born as institutions inspired by Sunnī Islam and emerged from an atmosphere of clashing legal schools of thought and competition among philosophical approaches on how to educate and train human beings. Naturally, all madrasahs in the Sunnī world were shaped by the Ghazālī school, which grounds Sunnī doctrine theoretically on a *kalam-fiqh-tasawwuf* axis.[41]

The ultimate goal of madrasahs was to produce a *faqīh*, defined as a person with an integrated personality. According to Islam, a *faqīh* is more than just a judicial operator in narrow sense; he is a developed person who is in harmony with his internal and external environment and his God, a person equipped with *ʿaqlī* and *naqlī* knowledge, and possessing the authority to give *fatwās*, lectures, and jurisdiction. The components of the academic needle that this person is expected to devise and the synthesis of these substances are the same in essence. The synthesis, which consists of the same substances (but different in width and depth), was put into practice at every level of the madrasahs. Thus, lower level madrasahs were academic platforms where only one lecturer would instruct his students. At the higher level Fatih and Süleymaniye Kulliyah madrasahs, the programme of education would be the same (differing, again, only in width and depth) but it would be taught by more than one lecturer. In short, different levels of madrasah education and the programs, according to their private goals, would be taught at different levels and be complementary in nature.[42]

When we examine how *fiqh* was taught in the Süleymaniye madrasahs, we should bear this educational approach in mind.

Students were supposed to graduate from all of the lower level madrasahs and present their *temessuk* from the lecturers to prove that they had been successful and desired admission to Süleymaniye madrasahs. A student who started his education and training at his district's *sibyan maktab* (junior school) when he was 6 years old would study the basics until he was 12. The main focus was learning how to read and write, recite the Qur'an properly with *tajwīd* (science of reciting the Qur'an) and memorize it, along with some courses like *'aqā'id* (science of belief) and *ilmihal* (science of daily life *fiqh*), and reading and memorizing a small dictionary in Turkish, Arabic, or Persian. The lecturers would guide outstanding student toward the Hâshiye-i Tecrid madrasahs, where they would *murattab*, *koltuk*, and similar courses. Eventually they would reach the Süleymaniye madrasahs. The entire process, based upon the student's capacity, would take a minimum 5 years and, normally, 6 to 7 years. Thus each student would study for 12 years before entering the Süleymaniye madrasahs where, two years later, they would graduate with the equivalence of a present-day Masters degree.[43]

In order to judge the level of knowledge and cultural background of the students studying at the Süleymaniye madrasahs, one should briefly list the subjects studied at lower grades. This can be done only by evaluating the programmes conducted at the madrasahs and the subjects taught. Unfortunately there is almost no well-organized, reliable, and formal documentation on the madrasahs' programmes until the reformation. Specialists working on this topic have tried to evaluate the programme by coordinating formal documents like *waqfiyyah* and *qānunnāme* in way related to madrasahs, scientific works, and biographies of lecturers who had taught in them.[44] Based upon their work, we can determine which book was taught in which madrasah.

The educational board, main resources, and methods

Süleymaniye madrasahs hired one lecturer for the Dār al-Ḥadīth and one for each of the four madrasahs. All lecturers there were required to have teaching experience at a lower level madrasah. It would take 25-30 years for a lecturer to attain a teaching post at these madrasahs. The Sahn-i Semân mardasahs (50 coins) or its equivalent madrasahs, as well as the Ḍār al-Ḥadīth from other four madrasahs within the Süleymaniye, would promote the lecturers to all four of its madrasahs. If there were multiple applications for a vacant post, candidates would be examined on a core book, like the *Hidāyah*, and be evaluated on their teaching as well as their lesson preparation. Those who passed were hired.

Many famous Ottoman scholars were lecturers at the Süleymaniye madrasahs. In his appendix, Sekâkik mentioned his discussion of Kınalızâde Ali Efendi's (979/1572) biography. Ataî states that when Çifte Medreseler (Twin Madrasahs) were completed in Muḥarram 966, Kınalızâde[45] was appointed to the northern madrasah and Shan Mehmed Efendi (978/1570) to the southern one.[46] Mimarzāde Mustafa Efendi (971/1565) and Qadızāde Efendi (988/1580) were appointed to the eastern madrasah, which was completed some 6 years later.[47] Baltacı provided the names and short biographies of 66 lecturers employed at these madrasahs.[48] The *Sekaik* mentioned that about 250 lecturers known to teach at Süleymaniye madrasahs. Those who were getting 60 coins would be promoted as judges to Makkah, Madīnah, Jerusalem, Damascus, Aleppo, Cairo, Edirne, Bursa, and other centres and be paid 500 coins. Later they could become military judges in Anatolia or the European side of today's Turkey. The ultimate post was the Shaykh al-Islām.[49] Based on our research on the lecturers' biographies, the average duration of teaching at the Süleymaniye madrasahs was 2.5-3 years for lecturers; however, the duration of their stay periodically differed. These madrasahs were one of the key positions for those who wanted to become high-ranking bureaucrats.

A list of all madrasahs, including the Süleymaniye madrasahs, as well as the subjects and books taught at each level,[50] is given below:

Madrasah & Its Ranking	Subjects Taught	Required Books
1) Hāshiye-i Tejrīd (20 coins)	Ṣarf, Naḥv, Qirā'ah, Balāghah, Kalām, Manṭiq	Emsile, Bina, Maqsûd, Ízzi, Merah, Mutawwal, Hāshiye-i Tecrīd, Sharḥ-i Shemsiyye
2) Miftāh (30 coins)	Ṣarf, Naḥv, Balāghah, Kalām, Ḥadīth	Ṣarf ve Naḥv cont'd with Sharḥ-i Miftāh, Hāshiye-i Tecrīd, Masābih
3) Telwīḥ Madrasahs (40 coins)	Balāghah, Ḥadīth, Kalām	Miftāhu'l-'Ulūm, Meshāriq, Masābiḥ, Sherḥ-i Mawāqif, Sharḥ-i Maqāṣid
4) Hāriç Elli (50 coins)	Ḥadīth, Kalām	Sharḥ-i Mawāqif, Masābih
5) Dāhil Elli (50 coins)	Ḥadīth, Tafsīr	Bukhārī, Kashshāf, Bayḍāwī
6) Mūsile-i Sahn and Sahn-i Seman (50 coins)	Ḥadīth, Tafsīr, Kalām, Manṭiq	Bukhārī, Kashshāf, Bayḍāwī, Matālī, Sharḥ-i 'Aḍūḍ.

If we arrange the list according to the types of *fiqh* taught, it would be as follows:

Madrasah & Its Ranking	Subjects Taught	Required Books
1) Hāshiya-i Tajrīd (20 coins)	1) Furū' al-Fiqh, 2) Uṣūl al-Fiqh	Furū': *Sharḥ-i Farâiz* Uṣūl: *Talwiḥ 'ala't-Tawdīḥ*

2) Miftâḥ (30 coins)	1) Furū' al-Fiqh, 2) Uṣūl al-Fiqh	Furū': Ṣadr al-Sharī'ah (*Sharḥ al-Wiqāyah:* until lesson on Buyu') Uṣūl: *Tanqiḥ al-Uṣūl; Tawḍīḥ al-Tanqīḥ*
3) Talwīḥ (40 coins)	1) Furū' al-Fiqh 2) Uṣūl al-Fiqh	Furū': Ṣadr al-Sharī'ah (*Sharḥ al-Wiqāyah:* from lesson on Buyu' until the end), Sharḥ-i Farāiḍ. Uṣūl: *Talwīḥ*, (as a whole)
4) Hāriç Elli (50 coins)	1) Furū' al-Fiqh	*Hidāyah* (from the beginning until the end of lesson on Zakāh)
5) Dāhil Elli (50 coins)	1) Furū' al-Fiqh 2) Uṣūl al-Fiqh	Furū': *Hidāyah* (from the lesson on Zakāh until the lesson on Ḥaj), Uṣūl: *Talwīḥ*, (from the beginning until the lesson on Taqsīm-i awwal).
6) Mūsile-i Sahn and Sahn-i Seman (50 coins)	1) Furū' al-Fiqh 2) Uṣūl al-Fiqh	Furū': *Hidāyah* (from the lesson on Nikāḥ until the end of the lesson on Buyu'), Uṣūl: *Talwīḥ*, (from the lesson on Taqsīm-i awwal until the lesson on Aḥkām).

Based on the above tables, a student would study books on *tafsīr*, *ḥadīth*, and *kalām* in addition to the pragmatic sciences of *ṣarf*, *naḥv*, *balāghah*, and *manṭiq* at different grades of madrasahs, at different levels of width and depth, as a whole or in portions to qualify for Süleymaniye madrasahs. In terms of *fiqh*, he would finish *tawḍīḥ*, *tanqīḥ*, and *talwīḥ* from *uṣūl*, and *farā'iḍ* and *wiqāyah* from *furū'* totally in addition to *'ilm al-ḥāl*. He would finish most parts of *hidāyah*, as well as its revised *sharḥ* (commentary) and *ḥāshiyah* (annotation), together with the other sources in the field. The Süleymaniye madrasahs provided a higher level of education based upon the traditional madrasah programmes and structured the academic institution, whereas professionalism was targeted for certain subjects. The subjects taught at the lower levels by various methods were combined in sum. These madrasahs prepared their graduates for authoritative positions in giving *fatwās*, lectures, and jurisdiction and furnished them with *ijâzetnâmah* (certificate) they needed to be promoted.

Consequently, if we combine the two tables given above, the final table would be the one given below:

7) Süleymaniye Traditional Madrasahs (60 coins)	Fiqh, Uṣūl al-Fiqh, Kalām, Tafsīr, Ḥadīth	*Hidāyah* (beginning from the lesson on Buyu' until the end); Sharḥ-i Farāiḍ (as a whole); *Talwīḥ*, (beginning from the lesson on Aḥkām until the end); Sharḥ-i Mawākif, Bukhārī, Kashshāf and other well-known 'aqlī and naqlī books.
8) Süleymaniye Ḍār al-Ḥadīth Madrasahs (50/100 C.)	Ḥadīth, Fiqh, Tāfsīr	Hidāyah, *Talwīḥ* and similar books on furu' and uṣūl, Mashāriq, Masābiḥ, Muslim, Bukhārī[51]

As these tables show, at least one subject related to *fiqh* was taught at each grade. The madrasah education system required that certain books be finished and that examinations for certain subjects be passed; therefore, the programmess were implemented in a way that suited the age and maturity of the audience from the simple and the concrete to the complicated and the abstract. The books mentioned in the table formed the backbone of the madrasah's programmes and were taught at the beginning and higher levels.[52] Below is a partial list of some of the writings pertaining to the texts, commentaries, and annotations on *fiqh* that were taught or recommended to be taught:

Furū'-i Fiqh

1. *Mukhtaṣar al-Qudūrī*	Qudūrī (428/1037)
2. *Tuḥfah al-Fuqahā'*	'Alā' al-Dīn al-Samarqandī (538/ 1144)
3. *al-Hidāyah*	Burhān al-Dīn al-Mirghinānī (593/1197)
4. *Farāiḍ*	Abū Ṭāhir Sirājuddīn es-Sajāvandī (596/1200)[53]
5. *al-Mukhtār*	Majd al-Dīn al-Mūṣilī (683/ 1284)
6. *al-Ikhtiyār li Ta'līl al-Mukhtār*	Majd al-Dīn al-Mūṣilī (683/ 1284)
7. *al-Wiqāyah*	Tāj al-Sharī'ah Maḥmūd (630/ 1232)[54]
8. *Majma' al-Baḥrayn wa Multaqā al-Nahrayn*	Ibn al-Sā'ātī (694/1295)
9. *Munyah al-Muṣallī*	Muḥammad b. 'Alī al-Kashgarī (705/1305)
10. *Kanz al-Daqā'iq fī al-Furū'*	Ḥāfiẓ al-Dīn al-Nasafī (710/ 1310)[55]
11. *Tabyīn al-Ḥaqā'iq Sharḥ Kanz al-Daqā'iq*	'Alī al-Zayla'ī (743/1342)
12. *Sharḥ al-'Ināyah 'alā al-Hidāyah*	Akmal al-Dīn al-Bābirtī (786/ 1384)
13. *Wiqāyah al-Riwāyah fī Masā'ili al-Hidāyah*	Tāj al-Sharī'ah (8/14. century)

14. *Ghurar al-Aḥkām*	Molla Khusraw (885/1480)[56]
15. *Multaqā al-Abḥur*	Burhanuddīn Ibrahim al-Ḥalabī (956/1594)[57]
16. *Tabyīn al-Ḥaqā'iq Sharḥ Kanz al-Daqā'iq*	Molla Miskīn (811/1408)
17. *Al-Baḥr al-Rā'iq Sharḥ Kanz al-Daqāiq*	Ibn Nujaym (970/1563)
18. *Radd al-Muḥtār 'alā al-Durr al-Mukhtār*	Ibn 'Ābdīn (1306/1888)

Uṣūl al-Fiqh

1. *Mukhtaṣar al-Muntahā*	(Text: Mālikī)	Ibn Ḥājib (646/ 1249)
2. *al-Mughnī*	(Text: Ḥanafī)	Khabbāzī (691/1292)
3. *al-Manār*	(Text: Ḥanafī)	Nasafī (710/1310)
4. *al-Tanqīḥ*	(Text: Ḥanafī)	Ṣadr al-Sharī'ah (747/1346)
5. *al-Tawḍīḥ*	(Sharḥ: Ḥanafī)	Ṣadr al-Sharī'ah (747/1346)
6. *al-Talwīḥ*	(Ḥāshiyah: Ḥanafī)	Taftazānī (792/1389)
7. *Fusūl al-Badā'i'*	(Text: Ḥanafī)	Molla Fanārī (834/1431)
8. *Taḥrīr*	(Text: Ḥanafī)	Ibn al-Humām (861/1456)
9. *Mirqāh al-Wuṣūl; Mirāh*	(Text+Sharḥ: Ḥanafī)	Molla Khusraw (885/1480)

Clearly, *al-Wiqāyah, al-Hidāyah*, and *Farā'iḍ* (all *furū' al-fiqh*) and *Tawḍīḥ, Tanqīḥ*, and *Talwīḥ* (all *uṣūl al-fiqh*) form the backbone of the *fiqh* programme. In order to understand these books' place in *fiqh* literature, let's examine them one by one:

Al-Wiqāyah

This compilation of selections from Burhān al-Dīn Marghinānī's (593/1192) *al-Hidāyah* on Ḥanafī *fiqh* was ordered by Tājushsharī'ah Omar b. Abdullah b. 'Ubaydullah for his grandson Ṣadrus Sharī'ah. It is considered one of the four notable sources[58] (*mutun-u erbaa*). Ṣadrus Sharī'ah summarized it as *an-Nuqāye* and wrote its commentary, *Sharḥ al-Wiqāyah,*[59] which was studied especially in 30 and 40 coin madrasahs. Taşköprülüzâde, the most famous madrasah lecturer, began to teach it when he was appointed as a lecturer at Istanbul's 30 coin Haji Hasanzāde Madrasah in 933/1527.[60] He taught this book up to the section on *bay'* (sale), and taught the rest of it when he was appointed to the 40 coin Üsküp Ishākiye Madrasah in 936/1529.[61]

Al-Hidāyah

This notable source of Ḥanafī jurisprudence was considered the essence of *fiqh* education at the 50 coin and higher madrasahs. Its author, Burhān al-Dīn al-Marghinānī (593/1192) of Turkistan, wrote his *Bidāyah al-Mubtadi'* based on Qudūrī's (439/1047) *al-Mukhtaṣar* and Abū Ḥanīfah's (150/767) student Muḥammad b. Ḥasan Shaybānī's (189/805) *al-Jāmi' al-Ṣahgīr.* He then wrote *Kifāyah al-Muntahī*, a large commentary on *Bidāyah al-Mubtadī.* Subsequently, he shortened some its chapters due to the difficulty in usage by preparing *al-Hidāyah.*[62]

He followed *al-Jāmi' al-Ṣaghīr's* format for *al-Hidāyah*, but increased the number of chapters from 40 to 56. When handling the various issues, Marhginānī first considered Abū Ḥanīfah's opinions and then those of his students: Abū Yūsuf and Muḥammad b. Ḥasan Shaybānī. He did, however, touch on Zufar b. Huzayl's opinion from time to time. Additionally, he mentions Imām Shāfi'ī and Imām Malik's approaches, together with those of Ḥanafī jurisprudential scholars, among them Ḥasan b. Ziyād al-

Lu'lu'ī, Ibn Sama'a, Ṭaḥāwī, Jaṣṣāṣ, Karkhī, and Sarakhsī. His way of listing different approaches and evidences is the same as that found in his contemporaneous Ḥanafī colleague Kāsānī's *Badā'i' al-Ṣanā'i'*.[63]

After Kalenderhāne Madrasah, Taşköprülüzâde was transferred to the 50 coin Mustafa Pasha Madrasah in 944/1537, where he taught *al-Hidāyah* up till the chapter on *zakāh*. He also taught it at the higher level madrasahs, such as the 60 coin Edirne Bayezid Han Medresesi. His biography states that he taught it, beginning from *Zakāh* until *Ḥajj* (*zakāh*, fasting, and *ḥajj*) at the 50 coin Edirne Uc Serefeli Madrasah, to which he moved in 945/1538.[64] These chapters consist of 42 pages (4.7% of the whole book). He continued lecturing till he was transferred to the Sahn-i Semaniye madrasahs in 946/1539, where he started with *nikāḥ* and finished with *buyū'* (*nikāḥ*, *talâq*, oath, *sharī'* punishments, theft, *fiqh al-sīrah*, *laqīt*, *luqatā*, *ibāq*, *mafqūd*, enterprise, and *waqf*).[65] In other words, he taught 290 pages (32.6% of the book), where the most important subjects on ruling the state and society falls at the Sahn-i Semaniye madrasahs. He kept teaching *al-Hidāyah* at the 60 coin Bayezid Han Madrasah, where he was transferred in 951/1544, from *buyū'* to *shuf'ah* (right of pre-emption) (*bay'*, *kafālah* [guarantee], *ḥiwālah* [transfer of debt], *wikālah* [contract of agency], *da'wah* [case], *iqrār* [confession], *ṣulḥ* [peace], *muḍārabah* [silent partnership], *wadī'ah* [deposit], *mukātabah* [a contract of manumission between a master and a slave], *ikrāh* [coercion], and *ḥajr*).[66] As we can see, 41.2% of the book was not taught.

Farā'iḍ

This book, which focuses solely on *farāiḍ* (Islamic inheritance jurisprudence), was written by Sajāvendī (596/1200). Many commentaries and summaries were written on it; poetic versions of it were written in Arabic, Persian, and Turkish and translated into English and Persian.[67] *Sharḥu's-Sirājiyye*, Sayyid Sharif Jurjani's commentary on the *Farā'iḍ*, was widely studied at the madrasahs. Taşköprülüzâde also taught Jurjani's commentary at the Dimekota Madrasah.

Tanqīḥ

Ṣadr al-Sharī'ah al-Thānī 'Ubaydullāh al-Maḥbūbī (745/1345) from Bukhārā wrote this book, which deals with *uṣūl al-fiqh*. *Tawḍīḥ* is the commentary on *Tanqīḥ*, written by the same author.[68] There is also another commentary on this book, the *Talwīḥ,* which was written by on Ṣa'd al-Dīn Taftazānī (792/1390), the famous scholar on the sciences of *balāghah, kalām*, and *fiqh*. *Uṣūl al-fiqh* was taught for the first time at the 40 coin madrasahs under the Ottomans. Taşköprülüzâde taught *Tawḍīḥ* at the 40 coin Üsküp İshakiye Madrasah in 936/1529 and *Talwīḥ* at the Edirne Üç Şerefeli Madrasah.[69]

These lectures were conducted in circles, where the students would gather around the lecturer in a circle. The assistant lecturers would also be present to help students revise and better understand the lesson during and after the class discussions. Good methodologies were applied to ensure the appropriate presentation, memorization, dictation, and discussion. Daily classes would start prayer, after which the lecturer would briefly go through the day's lesson and the students would present their work to either him or the assistant lecturer. The content of the madrasah programs relied heavily on the transmission of *naqlī* knowledge. Since this knowledge was in Arabic, succinct books had to be memorized. As with learning a foreign language, memorization remains a crucial method even today.

Dictation was not a routine recording activity, but a pedagogical activity, an interplay between the brain and the memory as a teaching-learning method. Students used this method to take notes during the lecturer's explanation and to copy the books in order to prepare for the lectures. Teaching by dictation formed the backbone of education and training, especially in the days before printing presses. The academic calendar was organized in such a way to let students have four days of classes and three days to spend in the library preparing for the upcoming lectures. At the higher levels, discussions consisted of three elements: *ikhtiṣār*, *iqtiṣād*, and *istisqā*. The lecturer would briefly introduce the lesson and ask tricky questions to stimulate the students' minds (*ikhtiṣār*). In-depth analysis would be provided based on the cause and effect relationship followed by brainstorming activities to produce new knowledge during question and answer sessions (*iqtiṣād*). *Istisqâ* refers to involving the students in teaching and explaining the lesson.

In short, the lecturer would start the lessons by reciting the *Basmalah*, the *Ḥamdalah*, and the *La ḥawla*. The lesson's general overview would be presented, and the lecturer would elaborate on other scholars' approaches and talk about their books. The students would give their opinion, thereby starting the question and answer session. The lecturer would guide the discussion in a pedagogical way iin order to reach a conclusion. The class would end when the discussion was finished.[70]

General evaluation and conclusion

Islam's educational and training activities began with the Prophet, who was appointed to convey its message, and still survives in our own time, albeit with modifications in its content, method, and locations. Madrasahs formed the backbone of educational system, especially during the Ottoman era, and the Süleymaniye madrasahs marked its highpoint. The madrasahs fulfil the expectations of an institution of higher learning by informing the society of the available cumulative knowledge and spreading it throughout society and training the personnel who would meet its needs. When we talk about the role of an institution of higher learning in *producing knowledge*, although there are many supporting and opposing ideas affirmed,[71] within the context of *fiqh* we cannot say that the madrasahs fully succeeded in its mission. If we consider the number of writings as proof of producing knowledge, then there is a huge difference between the establishment and advancement periods of the Ottoman empire and its later periods.[72] As a matter of fact, madrasahs failed to achieve this goal even after the *Tanẓīmāt* (reorganizations) was implemented in 1839, for laws were imported from Europe and European-style schools were set up to train the personnel while madrasahs were being reformed. In addition, the main reason for reforming the Ottomans' judicial governance system and compiling the *Majallah* and Judiciary Family Enactment (Huqūqi Â'le Qararnāmesi) act is that the level of *fiqh* education at madrasahs could not remedy the needs of the time.[73] In our opinion, there are two main causes for this: the dualist approach to the sciences and the non-internalized scientific mindset in the educational system.

The Ottoman madrasahs, which were philosophically founded on Khawarizmī and Gazālī's classification of knowledge, placed the *naqlī* sciences over the *'aqlī* sciences, and then education itself became devoted to memorization and other *'ilm al-ālāt* (supportive sciences), which dulled the students' minds. Despite this, neither the Qur'an nor the ḥadīth literature classifies knowledge into religious and non-religious sciences.

When we talk about the scientific mindset, the basic books studied in the Ottoman madrasahs, apart from *Kutub al-Sittah*, were written during the eleventh and thirteenth centuries. For example Marhgīnānī, the author of *Hidāyah*, died in 593/1192. This book could logically be taught in the early Ottoman madrasahs; however, it was written 3 centuries before the Conquer's order that it be retained as part of the madrasah's curriculum. The Lawgiver's tacit approval that such books be taught caused their contents to be accepted unconditionally. As a result the study programme, its contents and the books taught, remained almost the same at the Fatih madrasahs until the nineteenth century.

Another issue is the consistency of the knowledge that was taught and acted upon for centuries from the sources that this knowledge believed to have been originally derived. For example, according to all Sunnī legal schools the primary source to be consulted when conducting *ijtihād* (independent interpretation) was the Qur'an, followed by the Sunnah. When we refer to the *Hidāyah* on the issue of *talāq*, for instance, we can see that the theory is based on a ḥadīth rather than the Qur'an.[74] According to Zaylaʿī's (762/1361) statements in his *Naṣb al-Rāyah*, this particular ḥadīth is not qualified to be a source from which a legal decision can be derived.[75] He wrote his book one century before the Fatih madrasahs were even opened. It would be impossible to think that the lecturers of that time were ignorant of Zaylaʿī's opinion. This can only be explained as something non-internalized or a divergence from scientific mindset, whereas a notion refuted by a Ḥanafī scholar kept being taught and followed in Ḥanafī schools.

In conclusion, the madrasahs fulfilled an important function during the Ottoman period but went through a severe crisis because the cumulative knowledge and methods of producing knowledge could not keep up with the rapidly changing times.

Notes

1. Associate Prof Dr Servet Bayındır is a lecturer in the Department of Islamic Jurisprudence, Faculty of Theology, Istanbul University (e-mail: servetbayindir@hotmail.com).

2. Wahbah Zuḥaylī, *Uṣūl al-Fiqh al-Islāmī* (Damascus: Dār al-Fikr, 1986), p. 26.
3. Hayrettin Karaman, "Fıkıh," Diyanet İslam Ansiklopedisi (*DIA)* (Istanbul: TDIV, 1988), vol. 13, p. 1.
4. "معرفة النفس ما لها وما عليها": Molla Husrev, Husrev Mehmed Efendi, *Mir'āh al-Uṣūl Sharḥ Mirqāh al-Wuṣūl* (Istanbul: Shirket-i Sahafiye-i Osmaniye, 1321), p. 10.
5. Zayn al-Dīn Zakariyyā b. Muḥammad b. Aḥmad Zakariyyā al-Anṣārī Abū Yaḥyā, *Fatḥ al-Wahhāb bi Sharḥ Manhaji al-Ṭullāb*, vol. 1 (Beirut: Dār al-Kutub al-'Ilmiyyah, 1418/1998), p. 8; Shams al-Dīn Muḥammad b. Aḥmad b. Ḥamzah al-Anṣārī, Ramlī, *Nihāyah al-Muḥtāj ilā Sharḥ al-Minhāj*, vol. 1 (Beirut: Dār al-Fikr, 1404/1984), p. 31.
6. *Majallah*, Article, 1.
7. *Al-Mawsū'ah al-Fiqhiyyah*, vol. 23, Article "fiqh"; "العلم بالأحكام الشرعية العملية المكتسب من أدلتها التفصيلية"
8. Recep Şentürk, *İslam Dünyasında Modernleşme ve Toplumbilim* (Istanbul: İz Yayıncılık, 1996), pp. 114-115.
9. Abū Naṣr Muḥammad b. Muḥammad b. Ṭarkhān al-Fārābī, *Taḥṣīl al-Sa'ādah*, ed. Ja'far Āl Yāsīn, 2nd ed. (Beirut: Dār al-Andalus, 1983), p. 23.
10. Abū Naṣr Muallim-i Sānī Muḥammad b. Muḥammad b. Ṭarkhān Fārābī, *Iḥṣā' al-'Ulūm*, ed. 'Uthmān Muḥammad Amīn (Cairo: Maktabah al-Khānjī, 1350/1931), p. 1.
11. Abū 'Alī Ḥusayn b. 'Abdullah b. 'Alī Balkhī b. Sīna, *Rasāilu Ibn Sīna = İbn Sina Risaleleri = Les opuscules d'Ibn Sîna: 'Uyūnu'l-Ḥikmah: Risālatu Abu'l-Faraj b. at-Ṭayyib wa Risālatu'r-Rad li-Abū Ali b. Sīna*, ed. Hilmi Ziya Ülken, vol. 1 (Istanbul: Istanbul University, 1953), p. 13.
12. Abū 'Abdullah Muḥammad b. Aḥmad b. Yūsuf al-Hawārazmī, *Kitāb mafātiḥ al-'ulūm: text and studies = Kitābu mafātiḥu'l-'ulūm li-Âbū 'Abdullah Muḥammad b. Aḥmad b. Yūsuf al-Hawārazmî* (Collected and reprinted by Fuat Sezgin; collaboration with Carl Ehrig-Eggert, Eckhard Neubauer) (Frankfurt am Main: Institute for the History of Arabic-Islamic Science at the Johann Wolfgang

Goethe University, 2005), pp. 5-6, 131-132.
13. Abū Ḥāmid Muḥammad b. Muḥammad al-Ghazālī, *Iḥyā' 'Ulūm al-Dīn*, vol. 1 (Cairo: Muassasah al-Ḥalabī, 1387/1967), pp. 27-28; Hüseyin Atay, *Osmanlılarda Yüksek Din Eğitimi* (Istanbul: 1983), pp. 36-72.
14. Macdi Muhammed Efendī, *Ḥadāiqu'sh-Shaqāiq* (Istanbul: 1989), pp. 153-154.
15. Ibid., pp. 4-6.
16. Ahmed Çelebi, *Islam'da Eğitim-Öğretim Tarihi*, trans. Ali Yardım (Istanbul: Damla Yayınevi, 1976), p. 59.
17. Mustafa Baktır, *Islam'da İlk Eğitim Müessesesi: Asḥab-i Suffah* (Istanbul: Timaş Yayıncılık, 1990), pp. 20, 29-39, 43, 52-224.
18. Çelebi, ibid., pp. 35, 49, 53, 59, 95, 100; George Makdisi, *Ortaçağda Yüksek Öğretim: Islam Dünyası ve Hıristiyan Batı*, trans. Ali Hakan Çavuşoğlu-Hasan Tuncay Başoğlu (Istanbul: Gelenek Yayıncılık, 2004), p. 49-80.
19. Çelebi, ibid., pp. 108-109.
20. For further explanation, see F. Reşit Unat, *Türkiye Eğitim Sisteminin Gelişmesine Tarihi Bir Bakış* (Ankara: M.E.B., 1964), p. 3; Necdet Sakaoğlu, *Osmanlı Eğitim Tarihi* (Istanbul: İletişim, 1993), p.16; Ersoy Taşdemirci, "Medreselerin Doğus Kaynakları ve İlk Zamanları," *Erciyes Üniversitesi Sosyal Bilimler Dergisi*, vol. 2 (Kayseri: 1989), p. 269.
21. Mustafa Sanal, "Kuruluşundan Ortadan Kaldırılışına Kadar Olan Süre İçerisinde Medreseler" http://yayim.meb.gov.tr/dergiler/143/17.htm (11.11.2007).
22. Recep Cici, *Osmanlı Dönemi İslam Hukuku Çalışmaları: Kuruluştan Fatih Devrinin Sonuna Kadar* (Bursa: Arasta Yayınları, 2001), p. 18.
23. Cahid Baltacı, *XV-XVI. Asırlarda Osmanlı Medreseleri* (Istanbul: İrfan Matbaası, 1994), p. 43.
24. Yahya Akyüz, *Türk Eğitim Tarihi (Başlangıçtan 1993'e Kadar)* (Istanbul: Kültür Koleji Yayınları, 1994), p.43.
25. Mustafa Bilge, *İlk Osmanlı Medreseleri* (Istanbul: Istanbul Edebiyat Fakültesi Yayınları, 1984), pp. 5-7, 11-14.
26. Ayşe Zisan Furat, *XV. Ve XVI. YY.'larda Fatih ve Sülaymaniye*

Medreselerinde Verilen Din Eğitiminin Karşılaştırmalı Bir İncelemesi (Unpublished Master's Thesis, Istanbul University, Institute Social Sciences) (Istanbul: 2004), pp. 27-30, 87-95.

27. Akyüz, ibid., p. 247.
28. Mustafa Ergun, *II. Meşrutiyet Devrinde Eğitim Hareketleri (1908-1914)* (Ankara: Ocak Yayınları, 1996), pp. 348-349.
29. Sanal, p.6.
30. Doğan Kuban, "Sülaymaniye Külliyesi," *Dünden Bugüne İstanbul Ansiklopedisi*, vol. 7 (Istanbul: Tarih Vakfı, 1994), pp. 254-255.
31. Baltacı, pp. 518-519; Şennur Sezer and Adnan Özyalçıner, *Üç Dinin Buluştuğu Kent Istanbul* (Istanbul: İnkılap Kitabevi, 2003), pp. 121-129; Tahsin Öz, *Istanbul Camileri* (Ankara: Türk Tarih Kurumu, 1962), vol. 1, pp. 131-135.
32. Kemal Edip Kürkçüoğlu (prepared by), *Sülaymaniye Vakfiyesi* (Ankara: Posta Matbaası, 1962), pp. 22-26; Baltacı, ibid., pp. 518-519.
33. Yusuf Alemdar, *XV-XVI. Asırlarda İstanbul Darulkurraları* (Unpublished Master's Thesis, Ankara University, Institute Social Sciences) (Ankara: 1996), pp. 77-81.
34. Serpil Çelik, *Mevcut Belgeler Işığında Sülaymaniye Kulliyesinin Yapım Süreci* (Unpublished Doctorate Thesis, Istanbul Technology University, Institute Applied Sciences) (Istanbul: 2001), p. 296.
35. Kürkçüoğlu, ibid., pp. 32-33, 37.
36. Baltacı, ibid., p. 44.
37. Ali Gelibolulu, *Kuhnu'l-Ahbar* (prepared by Ahmet Uğur, Mustafa Çuhadır, Ahmet Gül, İbrahim Hakkı Çuhadır) (Kayseri: Erciyes Üniversitesi Yayınları, 1997), pp. 520-521.
38. Yaşar Sarıkaya, *Medreseler ve Modernleşme* (Istanbul: İz Yayıncılı, 1997), p. 45.
39. Ömer Özyılmaz, *Osmanlı Medreselerinin Eğitim Programları* (Ankara: Kültür Bakanlığı Yayınları, 2002), p.17.
40. Özyılmaz, ibid., pp. 4-5.
41. Hasan Akgündüz, *Klasik Dönem Osmanlı Medrese Sistemi: Amaç Yapı İşleyiş* (Istanbul: Ulusal Yayınları, 1997), pp. 372-376.
42. Akgündüz, ibid., p. 383.
43. Cevat İzgi, *Osmanlı Medreselerinde İlim* (Istanbul: İz Yayıncılık, 1997), pp. 50-51; Atay, ibid., p. 98; Özyılmaz, ibid., p. 7.

44. For further information, see Özyılmaz, ibid., pp. 4-17.
45. Nev'izade Atai, *Ḥadāi'q al-Ḥaqā'iq fī Takmilah al-Shaqā'iq* (Istanbul: 1989), p. 165.
46. Atai, ibid., p. 137.
47. Ibid., pp. 39-42.
48. Baltacı, ibid., pp. 519-534.
49. Yaşar Sarıkaya, ibid., p. 45; Furat, ibid., p. 111.
50. Atay, *Osmanlı'da Yüksek Din Eğitimi*, p. 100; Hüseyin Atay, "Fatih-Sülaymaniye Medreseleri Ders Programları ve İcazetnameler," *Vakıflar Dergisi*, vol. 8 (Vakıflar Genel Müdürluğü Yayınları, 1981), pp. 174-187; Akgündüz, ibid., pp. 403-405.
51. As regards the Süleymaniye madrasahs, Vakfiye states that books such as *Masābiḥ*, *Mashāriq*, *Bukhārī*, and *Muslim* were taught at Dār al-Ḥadīth (Kürküçüoğlu, pp. 31-32). Other sources mention that subjects like *tafsīr* and *fiqh* were taught at Dār al-Ḥadīth (Bilge, pp. 110, 232; Selahattin Yıldırım, *Osmanlı İlim Geleneğinde Edirne Ḍārulḥadīsi ve Müderrisleri* (Istanbul: Darulhadis, 2001), p. 42). Since appointments as central judges, military judges, and Shayh al-Islām were done from the Süleymaniye madrasahs, we have come to conclude that subjects like *fiqh* were being taught in addition to Ḥadīth .
52. İzgi, ibid., p. 171.
53. *Sharḥ al-Farā'id al-Sirājiyyah*. Sayyid Sharīf Jurjānī's (816/1413) commentary on this book became very famous and was taught repeatedly in madrasahs.
54. *Al-'Ināyah* was 'Alā' al-Dīn 'Alī al-Aswad (800/1397) commentary, and *al-Nuqāyah* was Ṣadr al-Sharī'ah 'Ubaydullāh b. Mas'ūd (747/1347) *Ḥāshiyah* (brief summary) on this book.
55. Ibn Nujaym wrote *al-Baḥr al-Rā'iq* as a commentary on this book.
56. The same author wrote *Durar al-Ḥukkām Sharḥ Ghurar al-Aḥkām* as a commentary on this book.
57. Shaykhzādah 'Abd al-Rḥmān b. Muḥammad b. Sulaymān (1078/1667) wrote *Majma' al-Anhur* as a commentary on this book.
58. The other three are Nasafi's *Kanzu'd-Daqāiq*, Mawsīlī's *al-Muḥtār*, and Ibnu's-Sa'ati's *Majma' al-Baḥrayn*.

59. Cengiz Kallek, "El-Hidaye," *DIA*, vol. 17 (Ankara: TDVIA, 1998), p. 471.
60. Mecdi Efendi, ibid., p. 556.
61. Ibid., p. 557.
62. For the content and the particulars of the writing, see Kallek, pp. 471-473.
63. Kallek, ibid., p. 471.
64. Mecdi Efendi, ibid., p. 558.
65. Ibid., p. 558.
66. Ibid., p. 558.
67. Ferhat Koca, "El-Feraiz es-Siraciyye," *DIA*, vol. 12 (Istanbul: TDV, 1995), pp. 367-368.
68. Ahmet Özel, *Hanefi Fikih Alimleri* (Ankara: Diyanet Vakfı Yayınları, 1990), p. 78.
69. Mecdi Efendi, ibid., p. 558.
70. Akgündüz, ibid., pp. 413-415; For more information on the methods applied in Islamic jurisprudence education, see Maqdîsî, pp. 162-229.
71. Osman Ergin, *Turkiye Maarif Tarihi 1, 2* (Istanbul: 1961), pp. 104-117; İzgi, ibid., pp. 133-159; Cici, ibid., p. 352.
72. According to Unan, 48 *fiqh*, 14 *tafsīr*, 25 *aqā'id* and *kalām*, 11 *akhlāq*, and 1 Ḥadīth . Together with the other areas, a total of 143 religiously oriented works were written during the period from the establishment of Sahn-i Saman Madrasahs in 1470 until 1730. For further information, see Fahri Unan, *Kuruluşundan Günümüze Fatih Kulliyesi* (Ankara: Türk Tarih Kurumu, 2003), pp. 359-363).
73. M. Akif Aydın, "Mecelle-i Akam-i Adliyye," *DIA*, vol. 28 (Ankara: TDV, 2003), pp. 231-235; ibid., "Hukuk-i Aile Kararnamesi," *DIA*, vol. 18 (Ankara: TDV, 2003), pp. 314-318.
74. Al-Marghinānī, *al-Hidāyah* (Istanbul: 1986), vol. 1, 226-227. For further information on judicial interpretations of verses and ḥadīth on *talâq*, see Abdülaziz Bayındır, *Kur'an Işığında Doğru Bildiğimiz Yanlışlar* (Istanbul: Süleymaniye Vakfı Yayınları, 2007), pp. 206-220.
75. Jamāl al-Dīn Abū Muḥammad al-Zayla'ī, *Naṣb al-Rāyah li Aḥādīth al-Hidāyah*, vol. 3 (Cairo: 1357/1939), p. 221.

7

Judicial pluralism in the Malaysian legal system

Saim Kayadibi

Abstract

Malay society, beside its determination to preserve its own traditions, has allowed other communities to live freely according to their own cultural values and traditions. Diversity is a source of cultural and social wealth that reflects an extraordinary degree of freedom in both legal and cultural richness. Such features resemble the Ottomans' approach. Malay society has apparently interiorized the value of diversity. Its people believe that for peace, freedom, tolerance, and strength between the different groups to continue, judicial pluralism must be maintained. In connection with this, the Malay legal system has been shaped by different legal systems, among them Islamic law, which has been implemented as per the society's request at will as a part of life in a natural way, the legal systems of Western colonial powers rather have been used by force on demand. In contrast, the Ottomans' *Majallah al-Aḥkām al-'Adliyyah*, the Ḥanafī legal code of Qadri Pasha (later called the *Majallah Ahkam Johor*), and the *Undang-undang Sivil Islam* were all used as the main source of judicial matters in the courts.

In this paper, the historical development of the Malay legal system is analyzed and the following themes are elaborated upon: Malaysia's constitutional law, customary law, and tribal legal systems; Sharīʿah and civil court procedures; the first contacts with Islamic law; the influence of Portuguese, Dutch, and English law; and the Turk-Malay connection and strong relationships.

Introduction

A multiethnic and multicultural county often confronts the question of how to deal with pluralistic legal system. Social engineers investigate the possibilities of whether it can govern the society in a peaceful atmosphere, might cause chaos, or might cause discrimination. Social harmony requires faithful and serious approaches.

In this time of globalization, people's material and spiritual needs are constantly changing. If these needs are not met, problems will arise. While material needs can be easily satisfied, this is not always the case with spiritual needs. In fact, not meeting the latter needs may result in a severe, wide-ranging crisis from which one may not recover. In addition, both sets of needs are in constant flux.

The basic needs of modern people are sufficient food and clothing, a place of residence, freedom of thought in order to devise and elaborate upon new ideas, and the freedom to believe in one's religion or to have no religion at all. Islam teaches that honouring the five essentials needs of life (viz., religion, life, intellect, lineage, and property) will ensure human happiness, security, and peace.

In the globalized world nothing can be hidden, for transparency is the main tool of a multi-cultural society. Human rights and the indispensable rights of each person have to be implemented and guaranteed in order to create a just, calm, and peaceful society. If such an environment cannot be created, the country may be dragged into anarchy and consider such concepts as peace, dialogue, integrity, harmony, justice, and unity to be no more than castles in the air. Society and its players must learn from history how peaceful societies have been maintained for centuries through internal harmony and unity. The Ottoman legal system might be a good example for multi-cultural society, and its *Majallah al-Aḥkām* was a viable approach for Muslim countries like Malaysia.

One of Malaysia's distinctive characteristics is to embrace different social structures within a multiracial, multireligious, and multi-judicial atmosphere. According to the Department of Statistics and Economic Planning unit, the country's population of 27.7 million (2008) is expected to reach 29 million by 2010. The population comprises no fewer than 178 ethnic groups.[1] Based upon Wikipedia, I calculate that there are about twenty-one different ethnics, 6 million members of which live in East Malaysia and the other 23 million are living in Peninsular Malaysia. Malay and other Bumiputera (indigenous non-Malay) groups make up 65% of the population, Chinese 26%, Indians 7.1%, and other unlisted ethnic groups 1%. Although Islam is the official religion, Malaysia is considered a multireligious society because its constitution guarantees religious freedom even if the country were secular. According to the Population and Housing Census 2000 figures, approximately 60.4% are Muslim; 19.2% are Buddhist; 9.1% are Christian; 6.3% are Hindu; and 2.6% are Confucian, Taoist, and other traditional Chinese religions (e.g., animism, folk religion, Sikhism, and atheist or "unknown" [0.9%]).[2]

Power in the Parliament is spread among the various religious and ethnic segments of the population. Although more than one-third of the Parliament and its Federal Cabinet are non-Malay and non-Muslim, the Malays occupy a dominant position in the government and in the ruling party UMNO (United Malays National Organization).[3] The Dewan Rakyat (House of the People, or. House of Representatives) consists of 222 seats (MPs) elected from single-member constituencies drawn based on population in a general election using the first-past-the-post system. The current National Front (Barisan Nasional) coalition, formed in 1973 as the successor to the Alliance (Perikatan) and which has been the ruling political party since independence, occupies 4,082,411 votes of 50.27% of 140 seats which represent s 63.1% of all seats in the parliament. The main opposition party, the Pan-Malaysian Islamic Party (PAS), occupies 1,140,676 votes of 14.05% of 23 seats which represents 10.4% of all seats in the parliament. Despite its multicultural composition, Malaysian society and politics are clearly defined as "Islamic." To the Malay people, "it is almost unthinkable to be anything but Muslim and they expect their government and its legal structure to protect that identity."[4] In the mind of citizens, being Malay or being Muslim are the same, for once you convert to Islam you are automatically considered Malay, based on the Federal Constitution. Article 160 defines "Malay" as "a person, who professes the religion of Islam, habitually speaks the Malay language, and conforms to Malay customs."[5] Beside this, a define of identity in Malaysian society, it has to be expressed that Muslims, from very historical realities, feel honoured to show peaceful cultural diversity and the Qur'an itself encourages Muslims to respect cultural and religious diversity and yet to retain their identities: "O people, surely We have created you of a male and a female, and made you tribes and families that you may know each other..."[6]

Finally, it could be said that a multi-legal system for a multi-cultural society would be the best way to unite different races and religions so that the society can avoid violence, chaos, and discrimination as much as possible.

The Malaysian legal system

Malaysia's long legal historical experience with a colourful environment is the result of a great deal of cultural diversity. Its legal history can be traced back to sometime around the fifth century, although its political history only started in 1963. As every human society has been based upon some sort of basic primordial rules before a codified legal system, Malay society was based on some legal foundations hidden within the community: the customary rules of the tribes, which relied upon belief in a common blood, patriarchal authority, and judicial organs operated by the tribal leader.[7]

Malaysian laws emanate from the five basic sources: the written law, the federal and state constitutions, and legislation passed by the Parliament and State Legislative Assemblies. This also includes prior legislation, the application of which has been extended and is still enforceable, judicial decisions, customary law; English law; and Islamic law.[8] Despite Malaysia's political unity, its distinct geographical regions (viz., Peninsular Malaysia, Sabah, and Sarawak), the country is governed by different set of laws and court systems in the interest of social harmony; however, the Federal Constitution is the supreme law of the federation. Malaysian law has been divided into three types: public law, international law, and private law. Generally, public law governs the individual-state relationship and is subdivided into constitutional law (deals with the Parliament's position of supremacy and the citizens' rights) and criminal law (deals with various offences committed by individuals against the state). International law, on the other hand, is divided into public and private. The laws that prevails between states is called public international law and the law, which may be called a conflict of laws or part of municipal laws, deals with cases involving more than one country; private law, which deals with the rights and duties of individuals amongst themselves, is considered under three divisions: contracts, tort, and trust. Contracts deal with the rights and obligations that arise due to agreements, tort involves offences committed against individuals, and trust governs the relationship between trustees and beneficiaries.[9]

Malaysian constitutional law

Although Article 3 of the Federal Constitution states that Islam is the state religion, Article 11 proclaims that other religions may be practised in peace and harmony in any part of the Federation. The Administration of Islamic law Act 1993 (Federal Territories) consists of eleven parts: preliminary; the Majlis Agama Islam Wilayah Persekutuan; Appointment of Mufti, Authority in Religious Matters and the Islamic Legal Consultative Committee; Sharīʿah Courts; Prosecution and Representation; Financial; Mosque; Charitable Collections; Conversion to Islam; Religious Education and General.[10] Historically, the modern constitutional move of the States of the Federation began when the first meeting of the first Council of State was officially opened on September 10, 1877; it is continued until the formation of the Federation of Malaya with two agreements: the State Agreement and the Federation of Malaya Agreement in 1948. With some essential amendments the 1948 Constitution remained in force until the independence of the Federation of Malaya in 1957.[11]

Article 4 states that the constitution is the supreme law of the Federation. Therefore, any law or regulation passed after the Merdeka (Independence) Day would be invalid if it was inconsistent with this Constitution. The Supreme Head of the Federation is to be called Yang di-Pertuan Agong (Article 32) and shall be elected by the Conference Rulers for a term of five years; however, the Conference Rulers can remove him from office and he can resign any time by confirming his intention to do so in writing.

The Parliament consists of 180 members with the House of Parliament (the Dewan Negara) and the House of Representatives (Dewan Rakyat), as well as the Head of the Federation (Yang di-Pertuan Agong). The Federation's legislative authority is vested in the Parliament. Article 66 states that the power of Parliament to make laws shall be exercised by Bills passed by both Houses (or, in the cases mentioned in Article 68, the House of Representatives) and, except as otherwise provided in this Article, assented to by the Yang di-Pertuan Agong.[12] According to Article 45/2, members of the Senate are appointed by the Head of the State for a three-year term. Following the constitutional development, however, the king's absolute power gradually diminished. He now functions as an advisory body that can only assent to the Parliament's decisions.

The Head of the Federation appoints the Prime Minister from the members of the House of Representatives. According to Article 43/7, a person who is a citizen by naturalisation or by registration under Article 17 shall not be appointed to this post. In contrast to the Head of the State, the Prime Minister shall hold office as long as he fulfils all of its requirements and has the vote of the majority of the members of the House of Representatives.

Malay customary law

From the fifth to the fifteenth centuries, foreign influence percolated into the Malay world. The customs and legal systems of neighbouring Sumatra and India penetrated into the country's legal system at various times. Over time, "early Malay customary law" emerged from these foreign influences. Furthermore, this early customary law survived in traditional proverbs and narratives. Besides Chinese traders and missionaries who settled in Malaya, Indian Hindus who migrated to the Malay states influenced their political, social, and institutional structures. This occurred mainly in the concept of kinship, tribal polities (which eventually changed), the paraphernalia of court ritual and ceremony still seen today, and their ideas and forms of worship. Naturally, the influence of Hindu and Buddhist (Indian and Chinese) custom and laws in legal matters and social affairs was obvious.[13] After Islam reached Malaya, its legal system made many contributions and became a significant part of Malay customary law.[14] These pre-modern bases of Malay customary law were nourished by *perpatih*[15] and *temenggong*.[16] The first is considered to be an extension of the tribal laws and the latter, by contrast, was adapted to a bilateral social system that emphases patriliny and endogamy.[17]

Archaeologists have found proof of the existence of human beings living in the area about 35000 years ago. This reflects the significance of customary law in the region; the excavations of human race in the limestone caves between 3000 and 2000 BC in the Malay Peninsula and the migration of people from southern or western China to this region between 2500 BC and 1500 BC.[18]

Tribal legal system

The aboriginal inhabitants of Peninsular Malaysia can be categorized as Negritoes, Senois, and Proto-Malays. The Negritoes were one of the least organized groups in these tribal nomadic societies. Every tribe was led by a powerful chief who was usually the oldest man. The chief of each tribe concerned would assemble and, assisted by a few advisers, settle inter-tribal disputes. He had absolute authority on his subjects. In small communities like Negritoes, crime and cheating were rare and thus the culprit would be fined, scolded by all tribal members, or whipped. The Senois, who were more settled and organized, called their leaders Penghulu. Upon his death his eldest son would inherit this name. If the leader died without leaving a direct male heir, anyone could be appointed to this post. Economic transactions were primitive and private property was unknown. Therefore the land was held in common; the production, harvesting, and processing of food were communal; and the harvests and products were shared among the tribe's members. In administrative terms, the

Proto-Malays were the most developed amongst the indigenous tribes. The head, known as Batin, was helped by the Jinang, Pengulu Balai, Jukra, and Pnaglima. The leader administered the law based upon his knowledge of the tribe's laws and custom. The penalties varied according to local interests: some tribes imposed the death penalty for murder and others would impose fines, as well as impale, drown, and expose offenders to the sun, depending upon the seriousness of their crime. Some of these penalties were the result of the contact with Hindu and Islamic law and civilization.[19]

The Portuguese and Dutch influence

Prior to the Portuguese and Dutch invasions, the Malacca region was ruled by the sultan, who administered justice in his capacity as the highest court. The ruler, portrayed as the source of law and the fountain of justice, determined which penalty fit the crime (e.g., killing, stabbing, slashing, assault and battery, robbery, theft, making false allegations, and lying); he could also decide not to impose any penalty. The administration of justice was carried out by the three offices: the Bendahara, the Temenggong, and the Laksamana. The first one was equated with the Prime Minister today as regards the amount of power he can wield; the second one, who had the power of a Chief of Police, led investigated criminal matters and was responsible for building and supervising prisons; and the last one, the Admiral, administered judicial affairs.[20] Hindu, Islamic and indigenous Malay laws were all recognized and implemented in the Sultanate of Malacca; the *Undang-undang Melaka* and the *Undang-undang Laut Melaka* served as the sultanate's two legal digests.[21] These digests were based upon the laws of *adat temenggong* and Shāfiʿī legal school. Some sections, however, were not really from that particular school but rather were taken from Islamic family law. In addition, the penalties were also derived from the Islamic local customary legal systems. The *Undang-undang Melaka*, a particular law of Malaysia, also has been strongly influenced by Islamic law.[22]

After the Portuguese invaded and conquered Malacca in 1511, they established a military and civil administration in the region. In civil affairs, the Governor was assisted by a Council composed of the Ovidor (Chief Justice), the Viador (Mayor), the Bishop or his deputy, and a Secretary of State. Despite this, however, it is not clear whether the Portuguese introduced their own laws or not, because the Portuguese judges introduced many ordinances without providing any specific details as to how they had been derived. On the other hand, Dutch influence began in the region as early as the seventeenth century. When Malacca was transferred to Dutch control, laws were issued by the central government in Holland and Batavia (Java) and the local executive. In order to unify the region's laws, the Dutch East India Company tried to introduce standard regulations that applied throughout the Indonesian Archipelago. Mainly an attempt to deal with Malacca, it was failure. In fact, only a guide for the Court of Justice in Malacca remained.[23] Some Indonesians migrated to Peninsular Malaysia while Malacca was under Portuguese and Dutch control. After a degree of law and order was established in the region, Malacca became a centre of trade.[24]

Contact with Islamic law

In the early years of the thirteenth century, relations between the traditional Islamic heartland and Malay world began to increase. Accordingly, Islamic law came into contact with the peninsula's customary life, which was embedded in the people's life and was considered the law of the land.[25] According to local historians, Islam reached Kelantan some time before 1181. The proof offered for this claim is a gold coin (*mas dinar*) found at Kota Kubang Labu with the inscription of "Al-Julus Kelantan" (The Government of Kelantan). The reverse side mentions the name of al-Mutawakkil and the date 577 AH, which corresponds to 1181 CE[26] The claim that Islam reached Southeast Asia no later than the end of the thirteenth century is beyond dispute.[27] The view of the local historians was verified by the *Kitab Jeoghrafi* (*The Manual of Geography*) and the *Tarikh Negeri Kelantan* (*The History of Kelantan*), both of which indicate that Islam had influenced the administration of the state since 1181.[28] In addition to these records, Ibn Batutah recounted his meeting with Queen Urduja, a Muslimah, in Kuala Krai, Kelantan, when Arab travellers sailed from India to China in 1297.[29]

After Malacca became a Muslim kingdom in the fourteenth century under Sultan Iskandar Shah, the region became a centre of Islamic civilizational life during the fifteenth century and played a significant role in firmly rooting Islamic values and laws in Southeast Asia. In fact, the presence of an Islamic Malacca caused a general weakening of the heretofore Hindu and Buddhist political, social, and cultural influence and even dominance over the life of the Peninsula's Malay population. In order to expand political relationships with other Muslims, Sultan Iskandar Shah welcomed Arab, Turk, Persian, and Chinese Muslims to Malaya; he went so far as to visit China to invite them to come to the region. Cheng Ho, a Muslim Chinese Commander, came with the Chinese fleet in 1409 in strengthen the China-Malacca relationship. Between 1403 and 1433, no less than seven naval expeditions visited the South Asian Sea, Malacca, and the Indian Ocean.[30]

Islamic law had a far-reaching influence upon local Malay custom in Pahang. Over time, many of its provisions became based upon Islamic law, such as *qiṣāṣ* (retaliation), fines, illegal sexual intercourse, sodomy, theft, robbery, apostasy, non-observance of the obligatory prayers, *jihād*, legal procedures, witnesses, oaths, trade, sales, security, investments, trusts, payment for labour, land, gifts, and *waqfs* (charitable foundations). The laws of Johor, especially, reflect the greatest incorporation of laws based upon Islamic law and principles. Traces and evidences of Islamic law and traditions are also embodied within the Malay law.[31] The *Majallah Ahkam Johor*, Undang-undang Sivil Islam[32] was the translated version of the Ottoman empire's *Majallat al-Aḥkam al-'Adliyyah.* Qadri Pasha's Ḥanafī code was translated and eventually became known as the *Ahkam Shariyyah Johor.* Islamic law influenced the Constitution of Terengganu (1911)[33] and the Constitution of Johor (1895).[34] Clearly, the law of the Malay land was Islamic before the coming of the British. The British colonialists replace Islamic law with British law administration, however, Islamic law was allowed to function in matters of family and inheritance, and some matrimonial and *ta'zīr* (punishment) offences.[35]

The Turk-Malay connection

The connections of the Turks, who originated in the steppes of Central Asia, with Southeast Asia are based on very significant values and solid relationships. The locations of their lands have several features in common: both are surrounded by three seas and semi-islands; however, their climates differ greatly and they are located far from each other. Notwithstanding these factors, Turks and Malays have strong cultural, religious, and historical relationships. The Turks played a great role in the Malay Archipelago in spreading Islam and helped the Malay people defend themselves against European colonialism and the ensuing negative (in the sense of anti-Islamic) influences.

The Turk-Malay relationship can be divided into three distinct historical stages: the beginning of the thirteenth century, the pan-Islamic era of Sultan Abdulhamid II, and after the Ottoman empire was replaced by the Republic of Turkey.

The first stage began with the coming of the Rumis (Asian Turks). After the great period of Islamization in Southeast Asia during the thirteenth century,[36] Islam acquired strong political power in several part of the Malay world. In terms of establishing Islam in the land, India was an influential country. It was followed by the Moghul-Turkish rule in this stage. In the course of this Pax Turcica, Sunnī Islam spread in the Indian sub-continent, particularly in the areas of modern-day Pakistan and Bangladesh, toward the Malay world via merchants, traders, Sufism, sheikhs and *murīds*, and dervishes.[37] An account by a French historian indicates this significant Turkish connection and role in the Malay world: "A great number of the Asian Turk, called Rumis, some of whom made themselves masters of some ports, as Meliques Az, who made a considerable settlement at Diu, where he was a long time troublesome to the Portuguese."[38]

Hurgronje identifies these Rumis as Ottoman Turks on the grounds that the Ottoman Sultan was traditionally known in Southeast Asia as "Raja Rum."[39] Historians have speculated that these Turks might have been the people of Seljuk empire (1040-1157). The Ottoman Sultan immediately sent naval and military aid to the Malays when the Portuguese attacked Malacca in 1511. After Malacca fell, the centre of Islam in the Malay world shifted to Aceh. The Ottomans continued to do what they could to protect the Malay world until the beginning of the twentieth century.[40] The Acehnese offered an annual tribute as a token for protection, but the Ottoman sultans always refused to accept it.[41] In mid-1850, this traditional Turkish protection was reconfirmed in two *firmans* issued by Sultan Abdulmejid and the region's independence was preserved against European penetration for over three hundred years starting from 16th century The Sultan of Aceh sent Abd ar-Rahman to Istanbul to seek the sultan's help when the Dutch made a last attempt to conquer Aceh in 1868. As a result, Mithat Pasha urged that the Ottoman fleet be dispatched to Sumatra.[42]

The second stage, that of Sultan Abdulhamid's pan-Islamic policy, opened a new relationship between the two peoples because it was a constant source of worry for the Dutch and British colonial powers in Southeast Asia. Holland's increasing penetration into Malay world in the 1890s caused the Malays to seek assistance and at least moral guidance from Istanbul.[43] The Ottoman Sultan, whom the Malays and Indonesians viewed as "God's Shadow on Earth,"[44] sent Muhammad Kamil Bey as his Consul General to Batavia (1897-1899). This official reawakened the connection between the Middle Eastern and Southeast Asian Muslims. In addition, one of his most important roles in Batavia was to foster closer links between the Southeast Asian and Middle Eastern presses, such as the Arabic-language publications *al-Malumat of Constantinople, Thamarat al-funun of Beirut,* and several Egyptian newspapers—all of which complained about the injustices and oppression visited upon the Muslims by the Dutch.[45] These efforts bore some fruit, as seen in the mutinies in Southeast Asia. Religious passions began to be aroused in those Muslims who sincerely believed that the Europeans were trying to undermine their beliefs. Britain's war against the Ottoman empire, as well as despotic Dutch colonialism, encouraged the region's Muslims to attack the colonial powers wherever and whenever they could.[46] One important element of Sultan Abdulhamid II's pan-Islam policy was reflected in the Singapore Mutiny of 1915, when Indian and Malay Muslims refused to obey the British order to deploy to the Middle East in order to fight the Turks.[47] As a result, 530 were arrested in connection with the ensuing conflicts, 47 were sentenced to death, 64 were exiled for life, 73 were exiled for lesser terms, 12 were imprisoned for rigorous terms, and 16 to shorter terms. The executions were considered barbaric.[48] Notwithstanding these executions, the mutiny was a potentially serious threat to the British colonial government.[49]

The third stage, which started after the caliphate was abolished, did not sever the strong connection between the two worlds. Undeniably, the main attraction for this relationship had always been the institution of caliphate as represented by the Ottoman sultan in his capacity as the symbol of Muslim unity. Hitherto, the vision of Ottoman magnitude power, and glory and the all-powerful caliph continued to exist among the Indian, Indonesian, and Malay Muslims. The masses of the Malay, as well as their political and intellectual leaders, looked to the Ottomans for inspiration and sympathized with them during the Turkish-Russian war of 1877, the First World War, the Turkish National Independence War, the Balkans wars, and in many other events.[50]

As with the other sultans of Johor, there was a unique connection between Istanbul and Johor. This was made especially clear when Sultan Abu Bakar of Johor, a new type of relationship had already started. Ruqayyah Hanım, a member of the Ottoman sultan's harem, was presented as an honorary gift to the Sultan. She married Ungku Abdul Majid after their arrival at Johor, and the couple had three sons, one of whom was Ungku Abdul Hamid, the father of Ungku Abdul Aziz, the former Vice-Chancellor of the University of Malaya. Upon her husband's death, Ruqayyah Hanım married Dato' Jaafar. Seven children resulted from this union, one of whom, Dato' Onn, founded UMNO; his son Tun Hussein was the third Prime Minister of Malaysia. After her second husband died, Ruqayyah Hanım was married to Abdullah al-Attas, a well known Yemeni Arab trader whose sole son, Ali al-Attas, had three sons, all of whom became leading personalities in their respective fields: Hussein al-Attas (d. 2007) was an outstanding Malay sociologist and a founding member of the Malaysian People's Movement Party; Naquib al-Attas (b. 1931) is a prominent Muslim Malay Sūfī philosopher and scholar, as well as the founder and director of International Institute of Islamic Thought and Civilization (ISTAC) and finally the current prime-minister of Malaysia Mohd Najib Abdul Razak (b. 1953) has also Turkish blood from the same family tree.

In sum, the Turk-Malay relationship is not a weak tie; rather, it is a very strong relationship rooted in both people's respect of religious, cultural, and family-oriented relationships. Notwithstanding the great distance that separates them, they are united by their shared Islamic values.

The introduction of British law

Both the West and the East originated legal systems that they tried to apply in the Malay Archipelago; nevertheless, these laws were often not welcomed and consequently faded away. For instance, the Portuguese and Dutch tried to apply their law in Malacca during their respective occupations of that land; however, their legal systems had little, if any, effect upon on the country as a whole. Despite these repeated failures, the British colonial administration also sought to introduce its legal system in the region. By the Royal Charter of Justice of 1826, British law was introduced in the Straits Settlements (a group of British territories in Southeast Asia); it was introduced in the Malay states through legislation. These laws were mostly related to private law of torts, contract, property, commercial and industrial law, all of which were governed by a unified system of law and organisation based on common law, equity, and local and imperial legislation; domestic relations were provided for in group personal law. In contrast, Islamic law mostly dealt with matters of religious observance, succession, matrimonial relations, and domestic affairs generally in the Malay territories and other Muslim countries.[51]

The British also were involved with slavery, forced labour, and land tenure, which came under the regulations dealing with these respective subjects. While they were dealing with the land's rulers as advisors on legal matters, they neither interfered with nor questioned the Malays' religion (Islam) or customs. Despite their assurances, however, the British did interfere with Islamic law and its administration in all of the states. This resulted in the introduction of British law on the Indian model in various field, such as the adoption of the Indian codification of the principles of British law; the Panel Code of the Straits Settlements; and the Indian Evidence Act, which was adopted in Selangor by the Courts Regulation (1893), in Perak (1894), and in the Federated Malay States with the Revised Edition (1936). The Criminal Procedure Code of India was adopted, and land enactments were enacted in the various states between 1897 and 1903. All of the principles underlying the Malay Muslim laws related to criminal law, evidence, criminal procedure, contract, and land were replaced by the principles of British law. In addition, the Judicial Commissioner's Regulations and Orders in Council abolished the Courts of the Residents and Sultans in Council in 1896, and the Final Court of Appeal for the Federation was introduced with the establishment of a Judicial Commissioner. Subsequently, all judges in the new legal system were trained according to the British legal system. The changes continued: the Malay States' Civil Law Enactment (1937), which was extended to the other Malay states; the Civil Law Ordinance established, which established British law throughout the whole Federation of Malaya (1956), including the Borneo states that shared British common law. After independence, however, many Acts (e.g., the Companies Acts [1965], the Insurance Act [1963], and the Hire Purchase Act [1967]) were changed and based on Australian models.[52] British law was practiced in the Malay states usually by the decisions of judges when they could not find any appropriate customary and local laws when British-trained judges were applying British law.[53]

The dual court system

Given that Malaysia contains different ethnic groups, the formation of a dual legal system was necessary. Even if these two systems have different judicial methods and principles, both of them have influenced each other and cooperate in many judicial matters. In fact, they continue to draw closer together. For example, "in recent years even the names of the courts, the manner of addressing the judges and their dress on the bench have been adapted from those of the civil court. New court complexes house both the civil and the Sharīʿah courts under the same roof. Some Muslim civil court judges sit in the Sharīʿah Courts of Appeal with Sharīʿah Appeal Court Judges, complementing each other. Civil court judges are often invited to speak at seminars meant for Sharīʿah court judges."[54]

Basically, the Sharīʿah consists of an enormous number of rules and maxims derived from the Qur'an, the Sunnah, *ijmāʿ* (consensus), and *qiyās* (analogy). Therefore, it refers to "commands, prohibitions, guidance and principles that God has addressed to mankind pertaining to their conduct in this world and in the next."[55] This legal system, as well as others, is a normative system that regulates and controls human behaviour and nature. The Sharīʿah courts function according to Islamic law as their philosophy is to implement every ruling within the Islamic legal framework.

As law is a social phenomenon, the society brings its needs. The emergence of law and a legal system, as well as their functions, in a society reflect the society's nature, as can be seen in the fact that different social structures demonstrate different forms of law and roles for the law. Despite many differences, the society gradually moves toward cooperation, consensus, the common good, peaceful social change, and social equilibrium.[56] The nature of Malaysian society, which is multi-religious, is reflected in the country's dual court system because the Sharīʿah court has no jurisdiction over non-Muslims. Bear in mind that if a non-Muslim citizen wants to have pursue a court case, where can he/she can go? Conversely, the conflict occurs in Muslim citizens if there is no Sharīʿah court.

The Sharīʿah court system

The Sharīʿah courts, according to the Administration of Islamic Law Act 1993, have three levels: the Sharīʿah Subordinate Court, the Sharīʿah High Court, and the Sharīʿah Appeal Court. A Chief Sharīʿah Judge is appointed by the Yang di-Pertuan Agong (Supreme Head of State) on the advice of the Minister after consulting with the Majlis. The qualified person must be a citizen and and must have been, for a period of not less than than ten years preceding his appointment, a Sharīʿah High Court Judge, a *Kadi*, a Registrar, or a Sharīʿah Prosecutor of a State; being learned in Islamic law is not a requirement for that post.[57] The Chief Sharīʿah Judge shall be the Chairman for proceedings of the Sharīʿah Appeal Court. The Yang di-Pertuan Agong may also appoint High Court Judge after consulting with the Majlis on the Minister's advice.[58]

A Sharīʿah High Court shall have jurisdiction throughout the Federal Territories, be presided over by a Sharīʿah judge and shall try any offence in its criminal jurisdiction committed by a Muslim. The guilty party shall be punished under the Enactment, the Islamic Family Law (Federal Territories) Act 1984, or any other written law prescribing offences against precepts of Islam that are currently in force. It may impose any punishment provided therefore; and hear and determine, in its civil jurisdiction, all actions and proceedings in which the parties are Muslim. A Sharīʿah Subordinate Court shall have also jurisdiction throughout the Federal Territories and be provided over by a judge of the Sharīʿah Subordinate Court. The Sharīʿah Appeal

Court shall also have the jurisdiction to hear and determine any appeal against any decision made by the Sharīʿah High Court in the exercise of its original jurisdiction and shall have supervisory and revisionary jurisdiction over the Sharīʿah High Court.[59]

Legal officers and lawyers (*peguam syar'ie*) are also required, besides competent judges for the Sharīʿah courts, as this is the norm in civil legal procedures. In order to pursue legal activities and help the litigating parties and the courts, professionals are needed who can better administer the Islamic law in the Sharīʿah-based procedures. Complementary units must also be provided, such as education and the training of future judicial and legal officers or lawyers. Some universities, among them the International Islamic University of Malaysia and the University of Malaya, provide educational, training courses, and moot trials for these aspiring professionals.

The civil court system

A multi-cultural and multi-religious society naturally requires a dual court system to fulfil its subjects' expectations. Malaysia's dual court system is successful in this regard. The Shariʿah-based legal system is for the Muslims, while the civil legal system, which is based on the fundamental requirement that one be judged by the appropriate legal system, is for the non-Muslims. Qur'an 2:256 clearly supports the idea of freedom of choice and non-coercion as regards belief or ideology or being judged by any legal system. Each human being is a holy creation whose values and beliefs must be respected.

The civil court system refers to the non-Sharīʿah-based legal system, which consists of criminal, civil, and other cases. After colonizing Malays, the British introduced new courts based on their own model with judges and lawyers trained in British common law of England. Interestingly, even though the land's traditional law was Islamic, there were no Sharīʿah courts before the British came.[60] Nevertheless, three Supreme Courts did exist before the formation of the Malay Federation in 1963: the Supreme Court of the Federation of Malaya; the Supreme Court of Singapore; and the Supreme Court of Sarawak, North Borneo, and Brunei. Each Supreme Court featured a High Court and a Court of Appeal, led by a Chief Justice. The Chief Justices are governed by the Article 122B of the Constitution of Malaysia; the Judges shall be appointed by the Yang-di Pertuan Agong (the supreme head of the federation) on the advice of the Prime Minister of Malaysia after consulting the Conference of Rulers (Majlis Raja-Raja).[61]

Upon independence, the Court of Appeal was replaced by the Federal Court and according to the Article 131 of the Federal Constitution; the Privy Council continued to function as the country's highest court, entrusted with advising the Yang-di Pertuan Agong formally on dealing with appeals from the Federal Court. The decisions of the higher courts bind lower courts, and some courts are bound by their own decisions. After the Privy Council was abolished in 1985, the Federal Court was renamed the Supreme Court of Malaysia and became the highest court.[62] In other words, the hierarchy of Civil Courts begins from the top: the Federal Court, the Court of Appeal, the High Court, the Session Court, the Magistrates' Court, and the Penghulu's Court. The first three courts are considered Superior Courts, whereas the others are considered Subordinate courts. These courts all have jurisdiction in both criminal and civil cases.[63] On the other hand, Sharīʿah Courts have jurisdiction only over matters related to Muslims. Over time, however some amendments have been made due to the occurrence of jurisdictional conflicts when deciding disputes involving Muslims. One example of this is the amendment of Article 121 (1A).[64] In the event of a conflict arising between the two courts, the Sharīʿah court's decision prevails over that of the civil court. As Habibullah wrote: "Once it is determined that Syariah courts have jurisdiction on a matter, civil courts' jurisdiction is excluded."[65] The Sharī'ah courts have no jurisdiction over non-Muslims in any matters.

Notes

1. Muhammad Hashim Kamali, *Islamic Law in Malaysia: Issues and Developments* (Selangor: Ilmiah Publishers, 2000), 1.
2. http://en.wikipedia.org/wiki/Demographics_of_Malaysia#cite_ref-islam01_22-0.
3. Chandra Muzaffar, *Tolerance in the Malay Political Scene*, in Syed Othman Alhabshi and Nik Mustafa Nik Hassan, *Islam and Tolerance* (Kuala Lumpur: Institute of Islamic Understanding, 1994), 143.
4. Muhammad Hashim Kamali, ibid., 5.
5. *Laws of Malaysia, Federal Constitution* as of 10 April 2002 (Selangor: International Law Book Services, 2002), 198.
6. Qur'an 49:13.
7. Abdul Majeed Mohamed Mackeen, *Contemporary Islamic Legal Organization in Malaya*, Monograph Series No. 13 (New Hawen: Yale University Southeast Asia Studies, 1969), 9.
8. Ahmad Ibrahim and Ahilemah Joned, *The Malaysian Legal System*, 2nd ed. (Kuala Lumpur: Dewan Bahasa dan Pustaka, 1995), 4-5.
9. Lee Mei Pheng, *General Principles of Malaysian Law* (Selangor: Penerbit Fajar Bakti, 2001), 3-13.
10. Ahmad and Joned, ibid., 47-49.
11. Ibid., 143.
12. Article 66.
13. Ahmad and Joned, ibid., 6-7.
14. Mackeen, ibid., 11.
15. See more about this system in B.J. Brown, "Justice and Adat Perpateh," in *Papers on Malayan History*, ed. K.G. Tregonning (Singapore: Journal of Southeast Asian History, 1962), 135-161; P.P. Buss-Tjen, "Malay Law," *AJCL*, 7 (1958), 260-262; M.G. Swift, *Malay*

Peasant Society (London: The Athlone Press, 1965), 12-22.

16. For more on this system, see P.P. Buss-Tjen, ibid., 262-263; R.J. Wilkinson, "Introductory Sketch: Law," in *Papers on Malay Subjects* (Kuala Lumpur: 1908), 34-45.
17. Mackeen, ibid., 11.
18. Ahmad and Joned, ibid., 6.
19. Ibid., 10-12.
20. Richard Winstedt, *Malaya and Its History* (Longon: Hutchinson's University Library, 1948), 14-100.
21. Liaw Yock Fang, ed., *Undang-undang Melaka: Laws of Melaka* (The Hague: M. Hijhoff, 1976), 62.
22. See Muhammad Yusof Hashim, *Islam Dalam Sejarah Perundangan Melaka* (*Islam in Malacca Legal History*) (Kuala Lumpur: Persatuan Sejarah Malaysia, n.d.)
23. Ahmad and Joned, ibid., 15-16.
24. Saw Swee Hock, *The Population of Peninsular Malaysia* (Singapore: Singapore University Press, 1988), 37.
25. Mackeen, ibid., 14.
26. Asa'ad Shukri b. Haji Muda, "*Sejarah Kelantan*" (Kota Bharu: Pustaka Aman Press, 1962), 13, qf. Abdullah Alwi Haji Hassan, *The Administration of Islamic Law in Kelantan* (Selangor: Percetakan Dewan Bahasa dan Pustaka, 1996), 1.
27. Peter Riddel, *Islam and the Malay-Indonesian World: Transmission and Responses* (Honolulu: University of Hawaii Press, 2001); Ahmad Ibrahim, Sharon Siddique, and Yasmin Hussain eds., *Readings on Islam and Southeast Asia* (Singapore: ISEAS, 1985); Mohamad Taib Osman, ed., *Islamic Civilization in the Malay World* (Kuala Lumpur: Dewan Bahasa dan Pustaka, 1997), qf. Eric Tagliacozzo, eds., *Southeast Asia and the Middle East Islam, Movement, and the Longue Durée* (Singapore: NUS Press, 2009), 2.
28. Asa'ad Shukri b. Haji Muda, *Detik-Detik Sejarah Kelantan* (Kota Bharu: Pustaka Aman Press, 1977), 20-30, qf. Abdullah Alwi, ibid., 1.
29. Ibn Batutah, *Rihlah,* ed. Dr Ali al-Muntasar al-Kattani, 2 vols. (Beirut: Muassasah al-Risalah, 1981), 714; Asa'ad Shukri b. Haji Muda, ibid., 30, qf. Abdullah Alwi, ibid., 1.
30. Ahmad and Joned, ibid., 7-8.

31. Abdullah Alwi, ibid., xlvii.
32. *Al-Aḥkām al-'Adliyah, Undang-Undang Sivil Islam*, trans. Akhir Haji Yaacob (Selangor: Dewan Bahasa dan Pustaka, 2002).
33. *Laws of the Constitution of Johor*, Malayan Constitutional Documents, vol. 2.
34. *Laws of the Constitution of Terengganu*, Malayan Constitutional Documents, vol. 2.
35. Ahmad and Joned, ibid., 43-47.
36. Sayyid Qudratullah Fatimi, *Islam Comes to Malaysia* (Singapore: Malaysian Sociological Research Institute, 1963), 4.
37. Mehmet Özay, *Islamic Identity and Development Studies of the Islamic Periphery* (Kuala Lumpur: Forum, 1990), 24.
38. Sayyid Qudratullah Fatimi, ibid., 81.
39. Snouck Hurgronje, *The Achehnese*, vol. 1 (Leyden: Brill, 1906), 208
40. Anthony Reid, *The Contest for North Sumatra, Atjeh, The Netherlands and Britain, 1858-1898* (Kuala Lumpur: University of Malaya Press, 1969), qf. Mehmet Özay, ibid., 25.
41. Hurgronje, ibid., 208-210.
42. Anthony Reid, "Indonesian Diplomacy: A Documentary Study of Atjehnese Foreign Policy in the Reign of Sultan Mahmud, 1870-1874," *Journal of the Malay Branch of the Royal Asiatic Society* (JAMBRAS) vol. 42, part 2, (1969), 121.
43. Selim Deringil, Legitimacy Structures in the Ottoman State: The Reign of Abdulhamid II (1876-1909), *International Journal of Middle East Studies*, vol. 23, No. 3 (Aug. 1991), 350 (345-359).
44. Anthony Reid, "Nineteenth Century Pan-Islam in Indonesia and Malaysia," *The Journal of Asian Studies*, vol. 26, No. 2 (Feb. 1967), 267 (267-283).
45. Reid, Nineteenth, ibid., 281 (267-283).
46. A.J. Stockwell, "Imperial Security and Moslem Militancy, with Special Reference to the Hertogh Riots inSingapore (December 1950)," *Journal of Southeast Asian Studies*, vol. 17, No. 2 (Sep. 1986), 331 (322-335).
47. R.W.E. Harper and Harry Miller, *Singapore Mutiny* (Singapore: Oxford University Press, 1984), 25.

48. Nicholas Tarling, "'The merest pustule.' The Singapore Mutiny of 1915," *Journal of the Malaysian Branch of the Royal Asiatic Society* LV, 2 (1982), 50.
49. Nadzan Haron, "Colonial Defence and British Approach to the Problems in Malaya 1874-1918," *Modern Asian Studies*, vol. 24, No. 2 (May 1990), 293 (275-295).
50. Zainal Abidin b. Ahmad Pendeta Za'ba, "A History of Malay Literature XIV: Modern Developments," *Journal of the Malay Branch of the Royal Society* (December 1939), 151-152, qf. Mehmet Özay, ibid., 27.
51. Mackeen, ibid., 17.
52. Ahmad and Joned, ibid., 17-26.
53. Ibid., 63-72.
54. Abdul Hamid Hajj Mohamad, *Civil and Shariah Courts in Malaysia: Conflict of Jurisdiction, in Islamic Law in the Contemporary World*, ed. Zainal Azam Abd. Rahman (Kuala Lumpur: IKIM, 2003), 14.
55. Muhammad Ḥashim Kamali, "Source, Nature and Objectives of Shariah," *The Islamic Quarterly*, vol. XXXIII, No. 4 (1988), 215.
56. Anwarul Yaqin, *Law and Society in Malaysia* (Selangor: International Law Book Services, 2002), 13.
57. *Administration of Islamic Law* (Federal Territories), 1992, 40-41, cf. Ahmad Ibrahim and Ahilemah Joned, *The Malaysian Legal System*, 2nd ed. (Kuala Lumpur: Dewan Bahasa dan Pustaka, 1995), 53.
58. Ibid., 53.
59. Ibid., 54-57.
60. Abdul Hamid, ibid., 9.
61. *Laws of Malaysia*, ibid., 148.
62. Ahmad and Joned, ibid., 123.
63. For more details on judicial decisions about these courts, see Ahmad and Joned, ibid., 123-137.
64. Farid Sufian Shuaib, Tajul A.A. Bustami, and Mohd Hisham Moh. Kamal, "Administration of Islamic Law in Malaysia," *Malayan Law Journal* (Kuala Lumpur: Butterworth Asia, 2001), 91.
65. Ibid., 135.

Conclusion

Despite the existence of different legal and judicial systems, the nature of the Malay people was very prone to Islamic law and tradition. Notwithstanding the Western influence and interference in such matters, the law of the land and its culture is revitalized very often and returns to its origin. For example, the Portuguese and Dutch invasions, as well as British colonialism, disappeared. In contrast to the Westerners, the Ottomans followed a different model because of their Muslim character. History shows that the Ottomans came to the Malay Archipelago only to protect them from European colonial attacks. The translation and long-term effects of the Ottoman *Majallah al-Aḥkām al-'Adliyyah* and the Ḥanafī code of Qadri Pasha is evidence for a significant degree of legal interaction between the Islamic values of both peoples.

Regardless of their Islamic character, the Malays are able to get along very well with others. In fact, incidents of discrimination toward minorities are very rare. In connection with this, the country's minorities are guaranteed the freedom of belief and religion practice. Establishing civil courts side by side with Sharī'ah courts provides equal opportunities for legal redress to Malaysia's non-Muslim citizens. The official protection of these rights, all of which are clearly stated in the Federal Constitution, provide them with peace of mind, trust, and confidence toward the government and the Malays. Therefore, multi-cultural societies may take the Malay legal system as a model for creating a peaceful and tranquil life among the country's subjects and between them and the government.

Bibliography

Abdul Hadi W.M. and Ara, L.K., *Hamzah Fansuri: Penyair Sūfī Aceh,* Jakarta: Lotkala, 1984.

Abdullah, Abd Rahman Hj., *Islam dalam sejarah Asia Tenggara Tradisional,* Kuala Lumpur: Pustaka Hj. Abdul Majid, 2006.

Abdullah, Auni Hj., *Tradisi Pemerintahan Islam & Kolonialisme dalam Sejarah Alam Melayu,* Kuala Lumpur: Darul Fikir, 2005.

Abdullah, Haci Wan Muhd Saghir. (ed), *Hadiqatul Azhar Wal Rayahin,* Kuala Lumpur: Khazanah Fataniah, 1998.

—*Penyebaran Islam Dan Silsilah Ulama Sejagat Dunia Melayu,* vol. 5, Kuala Lumpur: Persatuan Pengkajian Khazanah Klasik Nusantara & Khazanah Fathaniyah, 1999.

—*Penyebaran Islam dan Silsilah Ulama Sejagat Dunia Melayu,* vol. 7, Siri Ke-8, Kuala Lumpur: Persatuan Pengkajian Khazanah Klasik Nusantara & Khazanah Fathaniyah, 1999.

Abdullah, Taufik, "Political Images and Cultural Encounter: The Dutch in the Indonesian Archipelago," *Studia Islamika: Indonesian Journal for Islamic Studies,* vol I., No. 3, 1994, p. 7

Abramski, Irit Bligh, "The Judiciary (Qadis) as a Governmental-Administrative Tool in Early Islam," Journal of the Economic and Social History of the Orient 35, no. 1 (1992): 40-71.

Abū Yaḥyā, Zayn al-Dīn Zakariyyā b. Muḥammad b. Aḥmad Zakariyyā al-Anṣārī, *Fatḥ al-Wahhāb bi Sharḥ Manhaj al-Ṭullāb,* vol. 1, Beirut: Dār al-Kutub al-ʻIlmiyyah, 1418/1998.

Administration of Islamic Law (Federal Territories), 1992, 40-41

Aharon, Layish, "Shahādat Naql in the Judicial Practice in Modern Libya," in Masud, Peters, and Powers, *Dispensing Justice in Islam: Qadis and Their Judgments*, Leiden and Boston: Brill, 2006.

Akgündüz, Ahmed, *Mukayeseli Islam ve Osmalı Hukuku Kullīyāti*, Diyarbakir: Dicle University 1986.

—*Osmalı Qanunnameleri ve Hukuki Tahlilleri*, vol. 1-9, Istanbul: OSAV, 1989-1992.

—*Shar'iyyah Sijilleri*, vol. 1 (Private Law), vol. 2 (Public Law), Istanbul: Türk Dünyası, 1989.

Akgündüz, Hasan, *Klasik Dönem Osmanlı Medrese Sistemi: Amaç Yapı İşleyiş*, Istanbul: Ulusal Yayınları, 1997.

Akolawin, N.O., "Personal Law in the Sudan: Trends and Developments," *Journal of African Law* 17, no. 2 (1973): 150

Akyüz, Yahya, *Türk Eğitim Tarihi (Başlangıçtan 1993'e Kadar)*, Istanbul: Kültür Koleji Yayınları, 1994.

Al-'Ābidīn, Muḥammad Amīn b. 'Umar b., *Radd al-Muḥtār 'alā al-Durr al-Mukhtār*, vols. 1-6 vol. I, pp. 55, vol. 3, pp. 395-396, Cairo: Maktabah al-Ḥalabī, 1967.

Al-Aḥkām Al-'Adliyah, Undang-Undang Sivil Islam, trans. Akhir Haji Yaacob, Selangor: Dewan Bahasa dan Pustaka, 2002.

Al-Attas, Syed Muhammad Naquib, *A Commentary on the Hujjat Al-Siddiq of Nur al-Din Al-Raniri*, Kuala Lumpur: Ministry of Culture, 1986.

—*A General Theory of the Islamization of the Malay-Indonesian Archipelago*, Kuala Lumpur: Dewan Bahasa dan Pustaka, 1969.

—*Preliminary Statement on a General Theory of the Islamization of the Malay Indonesian Archipelago*, Kuala Lumpur: Dewan Bahasa dan Pustaka, 1969.

Alemdar, Yusuf, *XV-XVI. Asırlarda İstanbul Darulkurraları* (Unpublished Master's Thesis, Ankara University, Institute Social Sciences), Ankara: 1996.

Al-Fairusy, Tgk. M. Dahlan. and Zunaimar, Dra., *Katalog Manuskrip Perpustakaan Dayah Tanoh Abee*, Banda Aceh: Pusat Dokumentasi dan Informası Aceh, 1993.

Alfian, Teuku H. Ibrahim. Wadjah Rakjat Atjeh Dalam Lintasan Sedjarah", *Seminar Kebudajaan Dalam Rangka Pekan Kebudajaan*

Atjeh Ke-II, (The Second Atjeh Cultural Festival, 20 August-2 September 1972) Dan Dies Natalis Ke XI Universitas Sjiah Kuala, Panitia Pusat Pekan Kebudajaan Atjeh Ke-II, Banda Aceh: 1972.

—"Islam Dan Kerajaan Aceh Darussalam" (ed.), Taufik Abdullah, *Sejarah Dan Dialog Peradaban*, Jakarta: LIPI Press, 2006.

Al-Habsyi, Imām Syed Zain Hussien. Owner of an Arabic Bookstore in Wadi Hana, Johor Bharu. Interview on May, 8 2008, at 9:00 am.

Al-Jawziyyah, b. al-Qayyim, *I'lām al-Muwaqqi'īn 'an Rabb al- 'Ālamīn*, v. 1, Beirut: Dār al-Kutub al-Ilmiyyah, 1996.

Al-Khaṣṣāf, Aḥmad Abū Bakr, (874 CE), *Islamic Legal and Judicial System*, New Delhi: Adam Publishers, 2005.

—*Sharḥ Adab al-Qāḍī li al-Imām Abī Bakr Aḥmad b. 'Umar al-Khaṣṣāf*, Beirut: Dār al-Kutub al-'Ilmiyyah, 1994.

Al-Khawārazmī, Abū 'Abdullah Muḥammad b. Aḥmad b. Yūsuf, *Kitāb mafātiḥ al-'ulūm: text and studies = Kitābu mafātiḥu'l-'ulūm li-Âbū 'Abdullah Muḥammad b. Aḥmad b. Yūsuf al-Hawārazmî* (Collected and reprinted by Fuat Sezgin; collaboration with Carl Ehrig-Eggert, Eckhard Neubauer), Frankfurt am Main: Institute for the History of Arabic-Islamic Science at the Johann Wolfgang Goethe University, 2005.

Al-Marghinānī, *al-Hidāyah*, Istanbul: 1986.

Al-Māwardī, Abū al-Ḥasan 'Alī b. Muḥammad b. Ḥabīb, (d. 1058), *al-Ḥāwī al-Kabīr*, 23 vols., Beirut: Dār al-Fikr, 1994.

Al-Morr, 'Awad. "The Supreme Constitutional Court of Egypt and the Protection of Human and Political Rights," in *Islam and Public Law*, 229.

Al-Mūminī, Aḥmad Sa'īd, "Qaḍā' al-Maẓālim: al-Qaḍā' al-Idārī al-Islāmī," *Jam'iyyah 'Ummāl al-Maṭābi' al-Ta'āwuniyyah*, Amman: 1991.

Al-Rifā'ī, 'Abd al-Ḥamīd, *al-Qaḍā' al-Idārī bayn al-Sharī'ah wa al-Qānūn*, Beirut: Dār al-Fikr al-Mu'āṣir, 1989.

Alsagoff, A.M., "The Arabs of Singapore," *Genuine Islam* 6 (1941): 74.

Al-Sagoff, Syed Mohsen, *The al-Sagoff Family in Malaysia*, Singapore: Mun Seong Press, 1962.

Al-Subkī, *al-Ṭabaqāt al-Shāfi'īyāh al-Kubrā*, 6 vols. (Cairo: 1324 AH), 5:134.

Al-Ṭabarī, Abū Ja'far Muḥammad b. Jarīr, (838-923), *Ta'rīkh al-Umama wa al-Mulūk,* Cairo: 1939.

Al-'Umarī, *al-Ta'rīf bi al-Muṣṭalaḥ al-Sharīf,* Cairo: 1312 AH.

Al-Zarqā, Musṭafā Aḥmad, *al-Fiqh al-Islāmī fi Thawbih al-Jadīd,* vol. 1, Damascus: Dār al-Qalam, 1998.

Ambary, Hasan Muarif, "Kedudukan dan Peran Tokoh Sejarah Syeikh Abdulrauf Singkel in Birokrasi dan Keagamaan Kesultanan Acheh," *Makalah Seminar Festival Baiturrahman II,* Banda Acheh, 16 January, 1994, 8.

Amiruddin, M. Hasbi, *The Response of the Ulama Dayah to the Modernization of Islamic Law in Aceh,* Bangi: Penerbit Universiti Kebangsaan Malaysia, 2005.

Andaya, Barbara Watson. and Andaya, Y. Leonard. *A History of Malaysia,* London: Macmillan Press, 1986.

Anderson, J.N.D., "A Law of Personal Status for Iraq," *The International and Comparative Law Quarterly* 9, no. 4 (1960): 542

—"Law Reform in the Middle East," *International Affairs* 32, no. 1 (1956): 44.

—"Recent Developments in Sharī'a Law II," *The Muslim World* 41, no. 1 (1951): 34.

—"Reforms in Family Law in Morocco," *Journal of African Law* 2, no. 3 (1958): 146

—"The Family Law of Turkish Cypriots," *Die Welt des Islams* 5. nos. 3/4 (1958): 165.

—"The Significance of Islamic Law in the World Today," *The American Journal of Comparative Law* 9, no. 2 (1960): 189.

--"The Syrian Law of Personal Status," *Bulletin of the School of Oriental and African Studies* 17, no. 1 (1955): 34.

—"The Tunisian Law of Personal Status," *The International and Comparative Law Quarterly* 7, no. 2 (1958): 262

Angell, J.B., "The Turkish Capitulations," *The American Historical Review* 6, no. 2 (1901): 254-259.

Archer, Raymond LeRoy, *Muḥammadan Mysticism in Sumatra,* Montana: Kessinger Publishing, 1935.

Armajani, Yahya, *Middle East: Past and Present,* New Jersey: Prentice Hall, 1986.

Ar-Raniri, Nuruddin, *Bustan'us Salatin, Chapters II and III*, Transcription by Jelani Harun, Kuala Lumpur: Dewan Bahasa dan Pustaka, 2004.

Atai, Nev'izade, *Ḥadā'iq al-Ḥaqā'iq fī Takmilah al-Shaqā'iq*, Istanbul: 1989.

Atar, Fahreddin, *Islam Adliye Teşkilatı*, 4th ed., Ankara: Ministry of Religious Affairs of Turkey, 1999.

Atay, Hüseyin, "Fatih-Sülaymaniye Medreseleri Ders Programları ve İcazetnameler," *Vakıflar Dergisi*, vol. 8 (Vakıflar Genel Müdürluğü Yayınları, 1981), pp. 174-187

—*Osmanlılarda Yüksek Din Eğitimi*, Istanbul: 1983.

Aybay, R., "Some Contemporary Constitutional Problems in Turkey," *Bulletin: British Society for Middle Eastern Studies* 4, no 1 (1977): 24.

Aydın, M. Akif, "Mecelle-i Akam-i Adliyye," *DIA*, vol. 28 (Ankara: TDV, 2003), pp. 231-235.

Azra, Azyumardi, "Education, Law, Mysticism: Constructing Social Realities," *Islamic Civilization in the Malay World*, Istanbul: Ircica, 1997.

—*Jaringan Ulama Timur Tengah dan Kepulauan Nusantara abad ke 17 dan 18* (Jakarta: Prenada Media, 2004), 2-3.

—*Jaringan Ulama Timur Tengah dan Kepulauan Nusantara Abad XVII dan XVIII*, 1st edition, Jakarta: Penerbit Mizan, 1994.

—*Jaringan Ulama—Timur Tengah dan Kepulauan Nusantara Abad XVII dan XVIII*, 4th ed., Bandung: Penerbit Mizan, 1998.

—*Jaringan Ulama Timur Tengah dan Kepulauan Nusantara Abad XVII dan XVIII*, 4th edition, Jakarta: Penerbit Mizan, 1998.

—*The Transmission of Islamic Reformism to Indonesia: Networks of Middle Eastern and Malay-Indonesian 'Ulama' in the Seventeenth and Eighteenth Centuries*, Hawaii: Hawaii University Press, 1992.

Az-Zayla'ī, Jamāl al-Dīn Abū Muḥammad, *Naṣb al-Rāyah li Aḥādīth al-Hidāyah*, vol. 3, Cairo: 1357/1939.

Baer, G., "The Transition from Traditional to Western Criminal Law in Turkey and Egypt," *Studia Islamica* 45 (1977): 139.

Baktır, Mustafa, *Islam'da İlk Eğitim Müessesesi: Asḥab-i Suffah*, Istanbul: Timaş Yayıncılık, 1990.

Baloch, N.A., *The Advent of Islam in Indonesia*, Islamabad: National

Institute of Historical and Cultural Research, 1980.

Baltacı, Cahid., *XV-XVI. Asırlarda Osmanlı Medreseleri,* Istanbul: İrfan Matbaası, 1994.

Barkan, Ömer Lütfi, *XV ve XVI. Asırlarda Osmanlı İmparatorluğunda Ziraī Ekonominin Hukukī ve Malī Esastarı* (Legal and Financial Principles of Agricultural Economy in the Ottoman State in the XV and XVI Centuries), Istanbul: Introduction, 1943.

Bayındır, Abdülaziz, *Kur'an Işığında Doğru Bildiğimiz Yanlışlar,* Istanbul: Süleymaniye Vakfı Yayınları, 2007.

Bentwich, N, "The Abrogation of the Turkish Capitulations," *Journal of Comparative Legislation and International Law* 5, no. 4 (1923): 182-188.

Berkes, Niyasi, *The Development of Secularism in Turkey,* New York: Routledge, 1998.

Bey, Saffet, "Bir Osmanlı Filosu'nun Sumatra Seferi, *Tarihi-i Osmani Encümeni Mecmuası,* 1 Teşrin-i Evvel 1327 (1912 M), p. 605-606.

Bilge, Mustafa, *İlk Osmanlı Medreseleri,* Istanbul: Istanbul Edebiyat Fakültesi Yayınları, 1984.

Bonderman, D., "Modernization and Changing Perceptions of Islamic Law," *Harvard Law Review* 81, no. 6 (1968): 1176.

Bowen, John R., "Fairness and Law in an Indonesian Court," Masud, Peters, and Powers, *Dispensing Justice in Islam: Qadis and Their Judgments,* Leiden and Boston: Brill, 2006.

Brown, B.J., "Justice and Adat Perpateh," in *Papers on Malayan History,* ed. K.G. Tregonning, Singapore: Journal of Southeast Asian History, 1962.

Brown, N.J., "Sharia and State in the Modern Muslim Middle East," *International Journal of Middle East Studies* 29, no. 3 (1997): 363-367.

Brown, P.M., "The Lausanne Conference," *The American Journal of International Law* 17, no. 2 (1923): 290-296.

—"The Lausanne Treaty," *The American Journal of International Law* 21, no. 3 (1927): 503-505

Buang, Ahmad Hidayat, *Studies in the Islamic Law of Contracts: The Prohibition of Gharar,* Kuala Lumpur: International Law Book Services, 2000.

Buckley, C.B., *An Anecdotal History of Old Times in Singapore 1819-1967,* Singapore: University of Malaya Press, 1969.

Çelebi, Ahmed, *Islam'da Eğitim-Öğretim Tarihi,* trans. Ali Yardım, Istanbul: Damla Yayınevi, 1976.

Çelik, Serpil, *Mevcut Belgeler Işığında Sülaymaniye Kulliyesinin Yapım Süreci* (Unpublished Doctorate Thesis, Istanbul Technology University, Institute Applied Sciences), Istanbul: 2001.

Cici, Recep, *Osmanlı Dönemi İslam Hukuku Çalışmaları: Kuruluştan Fatih Devrinin Sonuna Kadar,* Bursa: Arasta Yayınları, 2001.

Cin, Halil, and Akgündüz, Ahmed, *Türk Hukuk Tarihi,* vol. I, Konya: Selçuk University, 1989.

Cin, Halil, *İslām ve Osmanlı Hukukunda Evlenme* (Marriage in Islamic and Ottoman Codes), Ankara: Ankara University, l974.

Consultation with Prof Dr Abu Bakar Ceylin and Prof Dr Hamit Kırmızı, on Jan 16, 2010, 4:00 pm.

Cortesao, Armando. (ed.), *The Suma Oriental of Tome Pires,* vol. I, New Delhi: Asian Educational Services, 1990.

Coulson, N.J., "Doctrine and Practice in Islamic Law: One Aspect of the Problem," *Bulletin of the School of Oriental and African Studies* 18, no. 2 (1956): 211-219.

Dabbaghzadah, Nu'man Effendi, *Jāmi' al-Sak,* Istanbul: Dersaadah, 1214.

Dāraquṭnī, 'Alī b. 'Umar, "*Sunan*", Delhi: Maṭba'ah al-Anṣārī, 1310 AH.

Das Gupta, Arun Komar, "Iskandar Muda and the Europeans, ed. Ali Hasjmy," *Sejarah Masuk Dan Berkembangnya Islam Di Indonesia,* 3rd ed., Percetakan Offset: 1993.

—*Acheh in Indonesian Trade and Politics: 1600-1641,* New York: Cornell University, 1962.

Daudy, Ahmed, *Syeikh Nuruddin Ar-Raniry: Sejarah Hidup, Karya dan Pemikiran,* Banda Aceh: Diterbitkan Oleh Pusat Penelitian Dan Pengkajian Kebudayaan Islam, 2006.

Davis, Fanny, *The Ottoman Lady: A Social History from 1718 to 1918,* America: Greenwood Press, 1986.

De Koninck, Rodolphe, *Aceh in the Time of Iskandar Muda,* Banda Aceh: Pusat Dokumentasi Dan Informasi Aceh, 1977.

Deringil, Selim, Legitimacy Structures in the Ottoman State: The Reign of Abdulhamid II (1876-1909), *International Journal of Middle East Studies*, vol. 23, No. 3 (Aug. 1991), 350 (345-359).

Di Tiro, Hasan, "The Legal Status of Acheh-Sumatra under International Law," www.asfnl.org.

Dion, Mark, "Sumatra through Portuguese Eyes: Excerpts from Joao de barros' Decadas Da Asia," Decada I, Livro IV, Capitulos, p. iii-iv.

Divekar, V.D., ed., "Maritime Trading Settlements in the Arabian Sea Region up to 1500 AD," *The Indian Ocean in Focus' International Conference on Indian Ocean Studies*, Section III: The History of Commercial Exchange & Maritime Transport, Perth: People Helping People, 1979.

Djajadiningrat, Raden Hoesein, *Kesultanan Aceh*, Seri Penerbitan Museum Aceh 2, Proyek Rehabilitasi dan Perluasan Museum Daerah Istemewa Aceh, 1979.

Djamil, M. Yunus, "Wadjah Rakjat Atjeh Dalam Lintasan Sedjarah," *Seminar Kebudajaan Dalam Rangka Pekan Kebudajaan Atjeh Ke-II* (The Second Atjeh Cultural Festival, 20 August-2 September 1972) Dan Dies Natalis Ke XI Universitas Sjiah Kuala, Panitia Pusat Pekan Kebudajaan Atjeh Ke-II, Banda Aceh, 1972, p. 5.

Drewes, G.W.J., "New Light on the Coming of Islam to Indonesia?" (ed.), Ahmad Ibrahim, Sharon Siddique, and Yasmin Hussain, *Readings on Islam in Southeast Asia: Social Issues in Southeast Asia,* Singapore: Institute of Southeast Asian Studies, 1990.

E. Lee, Dwight, "The Origin of Pan-Islamism," *The American Historical Review,* 47 (1942): 282.

Efendi, Mecdi Muhammed, *Ḥadāiqu'sh-Shaqāiq*, Istanbul: 1989.

Ergin, Osman, *Turkiye Maarif Tarihi 1, 2,* Istanbul: 1961.

Ergun, Mustafa, *II. Meşrutiyet Devrinde Eğitim Hareketleri (1908-1914),* Ankara: Ocak Yayınları, 1996.

Esposito, John L., *Islam in Asia, Religion, Politics, and Society,* New York: Oxford University Press, 1987.

—*The Oxford Dictionary of Islam*, New York: Oxford University Press, 2003.

Eugene, Morris E., *Islam and Politics in Aceh:-A Study of Center-Periphery Relations in Indonesia*, New York: Cornell University, 1983.

Fang, Liaw Yock, ed., *Undang-undang Melaka: Laws of Melaka,* The Hague: M. Hijhoff, 1976.

Fārābī, Abū Naṣr Muḥammad b. Muḥammad b. Ṭarkhān, *Iḥṣā' al-'Ulūm,* ed. 'Uthmān Muḥammad Amīn, Cairo: Maktabah al-Khānjī, 1350/1931.

—*Taḥṣīl al-Sa'ādah,* ed. Ja'far Āl Yāsīn, 2nd ed., Beirut: Dār al-Andalus, 1983.

Fathurahman, Oman, and Holil, Munawar, *Katalog Naskah Ali Hasjmy Aceh, Catalogue of Aceh Manuscripts: Ali Hasjmy Collection,* The 21st Century Center of Excellence Programme "The Center for Documentation and Area-Transcultural Studies, Tokyo: Tokyo University of Foreign Studies, 2007.

Fathurahman, Oman, "The Cultural Emergency Relief Action: The Rebuilding Manuscript Library in Dayah Tanoh Abee," Aceh, http://naskahkuno.blogspot.com/2006/09/cultural-emergency-relief-action.html.

Fatimi, Sayyid Qudratullah, *Islam Comes to Malaysia,* Singapore: Malaysian Sociological Research Institute, 1963.

Fred R. von der Mehden, *Two Worlds of Islam Interaction between Southeast Asia and the Middle East,* Gainesville: University Press of Florida, 1993.

Furat, Ayşe Zisan, *XV. Ve XVI. YY.'larda Fatih ve Sülaymaniye Medreselerinde Verilen Din Eğitiminin Karşılaştırmalı Bir İncelemesi* (Unpublished Master's Thesis, Istanbul University, Institute Social Sciences), Istanbul: 2004.

Gedikli, Fethi. *XVI. ve XVII. Asır Osmanlı Şer'iyye Sicillerinde Mudārebe Ortaklığı: Galata Örneği,* PhD dissertation, Istanbul: Istanbul University, 1996.

Gelibolulu, Ali, *Kuhnu'l-Ahbar* (prepared by Ahmet Uğur, Mustafa Çuhadır, Ahmet Gül, İbrahim Hakkı Çuhadır), Kayseri: Erciyes Üniversitesi Yayınları, 1997.

Ghazālī, Abū Ḥāmid Muḥammad b. Muḥammad, *Iḥyā' 'Ulūm al-Dīn,* vol. 1, Cairo: Muassasah al-Ḥalabī, 1387/1967.

Gibb, H.A.R., and Bowen, Harold, *Islamic Society and the West,* vol. 2 of *Islamic Society in the Eighteenth Century,* London: Oxford University Press, 1957.

Gleave, Robert, "The Qadi and the Mufti in Akhbari Shi'i Jurisprudence," in *The Law Applied: Contextualizing the Islamic Shari'a: A Volume in Honor of Frank E. Vogel*, ed. Peri Bearman, Wolfhart Heinrichs, and Bernard G. Weiss, London: I.B. Tauris, 2008.

Göksoy, İsmail Hakkı, "Endonezya'da Tasavvufi Hareketler ve Bazı Özellikleri," *Tasavvuf*, vol. 4, No. 11 (Istanbul: Temmuz-Aralık, 2003), p. 82-84.

—*Güneydoğu Asya'da Osmanlı-Türk Tesirleri*, Isparta: Fakülte Kitabevi, 2004.

Groeneveldt, W.P., *Historical Notes on Indonesia & Malaya—Compiled from Chinese Sources*, Jakarta: C.V. Bhratara, 1960.

Gülkhane Khatt-i Humayūnu (Imperial Edict of Gülhane), *Dustūr* I. Tartīb, vol. 1, pp. 4-7.

Hall, D.G.E., *A History of South-East Asia*, 3rd ed., London: The Macmillan Press Ltd., 1976.

Hallaq, W.B., *Authority, Continuity and Change in Islamic Law* (United Kingdom: Cambridge University Press, 2001), 167.

—"Model Shura Works and the Dialectic of Doctrine and Practice," *Islamic Law and Society* 2, no. 2 (1995): 123.

—*The Origins and Evolution of Islamic Law*, Cambridge, UK: Cambridge University Press, 2004.

—"The 'qāḍīs dīwān (sijill)' before the Ottomans," *Bulletin of the School of Oriental and African Studies* 61, no. 3 (1998): 415-436.

Hamid, Ismail, *Perkembangan Islam di Asia dan Alam Melayu*, Petaling Jaya: Heinemann Educational Books, 1986.

Hamzeh, A. Nizar, "Qatar: The Duality of the Legal System," *Middle Eastern Studies* 30, no. 1 (1994): 80-86.

Ḥanbel, Imām Ahmed b. *El-Müsned*, trans. Rıfat Oral 1:262, ḥadīth no. 13:210, Konya: 2003.

Haron, Nadzan, "Colonial Defence and British Approach to the Problems in Malaya 1874-1918," *Modern Asian Studies*, vol. 24, No. 2 (May 1990), 293 (275-295).

Harper, R.W.E., and Miller, Harry, *Singapore Mutiny*, Singapore: Oxford University Press, 1984.

Hashim, Muhammad Yusof, *Islam Dalam Sejarah Perundangan Melaka*

(*Islam in Malacca Legal History*), Kuala Lumpur: Persatuan Sejarah Malaysia, n.d.

Hasjmy, Ali. *Aceh dan Pahang*, Aceh: Documentation and Information Center, 1989.

—"Banda Aceh Darussalam Pusat Kegiatan Ilmu dan Kebudayaan," dalam Ismail Suny (ed.), *Bunga Rampai Tentang Aceh,* Jakarta: Bhratara Karya Aksara, 1980.

—"Banda Aceh Darussalam Pusat Kegiatan Ilmu dan Kebudayaan," *Seminar Sejarah Masut dan Berkembangnya Islam di Aceh dan Nusantara, Di Aceh Timur,* 25-30 September, 1980, p. 3.

—*Bunga Rampai Revolusi dari Tanah Aceh,* Jakarta: Bulan Bintang, 1978.

—*59 Tahun Aceh Merdeka,* Jakarta: Bulan Bintang, 1977.

—*Kebudayaan Aceh Dalam Sejarah,* Jakarta: Penerbit Beuna, 1983.

—*Sejarah Kebudayaan Islam di Indonesia,* Jakarta: Bulan Bintang, 1980.

—*Ulama Aceh,* Aceh: Mujahid Pejuang Kemerdekaan dan Pembangun Tamadun Bangsa, 1997.

Hasjmy, Ali, and Talsya, T.A. *Aceh dan Pahang,* Medan: Pencetak Prakarsa Abadi Press, 1989.

Hassan, Abdullah Alwi Haji, *The Administration of Islamic Law in Kelantan,* Selangor: Percetakan Dewan Bahasa dan Pustaka, 1996.

Hill, A.H., "Hikayat Raja-Raja Pasai," *JMBRAS*, vol. 33, Part 2, No. 190, June 1960, p. 32.

Hill, E., "Al-Sanhuri and Islamic Law: The Place and Significance of Islamic Law in the Life and Work of 'Abd al-Razzaq Ahmad al-Sanhuri, Egyptian Jurist and Scholar, 1895-1971," *Arab Law Quarterly* 3, no. 1 (1988): 40.

Hirsch, Leo, "A Journey in Hadramaut," *The Geographical Journal,* 3 (1894): 196-205.

Hock, Saw Swee, *The Population of Peninsular Malaysia,* Singapore: Singapore University Press, 1988.

Hooker, M.B., (ed.) *Islam in South-East Asia*, 2nd ed., Leiden: E.J. Brill, 1988.

Hoyle, M.S.W., "The Mixed Courts of Egypt: An Anniversary Assessment," *Arab Law Quarterly* 1, no. 1 (1985): 60.

http://en.wikipedia.org/wiki/Demographics_of_Malaysia#cite_ref-islam 01_22-0.

Hurgronje, Snouck, *The Acehnese*, trans. A.W.S. O'Sullivan, vol. I, Leiden: E.J. Brill, 1906.

Hurvitz, N., "Miḥna as Self-Defense," *Studia Islamica* 92 (2001): 93-111.

Husrev, Molla, (Husrev Mehmed Efendi) *Mir'āh al-Uṣūl Sharḥ Mirqāh al-Wuṣūl*, Istanbul: Shirket-i Sahafiye-i Osmaniye, 1321.

Hussain, Hj Shaharom, "Hubungan Johor Dengan Turki," *Jurnal Jauhar* 4 (2002): 55.

—*Tawarikh Johor*, Singapore: Al-Hamadiah Press, 1950.

Ibn 'Ābidīn, Muḥammad Amīn, (d.1252/1836), *Nashr al-'Urf fī Binā' ba'ḍ al-Aḥkām 'alā al-'Urf*, Beirut: n.d.

—*Ḥāshiyah Nasamāt al-Asḥār*, Cairo: Muṣṭafā Bābī al-Ḥalabī, n.d.

Ibn Baṭūṭah, *Riḥlah*, ed. Dr 'Alī al-Muntaṣir al-Kattānī, 2 vols., Beirut: Muassasah al-Risālah, 1981.

Ibn Hishām, Abū Muḥammad 'Abd al-Mālik, (d. 833 CE), *al-Sīrah al-Nabawiyyah*, ed. Muṣṭafā Ibrāhīm, Egypt: 1936.

Ibn Kathīr, Abū al-Fidā' Ismā'īl b. Abī Hafs, (701-774), *al-Bidāyah wa al-Nihāyah*, Cairo: 1932.

Ibn Sa'd, Muḥammad b. Manī' al-Baghdādī, (784-845 CE), *Ṭabaqāt al-Kubrā*, Leiden: 1917.

Ibn Sīna, Abū 'Alī Ḥusayn b. 'Abdullah b. 'Alī Balkhī, *Rasāilu Ibn Sīna = İbn Sina Risaleleri = Les opuscules d'Ibn Sîna: 'Uyūnu'l-Ḥikmah: Risālatu Abu'l-Faraj b. at-Ṭayyib wa Risālatu'r-Rad li-Abū Ali b. Sīna*, ed. Hilmi Ziya Ülken, vol. 1, Istanbul: Istanbul University, 1953.

Ibn Taghrī Birdī, *al-Nujūm al-Zāhirah*, 13 vols., Cairo: 1929-1956.

Ibrahim, A.A., "Tale of Two Sudanese Courts: Colonial Governmentality Revisited," *African Studies Review* 40, no. 1 (1997): 13-33.

Ibrahim, Ahmad, and Joned, Ahilemah, *The Malaysian Legal System*, 2nd ed., Kuala Lumpur: Dewan Bahasa dan Pustaka, 1995.

Ibrahim, Ahmad, et. al., eds., *Readings on Islam and Southeast Asia*, Singapore: ISEAS, 1985.

İnalcık, Halil. *Studies in Eighteenth Century Islamic History*, ed. Thomas Naff and Roger Owen, vol. 4: *Papers on Islamic History*, Philadelphia:

University of Pennsylvania: The Middle East Center, 1977.

Ingrams, W.H., "Hadramaut: Past and Present," *The Geographical Journal* 92 (1938): 291-297.

İpşirli, Mehmet, "The Ottoman Ulama," in Prof Kemal Çicek, *The Great Ottoman Turkish Civilization* 3, Ankara: Yeni Türkiye, 2000.

Ismail, Siti Zainon, *Warisan Seni Budaya Melayu-Aceh,* Kaitan Pemerian Teks Sastera dan Realiti Budaya, Selangor: National University of Malaysia, n.d.

İzgi, Cevat. *Osmanlı Medreselerinde İlim,* Istanbul: İz Yayıncılık, 1997.

Jakub, Ismail. *Teungku Chik Di Tiro (Muhammad Saman) Palawan Besar Dalam Perang Aceh (1881-1891),* Jakarta: Bulan Bintang, 1960.

Jalil, Tuanku Abdul, "Pengertian Adat Aceh," *Loka Karya Adat Dan Budaya*, Lho'Seumawe, 8-10 January, 1988, p. 3

Jamil, Fadhlullah. *Islam di Asia Barat modern: Penjajahan dan Pergolakan,* Kuala Lumpur: Karisma Publication, 2007.

Johansen, Baber, "The Constitution and the Principles of Islamic Normativity against the Rules of Fiqh: A Judgment of the Supreme Constitutional Court of Egypt," in Muhammad Khalid Masud, Rudolph Peters, David S. Powers, eds., "Qadis and Their Courts: An Historical Survey" in *Dispensing Justice in Islam: Qadis and Their Judgments,* Leiden and Boston: Brill, 2006.

John, Horace St., *The Indian Archipelago: Its History and Present State,* vol. I, London: Longman, 1853.

Johns, A.H., "Islam in Southeast Asia: Problems of Perspective," C.D. Cowan and O.W. Wolters (ed.), *Southeast Asian History and Historiography:-Essays Presented to D.G.E. Hall,* New York: Cornell University Press, 1976.

—"Islam in the Malay World: An Exploratory Survey with Some Reference to Quranic Exegesis," ed. Raphael Israeli and Anthony H. Johns, *Islam in Asia*, vol II: *Southeast and East Asia,* Jerusalem: The Magnes Press, The Hebrew University, 1984.

—"Malay Sufism," *JMBRAS*, vol. XXX, Part 2, No. 178, August 1957, p. 10.

—"Sufism as a Category in Indonesian Literature and History," *JSEAH*, 2 (1961): 10-23.

Joned, Ahmad Ibrahim and Ahilemah. *The Malaysian Legal System*, 2nd ed., Kuala Lumpur: Dewan Bahasa dan Pustaka, 1995.

Jurji, E.J., "Islamic Law in Operation," *The American Journal of Semitic Languages and Literatures* 57, no. 1 (1940): 38-39.

Juynboll, W., and Voorhoeve, P. "Atjeh," *The Encyclopaedia of Islam*, ed. H.A.R. Gibb and J.H. Kramers, vol. I, A-B, Leiden: E.J. Brill, 1979.

Kallek, Cengiz, "El-Hidaye," *DIA*, vol. 17 (Ankara: TDVIA, 1998), p. 471.

Kamali, Muhammad Hashim, "Appellate Review and Judicial Independence in Islamic Law," in *Islam and Public Law*, 50-52.

—*Islamic Law in Malaysia: Issues and Developments,* Selangor: Ilmiah Publishers, 2000.

—"Source, Nature and Objectives of Shariah," *The Islamic Quarterly*, vol. XXXIII, No. 4 (1988), 215.

Karakoç, Serkiz, *Külliyāt-i Qavānīn* (A Collection of Legal Codes), File 1, Ankara: TTK Library,

—*Tahşiyeli Qavānīn*, vols. 1-2, Istanbul: Cihān Matba' asi, 1911.

Karaman, Hayrettin, "Fıkıh," Diyanet İslam Ansiklopedisi *(DIA)* (Istanbul: TDIV, 1988), vol. 13, p. 1.

Kattānī, 'Abd a-Ḥayy b. 'Abd al-Kabīr, (d. 1962), *al-Tarātib al-Idāriyyah*, Rabat: 1346 AH.

Kayadibi Saim, and Buang, Ahmad Hiyadat, "Impact of Globalization on Higher Education from the Viewpoint of Islamic Law" (paper presented at the International Conference on Higher Education Research and Development, Dhurakij Pundit University, Bangkok, Thailand, 9-12 July 2009), 13.

Kayadibi, Saim, *Doctrine of Istihsan Juristic Preference in Islamic Law*, Konya: Tablet, 2007.

—"*Ijtihād* and Modernist Perspectives towards Islamic Law and Thought," *Journal of Islamic Law Studies* 11 (2008): 114.

Kechichian, Joseph A., "The Role of the Ulama in the Politics of an Islamic State: The Case of Saudi Arabia," *International Journal of Middle East Studies,* 18 (1986): 54.

Keddie, Nikki R., "Pan Islam as Proto-Nationalism," *The Journal of Modern History* 41 (1969): 17.

Kelly, Marjorie, (ed.) *Islam: The Religious and Political Life of a World*

Community, New York: Praeger, 1984.

Khādimī, Abū Saʿīd Muḥammad. (d.116/1755), *Manāfiʿ al-Daqāʾiq fī Sharḥ Majāmiʿ al-Ḥaqāʾiq,* Istanbul: 1305. AH.

Khoo, Gilber, and Lo, Dorothy, *Asian Transformation: A History of Southeast, South and East Asia,* Singapore: 1977.

Koca, Ferhat, "El-Feraiz es-Siraciyye," *DIA*, vol. 12 (Istanbul: TDV, 1995), pp. 367-368.

Kuban, Doğan, "Sülaymaniye Külliyesi," *Dünden Bugüne İstanbul Ansiklopedisi,* vol. 7, Istanbul: Tarih Vakfı, 1994.

Kürkçüoğlu, Kemal Edip, (prepared by), *Sülaymaniye Vakfiyesi,* Ankara: Posta Matbaası, 1962.

Lapidus, Ira M., *A History of Islamic Societies,* 2d edition, Cambridge: Cambridge University Press, 2002.

—*A History of Islamic Societies,* 7th ed., Cambridge: Cambridge University Press, 1995.

Lau, Martin, "The Islamization of Laws in Pakistan: Impact on the Independence of the Judiciary," in *The Rule of Law in the Middle East and the Islamic World: Human Rights and the Judicial Process,* ed. Eugene Cotran and Mai Yamani, London: I.B. Tauris in association with the Centre of Islamic Studies and Middle Eastern Law, School of Oriental and African Studies, University of London, 2000.

Laws of Malaysia, Federal Constitution as of 10 April 2002, Selangor: International Law Book Services, 2002.

Laws of the Constitution of Johor, Malayan Constitutional Documents, vol. 2.

Laws of the Constitution of Terengganu, Malayan Constitutional Documents, vol. 2.

Lewis, Bernard, "Politics and War" in *The Legacy of Islam,* ed. Joseph Schacht, 2d ed., Oxford: Clarendon Press, 1974.

—*The Emergence of Modern Turkey,* London: Oxford University Press, 1961.

Liebesny, Herbert J., *The Law of the Near and Middle East: Readings, Cases, & Materials,* Albany: New York State University Press, 1975.

Lobban, C. Fluehr, and Hillawi, H.B., "Circulars of the Sharīʿa Courts in the Sudan (*Manshūrāt El-Mahākim El-Sharī'ah fi Sūdān*) 1902-1979," *Journal of African Law* 27, no. 2 (1983): 80.

Lombard, Denys, *Kerajaan Aceh Zaman Sultan Iskandar Muda (1607-1636)*, trans. Winarsih Arifin, KPG (Kepustakaan Populer Gramedia) Forum, 2nd edition, Jakarta: Kepustakan Populer Gramedia, 2007.

Mackeen, Abdul Majeed Mohamed, *Contemporary Islamic Legal Organization in Malaya*, Monograph Series No. 13, New Hawen: Yale University Southeast Asia Studies, 1969.

Madelung, W. "The Origins of the Controversy Concerning the Creation of the Koran," in *Orientalia hispanica sive studia F.M. Pareja octogenario dicata*, ed. J.M. Barral, Leiden: E.J. Brill, 1974.

Majid, Mohamad Kamil Ab., "Gerakan Tajdid: Sejarah Dan Perspektif Masa Kini," *Jurnal Usuluddin*, 4 (1996), 98.

Makdisi, George, *Ortaçağda Yüksek Öğretim: Islam Dünyası ve Hıristiyan Batı*, trans. Ali Hakan Çavuşoğlu-Hasan Tuncay Başoğlu, Istanbul: Gelenek Yayıncılık, 2004.

Mallat, Chibli. "From Islamic to Middle Eastern Law: A Restatement of the Field (Part II)," *The American Journal of Comparative Law* 52, no. 1 (2004): 210.

Mardin, Abu al-Ula, "Development of the Sharia under the Ottoman Empire," Majid Khadduri and Herbert J. Liebesny, *Origin and Development of Islamic Law, Law in the Middle East*, Clark: The Lawbook Exchange, Ltd., 2008.

—*Medenī Hukuk Cephesinden Ahmed Jawdat Pasha*, Istanbul: Istanbul University, 1946.

Marrison, G.E., "Persian Influences in Malay Life: 1280-1650," *JMBRAS*, vol. 28, Part I, No. 169, 1955, p. 52-53, 55.

Marsden, William, *The History of Sumatra*, Kuala Lumpur: Oxford University Press, 1966.

Masailal Muhtadi li Ikhwanil Muhtadi in *Pusat Manuskrip Melayu*, Kuala Lumpur: Perpustakaan Negeri Malaysia, MSS 3662.

Masud, Muhammad Khalid, et. al., eds., "*Qāḍīs* and Their Courts: An Historical Survey" in *Dispensing Justice in Islam: Qadis and Their Judgments*, Leiden and Boston: Brill, 2006.

McAmis, Robert Day, *Malay Muslims: the History and Challenge of*

Resurgent Islam in Southeast Asia, UK: William B. Eerdmans Publishing Company, 2002.

Mehmed Ziya, *Açe Tarihi,* Istanbul: 1312.

Mersinli, Cema, "Roma-Rum Kelimeleri," *TTK Bulleten,* vol. 5, No. 17-18, April (Ankara: 1941), p. 160

Meuraxa, Dada, *Sejarah: Masuknya Islam ke Bandar Barus Sumatera Utara,* Bandung: Penerbit Sasterawan, 1963.

Milner, A.C., "Islam and the Muslim State, ed. M.B. Hooker, *Islam in South-East Asia,* 2nd edition (Leiden: E.J. Brill, 1988), p. 44.

Minahan, James, *Nations without States A Historical Dictionary of Contemporary National Movements,* Connecticut: Greenwood Press, 1996.

Misiroglu, Kadir, *Lozan Barış mı Hezimet mi?,* Istanbul: Sebil Yayınevi, 1965.

Mitsuo, Nakamura, "Introduction," *Islam & Civil Society in Southeast Asia,* Singapore: Institute of Southeast Asian Studies, 2001.

Mobini-Kesheh, Natalie, *The Hadrami Awakening: Community and Identity in the Netherland East Indies, 1900-1942,* New York: Cornell University, 1999.

Mohamad, Abdul Hamid Hajj, *Civil and Shariah Courts in Malaysia: Conflict of Jurisdiction, in Islamic Law in the Contemporary World,* ed. Zainal Azam Abd. Rahman, Kuala Lumpur: IKIM, 2003.

Mokhtar, Ahmad Baha, "Syarh Latif Ala Arba'in Ḥadithan li al-Imām al-Nawawi Karangan Syeikh Abd Rauf al-Fansuri: Satu Kajian Teks," Ph.D. dissertation, Jabatan Al-Qu'ran dan Al-Ḥadith, Kuala Lumpur: Akademi Pengajian Islam, Universiti Malaya, 2008.

Morley, J.A.E., "The Arabs and the Eastern Trade," *JMBRAS* 22 (1949): 175.

—"The Arabs and the Eastern Trade," *JMBRAS,* vol. XXII, 1949, p. 150.

Moustafa, T., "Law versus the State: The Judicialization of Politics in Egypt," *Law & Social Inquiry* 28, no. 4 (2003): 883-930.

Muda, Asa'ad Shukri b. Haji, *Detik-Detik Sejarah Kelantan,* Kota Bharu: Pustaka Aman Press, 1977.

—"*Sejarah Kelantan*", Kota Bharu: Pustaka Aman Press, 1962.

Muzaffar, Chandra, *Tolerance in the Malay Political Scene,* in Syed

Othman Alhabshi and Nik Mustafa Nik Hassan, *Islam and Tolerance,* Kuala Lumpur: Institute of Islamic Understanding, 1994.

Nadolski, Dora Glidewell, "Ottoman and Secular Civil Law," *International Journal of Middle East Studies* 8, no. 4 (1977): 517-518.

Nagata, Judith, "Islamic Revival and the Legitimacy among Rural Religious Elites in Malaysia," *Man: The Journal of the Royal Anthropological Institute* (N.S.), 17, 1 (1982): 44.

Nawas, J.A., "A Reexamination of Three Current Explanations for al-Ma'mun's Introduction of the Mihna," *International Journal of Middle East Studies* 26, no. 4 (1994): 615-629.

— "The Miḥna of 218 AH/833 AD Revisited: An Empirical Study," *Journal of the American Oriental Society* 116, no. 4 (1996): 698-708.

Nielsen, Jorgen S., "Maẓālim," *The Encyclopedia of Islam,* new edition, Leiden: E.J. Brill, 1991.

—"Sultan al-Ẓāhir Baybars and the Appointment of Four Chief Qāḍīs, 663/1265" *Studia Islamica* 60 (1984): 167.

Nor, Mohd Yusof Md., "Syair Sultan Abu Bakar Dokumentasi Sejarah Negeri Johor," in Obe Seminar Sejarah Dan Budaya Johor, *Yayasan Warisan Johor & Gabungan Persatuan Penulis Nasional Malaysia (GAPENA),* 3-6 May 2000, 10-11.

Osman, Mohamad Taib, ed., *Islamic Civilization in the Malay World,* Kuala Lumpur: Dewan Bahasa dan Pustaka, 1997.

Osman Nuri Ergin, *Majalla-i Umur-i Baladiyyah* (Istanbul: 1922), vol. I, pp. 265ff.

Othman, Mohammad Redzuan, *Islam dan Masyarakat Melayu Peranan dan Pengaruh Timur Tengah,* Kuala Lumpur: Penerbit Universiti Malaya, 2005.

Öz, Tahsin, *Istanbul Camileri,* Ankara: Türk Tarih Kurumu, 1962.

Özay, Mehmet, *Açe Kitabı,* Istanbul: Fide Yayınları, 2006.

—*Islamic Identity and Development Studies of the Islamic Periphery,* Kuala Lumpur: Forum, 1990.

Özel, Ahmet, *Hanefi Fikih Alimleri,* Ankara: Diyanet Vakfı Yayınları, 1990.

Öztürk, Osman, *Majalla,* Istanbul: 1973.

Özyılmaz, Ömer, *Osmanlı Medreselerinin Eğitim Programları,* Ankara: Kültür Bakanlığı Yayınları, 2002.

PA, YEE, no. 14-1540, *Devlet-i Aliyye'deki Islahât-ı Kanuniye* (Legal Reforms in the Ottoman State), pp. 5ff, 26-27.

—*Ottoman Archives*, YEE-14-1540, p. 14.

—*Tapu Tahrīr Defterleri* (Title-Deed Office Registry Books).

Pamuk, Şevket, "The Ottoman Empire in the 'Greatest Depression' of 1873-1896," *The Journal of Economic History* 44 (1984): 108.

Pasha, Ahmed Jawdat, *Ma'rūdhāt* (Petitions), Istanbul: Enderun, 1980.

—*Tadhakir*, vol. 4, Ankara: TTK, 1967.

Patton, W.M., *Ahmad ibn Hanbal and the Mihna*, Leiden: 1897.

Paulus, J., (ed.), 'Asal Usul Raja Raja Aceh," *Encyclopedie van N.I.*, Leiden: 1917.

Pet, Na Tien, and Mohamed, Noriah, (ed) *Syair Almarhum Baginda Sultan Abu Bakar di Negeri Johor*, Johor: Yayasn Warisan Johor, 2001.

Peter, G., "Riddel, Religious Links between Hadramaut and the Malay-Indonesian World, C.1850 to C. 1950," *Hadrami Traders, Scholars and Statesmen in the Indian Ocean, 1750s-1960s*, ed. Ulrike Frietag and William G. Clarence-Smith, Leiden: E.J. Brill, 1997.

Peters, Francis E., "The Early Empires: Umayyads, Abbasids, Fatimids," ed. Marjorie Kelley, *Islam: The Religious and Political Life of a World Community*, New York: Praeger, 1984.

Pheng, Lee Mei, *General Principles of Malaysian Law*, Selangor, Malaysia: Penerbit Fajar Bakti Sdn. Bhd., 1990.

—*General Principles of Malaysian Law*, Selangor: Penerbit Fajar Bakti, 2001.

Phillips, Lord, "Equality before the Law" (speech of Lord Chief Justice, East London Muslim Centre, 3 July 2008), 9.

Pintado, M.J., ed., *Portuguese Documents on Malacca*, vol. 1: 1509-1511 (Kuala Lumpur: National Archives of Malaysia, year), p. 341, 407.

Ramlī, Shams al-Dīn Muḥammad b. Aḥmad b. Ḥamzah al-Anṣārī. *Nihāyah al-Muḥtāj ilā Sharḥ al-Minhāj*, vol. 1, Beirut: Dār al-Fikr, 1404/1984.

Razi, Syahbuddin, "Dayah Cot Kala," *Seminar Sejarah Masuk Dan Berkembangnya Islam Di Aceh Dan Nusantara*, Majelis Ulama Propinsi Daerah Istimewa Aceh Dan Pemerintah Daerah TK. II, Aceh Timur: 1980.

Rebstock, U., "A Qāḍī's Errors," *Islamic Law and Society* 6, no. 1 (1999): 1-37.

Reid, Anthony, *An Indonesian Frontier: Acehnese and Other Histories of Sumatra,* Singapore: Singapore University Press, 2005.

—"Colonal Transformation: A Bitter Legacy," ed. Anthony Reid, *Verandah of Violence: The Background to the Aceh Problem,* Singapore: Singapore University Press, 2006.

—"Indonesian Diplomacy: A Documentary Study of Atjehnese Foreign Policy in the Reign of Sultan Mahmud, 1870-1874," *Journal of the Malay Branch of the Royal Asiatic Society* (JAMBRAS) vol. 42, part 2, (1969), 121.

—"Islamization and Christianization in Southeast Asia: The Critical Phase, 1550-1650, ed. Anthony Reid, *Southeast Asia in the Early Modern Era: Trade, Power and Belief,* Ithaca: Cornell University Press, 1993.

—"Nineteenth Century Pan-Islam in Indonesia and Malaysia," *The Journal of Asian Studies,* vol. 26, No. 2 (Feb. 1967), 267 (267-283).

—*Southeast Asia in the Age of Commerce 1450-1680,* vol. I: *The Lands below the Winds,* New Hawen, London: Yale University Press, 1988.

—*Southeast Asia in the Early Modern Era,* Ithaca: Cornell University Press, 1993.

—*The Blood of the People: Revolution and the End of Traditional Rule in Northern Sumatra,* Kuala Lumpur: Oxford University Press, 1979.

—*The Contest for North Sumatra, Atjeh, The Netherlands and Britain, 1858-1898,* Kuala Lumpur: University of Malaya Press, 1969.

—*The Making of an Islamic Political Discourse in Southeast Asia,* Clayton-Victoria, Australia: Aristoc Press Pty, Centre of Southeast Asian Studies, Monash University, 1993.

—*Witnesses to Sumatra: A Travellers's Anthology,* Kuala Lumpur: Oxford University Press, 1995.

Riddell, Peter G., "Aceh in the Sixteenth and Seventeenth Centuries: Serambi Mekkah and Identity," ed. Anthony Reid, *Verandah of Violence: The Background to the Aceh Problem,* Singapore: Singapore University Press, 2006.

—*Islam and the Malay-Indonesian World: Transmission and Responses,* Honolulu: University of Hawaii Press, 2001.

—*Islam and the Malay-Indonesian World: Transmission and Responses,* London: Hurst & Company, 2001.

Rimba, H. Abdullah Ujong, "Daerah Manakah Yang Mula Mula Menerima Agama Islam di Indonesia," *Seminar Sejarah Masuk Dan Berkembangnya Islam Di Aceh Dan Nusantara,* Majelis Ulama Propinsi Daerah Istimewa Aceh Dan Pemerintah Daerah TK. II, Aceh Timur, 1980.

Rinkes, D.A., *Nine Saints of Java* trans. H.M. Froger, Kuala Lumpur: Malaysian Sociological Research Institute, 1996.

Roberson, B.A., "The Emergence of the Modern Judiciary in the Middle East: Negotiating the Mixed Courts of Egypt," in *Islam and Public Law,* ed. Chibli Mallat, London: Graham &Trotman, 1993.

Roff, "Kaum Muda-Kaum Tua: Innovation and Reaction amongst the Malays, 1900-1941," K.G. Tregonning, ed., *Papers on Malayan History,* Singapore: University of Singapore, 1962.

Roff, Wiiliam R., "The Malay-Muslim World of Singapore at the Close of the Nineteenth Century," *The Journal of Asian Studies* 24 (1964): 80.

Rosen, L., "Equity and Discretion in a Modern Islamic Legal System," *Law & Society Review* 15, no. 2 (1980): 217-218.

Safran, N., "The Abolition of the Shar'i Courts in Egypt," *The Muslim World* 48 (1958): 20-28 and 125-135.

Şah, Rızaulhak, "Açe Padişahı Sultan Alaaddin'in Kanuni Sultan Süleyman'a Mektubu," Tarih Araştırmaları Dergisi, AÜDTCF, *Tarih Araştırmaları Enstitüsü,* S. 8-9, vol. V, 1967, Ankara Üniversitesi Basımevi, p. 385

Said, Saadiah Bt, "Penglibatan Keluarga al-Sagoff Dalam Ekonomi Johor 1878-1926," *Jurnal Jauhar* 2 (1983): 6-7.

Sakaoğlu, Necdet, *Osmanlı Eğitim Tarihi,* Istanbul: İletişim, 1993.

Sanal, Mustafa, "Kuruluşundan Ortadan Kaldırılışına Kadar Olan Süre İçerisinde Medreseler" http://yayim.meb.gov.tr/dergiler/143/17.htm (11.11.2007).

Sarıkaya, Yaşar, *Medreseler ve Modernleşme,* Istanbul: İz Yayıncılı, 1997.

Schacht, Joseph, *An Introduction to Islamic Law,* London: Oxford University Press, 1964.

—"Islamic Law in Contemporary States," *The American Journal of Comparative Law* 8, no. 2 (1959): 136.

Schrieke, B., *Indonesian Sociological Studies*, Part I, Bandung: W. Van Hoeve Ltd—The Hague, 1955.

Schrieke, B.J.O., *Indonesian Sociological Studies* 1 (1955); D.G.E. Hall, *A History of South East Asia* (London: McMillan, 1964), 190-191.

Sciolino, Elaine, "Britain Grapples with Role for Islamic Justice," *New York Times*, November 18, 2008.

Seljuq, Affan, "Relations between the Ottoman Empire and the Muslim Kingdoms in the Malay-Indonesian Archipelago," *Der Islam*, 57, 1980, p. 302-303.

Şenturk, Recep, *İslam Dünyasında Modernleşme ve Toplumbilim*, Istanbul: İz Yayıncılık, 1996.

Serjeant, R.B., "Materials for South Arabian History: Notes on New MSS from Hadramaut," *Bulletin of the School of Oriental and African Studies* 13 (1950): 283.

Sezer Şennur, and Özyalçıner, Adnan, *Üç Dinin Buluştuğu Kent Istanbul*, Istanbul: İnkılap Kitabevi, 2003.

Shaffer, Lynda Norene. *Maritime Souhtheast Asia to 1500*, New York: M.E. Sharpe, 1996.

Shuaib, Farid Sufian, et. al., "Administration of Islamic Law in Malaysia," *Malayan Law Journal* (Kuala Lumpur: Butterworth Asia, 2001), 91.

Siegfried, N.A., "Legislation and Legitimation in Oman: The Basic Law," *Islamic Law and Society* 7, no. 3 (2000): 377-378.

Singapore Free Press Weekly, dated 11.4.1885, p. 195.

Soebardi, S., and Lee, C.P. Woodcroft, "Islam in Indonesia," *The Crescent in the East: Islam in Asia Major*, ed. Raphael Israeli, London: Curzon Press, 1982.

Sofyan, İsmail, (ed.), *Perang Kolonial Belanda Di Aceh: The Dutch Colonial War in Aceh*, Banda Aceh: The Documentation and Information Center of Aceh, 1990.

Stiles, Erin, "Broken Edda and Marital Mistakes: Two Recent Disputes from an Islamic Court in Zanzibar" in Masud, Peters, and Powers, *Dispensing Justice in Islam: Qadis and Their Judgments*, Leiden and Boston: Brill, 2006.

—"When Is a Divorce a Divorce? Determining Intention in Zanzibar's Islamic Courts," *Ethnology* 42, no. 4 (2003): 274

Stockwell, A.J., "Imperial Security and Moslem Militancy, with Special Reference to the Hertogh Riots in Singapore (December 1950)," *Journal of Southeast Asian Studies*, vol. 17, No. 2 (Sep. 1986), 331 (322-335).

Sūfi, Rusdi, (ed.), *Biografi Pejuang-Pejuang Aceh*, Dinas Kebudayaan Propinsi Nanggroe Aceh, Darussalam Proyek Pembinaan dan Pengembangan Suaka Peninggalan Sejarah kepurbakalaan, Banda Aceh: Kajian dan Nilai Tradisional, 2002.

Sulaiman, Mohd Said b. Hj., *Hikayat Johor,* Johor: Johor Government Publishing Office, 1930.

Sulaiman, Muhd Said b. Hj. *Hikayat Johor II,* Johor: Peninsular Tax And Management Services, 1950.

Supplementary Sheet, Vācibat Komisyonu Zabıtları (Minutes of Wājibat Commission); al-Zarqā, *al-Fiqh al-Islāmī fī Thawbih al-Jadīd*, vol. 1, pp. 219ff.

Swift, M.G., *Malay Peasant Society,* London: The Athlone Press, 1965.

Tagliacozzo, Eric. eds., *Southeast Asia and the Middle East Islam, Movement, and the Longue Durée,* Singapore: NUS Press, 2009.

Takeshi, Ito, *The World of the Adat Aceh: A Historical Study of the Sultanate of Aceh*, Ph.D. dissertation, Australian National University, 1984.

Tarling, Nicholas, "'The merest pustule.' The Singapore Mutiny of 1915," *Journal of the Malaysian Branch of the Royal Asiatic Society* LV, 2 (1982), 50.

Taşdemirci, Ersoy, "Medreselerin Doğus Kaynakları ve İlk Zamanları," *Erciyes Üniversitesi Sosyal Bilimler Dergisi*, vol. 2 (Kayseri: 1989), p. 269.

Testa, Baron de, *Recucil des Traites de la Porte Ottomane*, vol. VII, Paris: 1892.

Teuku Iskandar, *Hikayat Aceh,* trans. Abu Bakar, Aceh: Departemen Pendidikan Dan Kebudayaan Direktorat Jenderal Kebudayaan Museum Negeri Aceh, 1986.

Teungku Anzib, *Adat Aceh,* Manuscript India Office Library in

Verhandelingen Lamnyong, van het Koninklijk Instituut voor Taal-, Land-, en Velkendunde. Jilid XXIV, Gravenhage: Martinus Nijhoff, 1958, Aceh: Pusat Latihan Penelitian Ilmu-Ilmu Sosial, 1976.

Thaib, Lukman, *Acheh's Case: A Historical Study of the National Movement for the Independence of Aceh-Sumatra,* Kuala Lumpur: University of Malaya Press, 2002.

Thayer, L.E., "The Capitulations of the Ottoman Empire and the Question of Their Abrogation as it Affects the United States," *The American Journal of International Law* 17, no. 2 (1923): 207-233

The Committee, *Majalla-i Aḥkām-i ʿAdliyyah* (The Ottoman Courts Manual [Ḥanafī]), Article: 1801.

The Mejelle, trans. C.R. Tyser, D.G. Demetriades, and Ismail Haqqi Efendi, Kuala Lumpur: The Other Press, 2001.

Tjandrasasmita, Uka, *Aceh Dalam Retrospeksi Dan Refleksi Budaza Nusantara,* Jakarta: INTIM Informasi Taman Iskandar Muda, 1988.

Tjen, P.P. Buss, "Malay Law," *AJCL,* 7 (1958), 260-262.

Tsafrir, Nurit, "The Beginnings of the Ḥanafī School in Iṣfahān," *Islamic Law and Society* 5, no. 1 (1998): 10.

Tuğ, Salih. *İslam Ülkelerinde Anayasa Hareketleri,* Istanbul: İrfan Yayınevi, 1969.

Türkgeldi, Ali Fuad, *Rijal-i Muhimma-i Siyasiyyah* (High Officials of Politics), Istanbul: TTK, 1928.

Tyan, Emile, *Histoire de l'organization judiciaire en pays d'Islam,* Paris: 1938.

Ukūd ve Vācibāt Komisyonları īalışma Esasları (Working Principles of Commissions of Uqud and Wājibat), *Jarida-i Adliye* (Judicial Gazette), 2nd Series, Issues 12-21, Supplementary Sheets, pp. 3ff

Unan, Fahri, *Kuruluşundan Günümüze Fatih Kulliyesi,* Ankara: Türk Tarih Kurumu, 2003.

Unat, F. Reşit, *Türkiye Eğitim Sisteminin Gelişmesine Tarihi Bir Bakış,* Ankara: M.E.B., 1964.

Veer, Paul Van't, *Perang Aceh: Kisah Kegagalan Snouck Hurgronje,* Jakarta: Grafiti Pers, 1985.

Vikør, Knut S., *Between God and the Sultan: A History of Islamic Law,* Oxford: Oxford University Press, 2005.

Wilkinson, R.J., "Introductory Sketch: Law," in *Papers on Malay*

Subjects, Kuala Lumpur: 1908.

Willer, Thomas F., "Malayan Islamic Response to British Colonial Policy," *Jurnal Sejarah*, 10 (1973): 82.

Wilson, H.E., "The Islamization of South East Asia," *Journal of Historical Research (Ranchi)* 15 (1972): 1.

Windstedt, R.O., *A History of Classical Malay Literature*, Kuala Lumpur: Oxford University Press, 1977.

—"A History of Malaya," *JMBRAS* 13 (1935): 29.

—*Malaya and Its History*, Longon: Hutchinson's University Library, 1948.

—"Muslim Theology, Jurisprudence and History," *JMBRAS*, vol. XXX. Part 3, 1961, p. 112.

—*The Malay Annals or Sejarah Melayu*, London: School of Oriental Studies, 1938.

Yahya, Mahyuddin Hj., *Sejarah orang Syed di Pahang*, Kuala Lumpur: Dewan Bahasa dan Pustaka, 1984.

Yanagihashi, H., "The Judicial Functions of the Sulṭān in Civil Cases According to the Mālikīs up to the Sixth/Twelfth Century," *Islamic Law and Society* 3, no. 1 (1996): 41-74.

Yaqin, Anwarul, *Law and Society in Malaysia*, Selangor: International Law Book Services, 2002.

Yatim, Othman Mohd, *Epigrafi Islam Terawal Di Nusantara*, Kuala Lumpur: Dewan Bahasa dan Pustaka, 1990.

Yazbak, Mahmoud, "Nabulsi Ulama in the Late Ottoman Period, 1864-1914," *International Journal of Middle East Studies*, 29 (1997): 74.

Yegar, Moshe. *Islam and Islamic Institutions in British Malaya*, Jerusalem: Magnes Press, 1979.

Yıldırım, Selahattin, *Osmanlı İlim Geleneğinde Edirne Ḍārulḥadīsi ve Müderrisleri*, Istanbul: Darulhadis, 2001.

Yule, Henry, and Cordier, Henri, *The Book of Ser Marco Polo The Venetian: Concerning the Kingdoms and Marvels of the East*, vol. 2, 3rd edition, New Delhi: Munshiram Manoharlal, 1920.

Za'ba, Zainal Abidin b. Ahmad Pendeta, "A History of Malay Literature XIV: Modern Developments," *Journal of the Malay Branch of the Royal Society* (December 1939), 151-152

Zainuddin, H.M., *Tarich Atjeh dan Nusantara*, 1st edition, Medan: Pustaka Iskandar Muda, 1961.

Zaman, Muhammad Qasim, "The Caliphs, the 'Ulamā', and the Law: Defining the Role and Function of the Caliph in the Early 'Abbāsid Period," *Islamic Law and Society* 4, no. 1 (1997): 1-36.

—"The Ulama in Contemporary Islam: Custodians of Change," *British Journal of Middle East Studies*, 31 (2004): 265.

Zarqā, Muṣṭafā Aḥmad, *al-Fiqh al-Islamī fī Thawbih al-Jadīd*, vol. 1, Damascus: Dār al-Kutub, 1964.

Ze'evi, D., "The Use of Ottoman Sharī'a Court Records as a Source for Middle Eastern Social History: A Reappraisal," *Islamic Law and Society* 5, no. 1 (1998): 38

Zuḥaylī, Wahbah, *al-Fiqh al-Islāmī wa Adillatuh*, 8 vols., Damascus: Dār al-Fikr, 1996.

Zuḥaylī, Wahbah, *Uṣūl al-Fiqh al-Islāmī*, Damascus: Dār al-Fikr, 1986.

Index

'Abbāsid(s), 9, 56, 61, 121-124, 143, 146
'Abduh, Muḥammad, 17
Abdulaziz Shah, 35
Abdulaziz Ujung, Teungku, 43
Abdulhamid II, Sultan, xi, 7, 15, 17-21, 197, 199, 209
Abdulhamid Khan, Sultan, 19, 21
Abdullah as-Shams, Shaikh, 40
Abdullah Kan'an, Shaikh, 36
Abdulmejid, Sultan, 100, 198
Abdurrahim (Menteşezade) Effendi, 92
Abdurrahman al-Pasi, 36
Abdurrauf al-Fansurî, 42
Abdurrauf as-Singkilī, xii, 32, 35, 41, 42, 63, 68, 83
Abee, xii, 39, 45, 56, 67, 69, 72-75, 77, 80, 82, 84
Abu al-Su'ûd Effendi, 92
Abu Bakar, Sultan, xi, 15, 18-21, 200
Abū Ḥanīfah, 119, 154, 175
Abū Mūsā al-Ash'arī, 120
Abū Qulābah, 119
Abū Yūsuf, 121, 175
Aceh, xii, 2, 3, 5, 10, 16, 32-47, 49-76, 78-84, 198; as entrepots, 57; Doorway to Makkah, 34; known as Serambi Mekah, 58; pioneer of Islamic educational centres, 58; written culture in, 33
Aceh Darussalam Sultanate, 32, 35, 37, 51; region's most important Islamic state, 37
Acehnese, xii, 16, 32, 35, 37, 38, 40, 41, 48, 51-54, 57, 58, 60, 65, 67-69, 72-74, 77, 198; first to be introduced to Islam in region, 58
adālatnamahs, 99
Adat, 49, 50, 52, 66, 81, 82, 207
Afghānī, Jamāl al-Dīn al-, 17
Africa, 8, 10, 28
Agong, 191, 204, 206
aḥkām, 115, 134
Ahl al-Bayt, 8, 9, 26

Ahmad III, 94
Ahmed Akgündüz, xii, 85, 110-112
Ahmed b. Muhammad Zain al-Patani, Shaikh, 45
Ahmed Jawdat Pasha, 107, 110, 112, 113
Ahmet Kasturi, Haji, 39
aḥwāl al-shakhṣiyyah, 97, 102
akhlāq, 154
Alaaddin Mughayat Shah, 37
al-Attas, Hussein, 200
al-Attas, Syed Abdullah, 20, 200
al-Attas, Syed Ali, 20
al-Attas, Syed Muhammad Naquib, 4, 20, 24, 48-50, 79, 80, 82
Alauddin Riayat Shah al-Kahar, Sultan, 16, 38
Alauddin Riayat Shah II, Sultan, 2
'Alawiyyīn, 8, 9
Albania, 108, 139
al-diyah, 98
Algeria, 134
alghāz, 155
Al-Hidāyah, 175
'Alī b. Khayrān, 119
Ali Kuşçu, 161
Ali Mughayat Syah, 37, 63
Ali Pasha, 107, 134
Allah, ix, xiv, 87, 91, 116, 120, 126, 127, 158
Alparslan, 160
'āmil, 118
amīn, 127
amīr, 118
'Amr b. al-'Āṣ, 126
amwāl, 155
Andalucia, 108, 124
Arab(s), xi, 4-8, 10-15, 18, 19, 22, 25, 30, 34, 39, 60, 61, 65, 83, 120, 150, 196, 200; in Java and Madura, 10; residents of Johor, 13; settlements along west Sumatra, 6
Arab empire, 120
Arabia, xi, 4, 35, 36, 40, 42, 57, 62, 65, 83, 139
Arabs, Ḥaḍramī, 3, 6-8, 13, 15, 22; brought Islamic culture to China, 10; in Singapore, 11-12; marrying local women, 6; migrate to nearby islands, 10; residents of Singapore, 12; sailed wooden ships to Archipelago, 5; settled in India and spread Islam, 4
Archipelago, xi, 2-7, 9-11, 15, 17, 24, 28, 34, 36, 44, 46, 48, 50, 52, 53, 58, 60, 64, 76, 78, 79, 81-83, 195, 197, 201, 211
aristocratic, 14
Aristotle, 127
Arqam, 158
Aru, 16, 37
âshir, 95
Asian, xii, 26, 48-50, 52, 54, 57, 58, 62, 77, 82, 196, 198, 199, 209, 210
Atatürk, Kemal, 22
atheist, 188
Azyumardi, 4, 6, 24, 25, 27, 42, 51, 53, 54, 79-81, 83,

Baba Davud, xii, 32, 33, 39, 42-47, 53, 54, 83; had a Turkish ancestor, 47; tomb, 46
Baghdad, 36, 56, 58, 59, 61, 64, 66, 67, 76, 82, 124, 160
Baghdadi, Nayan al-, 45
Baghdadi, Shaikh Abdulwahab al-, 72
Baghdadi, Shaikh Abdurrahim Hafız al-, 71
Baghdadi, Shaikh Muhammad Ali al-, 74
Baghdadi, Shaikh Muhammad Said al-, 74
Baghdadi, Shaikh Muhammad Salih al-, 71
Baiturrahman mosque, 40, 41, 75
Balkans, 16, 108, 200
Baluchistan, 34
Banda Aceh, xii, 32, 33, 36, 49, 51, 52, 56, 69, 82, 83
Bangladesh, 134, 139, 198
Barisan Nasional, 189
Barus, 5, 24
Baṣrah, 119, 142, 146, 160
Batavia, 11, 18, 26, 195, 199
bāṭinī, 157
bay'a, 2
Baybars, Sultan, 124, 143
Bayezid II, 98
bayt al-māl, 118
Bayt al-Maqdis, 38
Beirut, 111, 144, 146, 149, 181, 199, 208
Bek, 20
Bendahara, 194
Bengal, 34, 134
Betawi, 20, 75
Beunua, 37
Bey, 52, 150, 161, 163, 199
Borneo, 202
Bosnia, 108
Boyanese, 11
Britain, 136, 137, 151, 199, 209, 232, 234; war against Ottoman Empire, 199
British, 5, 13, 16, 18, 24, 29, 40, 64, 78, 79, 134, 137, 139, 153, 197, 199, 201, 205, 210, 211; colonialism, 211; interference in Islamic affairs, 202; involved with slavery, 201; sought to introduce its legal system in region, 201
Bruas, 4
Buddhism, influence on legal matters, 192
Buddhist(s), 2, 6, 188, 192, 196
Bugis, 11
Bukhara, 108
Bumiputera, 188
bureaucratization, 132
Bursa, 161, 165, 169, 182
Byzantine empire, 43

Cairo, 15, 28, 36, 45, 111, 124, 144, 147, 148, 159, 165, 169, 181, 182, 185
Caliph, 2, 146, 161, 238; as Allah's vicegerent, 87
Cambay, 4, 34
Canonical, 89

Cavi, 46, 53
Central Asia, 197
chastity, 100
China, 4-6, 10, 34, 40, 57, 62, 193, 196
Chinese, xii, 6, 11, 21, 26, 48, 188, 192, 196; traditional religions, 188
Christianity, 17
Christianization, 51, 80, 232
Christians, 2, 120, 132, 137, 143
civil law, 102, 104, 105
civilization, ix, 23, 27, 48, 77, 79, 200, 208
codification, 94, 101, 105, 110, 112
colonial, xiii, 7, 16, 17, 39, 72, 114, 134, 136, 141, 186, 199, 201, 211
colonialism, xi, 37, 66, 139, 197, 199, 211; British, 211; European, xi, 37, 66, 197
commercial law, 101
Confucian, 188
Constantinople, 19, 83, 110, 199
Coromandel, 4, 34
court, 92, 107, 109, 140, 141, 148, 149, 152, 195, 202-204, 206; dual system in Malaysia, 203
customary law, xiii, 91, 94, 109, 186, 190, 192, 193
Cyprus, 108

da'wah, 9, 47, 155, 176
Dāmād, 92
Damascus, 15, 28, 111, 112, 120, 149, 159, 161, 165, 169, 181, 238
Darawardī, 'Abd al-'Azīz al-, 119
Darussalam, xii, 32, 35-38, 49-53, 56, 63, 79, 81, 82
Dato' Bahaman, 16
Davud b. Agha Ismail b. Agha Mustafa al-Javi ar-Rumi, 42
Davud b. Ismail al-Patani, Shaikh, xii, 32, 45, 46, 83
Davud-i Kayseri, 161
Day of Judgement, 117, 125
Daya, 37
dayah, 58, 65, 68-71, 73, 75, 76
Dayah Tanoh Abee, xii, 39, 45, 56-59, 67-71, 75, 77, 80, 82, 84
Delhi, 4, 48, 50, 54, 60, 79, 144, 148, 238
Delhi Sultanate, 4
Devlet-i Aliyye, 110, 231
Dewan Negara, 191
Dewan Rakyat, 188, 191
dhimmīs, 97
Divan-i Humayun, 92, 103
diversity, xiii
Dīwān-i Aḥkām-i 'Adliyyah, 107, 108
Durar al-Ḥukkām Sharḥ Majallah al-Aḥkām, 110
Dutch, 4, 5, 7, 8, 10, 11, 18, 37, 39, 51, 59, 60, 68, 69, 72-75, 77, 79, 187, 194, 195, 198, 199, 201, 211, 235; destructive impact of – invasion, 69; colonial invasions, 7; holy war against, 59, 73; navy occupying Aceh, 72; resented the Arabs' presence, 10; tried to apply law in Malacca, 201

Dutch East India Company, 195

East Africa, 8, 10
Ebussuūd Efendi, 163
economic institutions, 6
Egypt, 13, 29, 35, 38, 108, 123, 131, 134-136, 138-140, 143-145, 148-153
Elizabeth I, Queen, 35, 64
Engku Abdul Majid, 20, 30
English law, 137, 187, 190
European, xi, 16-18, 37, 52, 58, 61, 66, 81, 87, 89, 101, 102, 112, 131, 133, 134, 136, 138, 169, 179, 197-199, 211; colonialism, xi, 37, 66, 197

falsafah, 157
family law, 86, 90, 97, 100, 102, 112, 132, 134, 139, 194
Fansuri, Sheikh Abdul Rauf Ali al, 22
faqīh, 89, 167
Faqih Jalaladdin b. Kamaluddin al-Asyi, Shaikh, 42
Fārābī, 155, 156, 181
farḍ ʻayn, 126
fāsiq, 129
fatāwah, 155
Fatih Sultan Mehmet, 162
Fatimi, S.Q., 4, 24
Fāṭimīds, 123, 124
fatwa(s), 2, 6, 14, 86, 88, 89, 101, 103, 167, 172
Federated Malay States, 202
fermans, 99, 198
fiqh, xiii, 42, 85, 92, 101, 104, 111, 112, 149, 154-158, 170-174, 181; defined, 154
fiqh al-sīrah, 155, 158, 176
firmans, 99, 198
First World War, 200
Firus al-Baghdadi, al-, 39, 45, 56, 58, 64, 66, 67, 69, 76
France, 107, 134, 136, 137, 150
freedom, of thought, 187, of religion, 187
French, 5, 107, 139, 198; civil law, 107
furūʻ al-fiqh, xiii, 155, 174
Fusṭāṭ, 119, 142

Gazi, 161
Germany, 22, 137
Ghazālī, Imam al-, 2, 155-157, 167, 182
Ghaznalis, 160
Greek, 127
Gresik, 4
Gujarat, 4, 34, 36, 60, 62
Gülhane Khatt-i Humayunu, 100

ḥadd, 95, 98, 102; *al-baghy*, 98; *al-qadhf*, 98; *al-shirb*, 98; *al-sirqah*, 98; *al-zinâ*, 98
Ḥadīth, 145, 149, 156-158, 161, 171, 179, 180, 185; literature, 98, 99
Ḥaḍramawt, 8-11, 25, 26, 34
Ḥaḍramī, xi, 3, 6-8, 10, 15, 18, 19, 22; Arabs, 3, 6-8, 13, 15, 22
ḥāfiẓ, 164

ḥajar al-aswad, 117
ḥajj, 176
Hajji Khalifa, 15
ḥajr, 89, 176
ḥakams, 118, 142
Hamzah Fansurī, 35, 63
Ḥanafi(s), xiii, 86, 89-91, 101, 102, 104-106, 110, 111, 123, 124, 132, 134, 139, 143, 147, 174, 175, 180, 186, 197, 211, 236
Ḥanbalī, 124
Harem, 30
Hārūn al-Rashīd, 122
Hatice Hanım, 20
heterodox, 3
hijrah, 158
Hikayat Johor, 19-21
ḥikmah al-tashrī', 155
ḥimārīyatayn, 121
Hindu(s), 6, 134, 188, 192, 194, 196; influence on legal matters, 192
hirābah, 98
ḥiyal, 155
Hocazâde Muslihuddin Mustafa, 156
Holland, 134, 195, 199
Horasan, 160
Hourani, Albert, 14, 27, 28
ḥudūd, 90
ḥukm, 130
human rights, 187
Hurgronje, Snouck, 29, 34, 48, 51, 52, 77, 84, 198, 209, 237
Hüseyn Efendi 16
Hussein Onn, 20
'ibādah, 97
'ibādāt, 154
Ibn al-'Ābidin, 111
Ibn al-'Arabī, 64
Ibn al-Qayyim, 111
Ibn Fārūq, 119
Ibn Sīna, 155, 181
Ibn Tagrī Birdī, 123
Ibn Wahb, 119
Ibrahim of Aleppo, 89
Ibrahim, Sultan, 18, 21, 22, 31
iddah, 102
Idris b. Hussein Kelantanam, Shaikh, 45
ijāzah, 68, 70
ijmā', 86, 88, 121, 130, 203
ijtihād, 104, 126, 130, 154, 180
'ilm al-farā'iḍ, 97
imām, 88, 118
Imām-i Mashrû', 87
Imperial Council, 92
India, 4, 5, 8-10, 35, 36, 40, 47, 50, 51, 57, 60, 61, 63, 67, 124, 134, 139, 192, 196, 198, 202, 236
Indian, 4, 6, 11, 25, 34, 60, 65, 81, 192, 198-200, 202
Indian Ocean, 8, 25, 61, 62, 78, 196
Indonesia, 2
Indra Purpa, 36
inheritance, 105
iqṭā', 121
iqtiṣād, 155, 178
Iran, 34-36, 40, 51, 57, 124, 139
Iraq, 13, 28, 34, 108, 139, 152
Iskandar Muda Mahkota Alam,

Sultan, 3, 35, 39, 40, 50, 52, 56, 58, 64, 66, 81; and Sufism, 66
Iskandar Shah, Sultan, 196
Iskandar Tsani, 41
Islam, adoption by indigenous people, 47; arrival to Archipelago, 3; came from Arabs, 4, 6; from the Arabian peninsula, 4; in Johor, 1, 7; pan-, xi, 7, 15, 17, 197, 199, 209, 232; spread by Arab, Indian, Chinese and Sūfīs, 6; spread through trade, 6
Islamic, banking, 137, education, 58, 76; empires, 2; government, 2; jurisprudence, 92; state, 117; values, 68
Islamic law, xi-xiii, 41, 57, 66, 72, 85-87, 91-94, 98, 103-106, 108, 110, 112, 115, 118, 119, 121, 131, 133-135, 138-140, 186, 187, 190, 191, 194-196, 201-205, 211
Islamization, 24, 28, 32, 34-36, 44, 47, 48, 50, 51, 53, 56-58, 60, 67, 79, 80, 82, 153, 198
ISTAC, 200
Istanbul, ix, 14-16, 19, 21, 43-45, 51, 54, 79, 84, 107, 110-113, 144, 145, 151, 162, 165, 175, 180-185, 198-200
iṣṭilāḥāt, 155
Italy, 134
i'tiqād, 154, 158
İzzet Pasha, 14
Ja'far al-Ṣādiq, 9
Jambi, 5, 16
Java, 4, 5, 10, 30, 53, 72, 80, 83, 195, 233
Javanese, 11
Jawi, 60, 74
Jawi Peranakan, 11
jazā al-siyāsah al-Shar'iyyah, 98
jazā al-ta'zīr, 98
Jerusalem, 28, 64, 77, 78, 149, 165, 169
Jews, 120, 137
jihād, 73, 74, 196
jilwāz, 127
jināyāt, 90
Johor, xi, xiii, 1-3, 5, 7, 8, 12, 13, 15-24, 26-31, 65, 186, 197, 200, 209; Sultanate, 2
Johor Religious Department, 21
Judicial, xii, xiii, 112, 134, 144, 145, 147, 149, 153, 186, 202
jurists, 101

kadi, 204
kalām, 155-158, 171, 177, 185
Kashf al-Ẓunūn, 15
kātib, 118, 127
kaum muda, 17
kaum tua, 17
Kayadibi, Saim, x-xiv, 1, 3, 4, 23, 114, 144, 148, 151, 186
Kedah, 5, 65, 74, 75
Kelantan, 45, 46, 196, 208
Keling, 40
khalīfah, 1, 68, 70, 83, 120
kharāj, 95, 118

Khawārizmī, 155-157
Khedive Ismāʿīl, 135
khitāb, 130
Khoja Emin Efendi Zadeh Ali Haydar, 110
Khurmuz, 61
Khusraw, Molla, 92
Kınalızâde Ali Efendi, 169
Kindī, al-, 123
Kitāb al-Buyūʿ, 107
Kitāb al-Kharāj, 122
Kitāb al-Qaḍāʾ, 107
Kuala Krai, 196
Kūfah, 119, 120, 142, 146
Kurds, 13
Kuwait, 108

Laksamana, 194
Lamuri, 37
Lancaster, James, 35, 64
Lebanon, 13, 108, 139, 140
Libya, 134, 149
Lingga, 37

Ma'mūn, al-, 9, 122, 143
Maʿrūḍāt, 107, 112, 113
madhhab, 123-124
Madīnah, 36, 65, 72, 117, 159, 165, 169
madrasah(s), xiii, 6, 92, 161-165, 167-171, 175-180, 184; defined, 160; management of, 162; philosophical grounds for, 166; specialization in, 161
Madura, 10
maghāzī, 155
mahārij, 155
Mahḍars, 128
Mahdī, al-, 121
maḥkamah, 114
Mahkama-i Nizāmiyyah, 104
maḥmūd, 158
Mahmud II, Sultan, 100, 109
Majallah, xi, xiii, 22, 85, 86, 93, 101-108, 110, 155, 186, 188, 197, 211; see also *Mecelle*
Majlis Agama, 191
Majlis al-Mabʿūsān, 103
Majmaʿ al-Anhur, 92
Makkah, 8, 15, 33, 34, 36, 45, 47, 58, 62, 64, 65, 72, 117, 165, 169
Malabar, 4, 5, 34
Malabari, al-, 36
Malacca, 2, 5, 7, 10, 37, 39, 40, 57, 62, 63, 79, 80, 194-196, 198, 201, 208; centre of trade, 195; captured by Portuguese, 37; Dutch tried to apply their law in, 201
Malacca Straits, 5, 39, 40, 57
Malay(s), xi-xiv, 1-11, 15, 17, 24-26, 28, 29, 32, 34, 36, 40, 42-46, 48-50, 52-54, 58, 60, 63-66, 76-83, 186, 188, 190, 192-202, 206-212; customary law, 192; defined, 189; language, 66, 189; nature of, 211; Proto-, 193
Malaya, 191, 192, 202, 206
Malaysia, ix, x, xiii, 2, 4, 23, 24, 29, 30, 45, 48, 50, 52, 54, 55, 77, 79,

81, 84, 139, 140, 144, 152, 153, 186, 188-190, 193, 195, 200, 203, 205-211; constitutional law, 186, 191; Federal Constitution, 190; legal system, xiii, 189; society defined as 'Islamic', 189
Malik az-Zahir, Sultan, 3, 36
Malik Ibrahim, Maulana, 4
Malik us-Saleh, 36
Mālikī(s), 123, 124, 134, 139, 143, 174
Mamlūks, 124
Marco Polo, 34, 48, 79, 238
Mardin, 113
masāil, 155
Masjid Nabawī, 159
Māwardī, al-, 122, 149
Mawqūfāt, 89
maẓālim, 121, 146
McAmis, Robert Day, 10, 24- 26
mecalis, 132, 143
Mecelle, 112, 132, 133, 135, 139, 143, 185; see also *Majallah*
Medrese, 161, 183
Mehmed II, 109; see also *Mehmed the Conqueror*
Mehmed the Conqueror, 95, 98, 164; see also *Mehmed II*
Mehmet Özay, ix, xii, 32, 48, 54, 56, 77, 209, 210
Mekteb-i Kuzat, 162
Melaka, see *Malacca*
Melikshah, 160
Merdeka, 191
metaphysics, 62
Meurah Johan Shah, 36
Meurah Shah Nuwi, 9
Mi'yār al-'Adālah, 98
Middle East, 3, 4, 8, 17, 19, 23, 24, 27, 34, 47, 54, 56, 61, 63, 76, 79, 83, 110-112, 124, 135, 138, 143, 145, 147, 148, 150-153, 199, 208, 209; relationship with Malay region, 3
miḥnah, 122, 143, 147
military, 16, 29, 38, 39, 41, 56, 61, 63, 73, 74, 87, 90, 95, 96, 99, 118, 120, 124, 141, 142, 165, 169, 184, 195, 198
Mimarzāde Mustafa Efendi, 169
Moḥammad Yamanī, Shaikh, 35
Mongol, 39
Morocco, 51, 139, 152
mu'allim, 6, 118
mu'āmalāt, 80, 91, 95, 97, 101, 148, 152, 154, 158
Mu'āwiyah, 119, 120, 142
mu'āyanah, 129
Mu'taḍid, 122
Muḍārabah, 99
mudda'ā 'alayhi, 128
mudda'ī, 128
muftī, 1, 2, 14, 15, 22, 23, 89, 108, 119, 120, 124
Mughal (*also* Moghul), 124, 134, 198
Muhammad IV, 89
Muhammad Amin, Teungku , 36
Muhammad Azhari, Shaikh, 41
Muhammad Dahlan al-Fairus al-Baghdadi, Teungku, 59
Muhammad Davud, 37
Muhammad Jailani b. Hasan b. Hamid, 41

Muḥammad (Prophet), 26, 87, 117, 118, 121, 126, 158, 178
Muhammad the Conqueror, 94
Muhammad Yamani, Shaikh, 62
muḥtasib, 118
mujtahid, 89
mujtahids, 87-89
Mukalla, 5, 8
mukattib, 118
Mukhtâr, 111
Mul Jawa, 5
Multaqā al-Abḥur, 89, 92, 104, 174
multi-cultural, 189
Muntasir, al-, 60
murīd, 68
Muṣʿab b. ʿImrān, 119
musallam, 95
Mustanṣir, 161
mustashār, 118
Mutawakkil, al-, 122

Nabawī, 159
nāḥiyah, 124
naḥū, 157
Naina b. Naina al-Malabari, Mevlana, 36
Napoleon, 135
Napoleonic Code, 106
Naqshbandiyyah, 57, 63, 70
Naquib al-Attas, Syed, 4
Nayan al-Firus al-Baghdadi, Shaikh, 70
naẓarī, 155, 156
Negritoes, 193
Nigeria, 134
Niẓām al-Mulk, 160
nizamiye, 132, 133, 135, 143
nobility, 72
Nubar Pasha, 135, 150
Nur Alam Naqiyatuddin, Queen, 68
Nuruddin ar-Raniri, 35, 41, 63

Oman, 34, 49, 53, 61, 80, 82, 84, 139, 140, 153
Omar b. Ali al-Junied, Syed, 19
Onn Jaafar, 20, 200
Orhan Gazi, 161
Orientalists, 4, 7, 29
Osman I, 90
Ottoman, xi-xiii, 1, 3, 4, 7, 12-19, 21-23, 27, 28, 31, 33, 38-40, 43, 44, 51, 56, 59, 61, 62, 71, 78, 82, 83, 85-92, 94-100, 102, 103, 105, 107-112, 118, 125, 131-133, 136, 138, 139, 143, 148, 150, 151, 154, 156, 157, 160, 161, 163-165, 169, 178-180, 188, 197-200, 209, 211; bureaucracy, 165; Civil Code, 103; codices, 89; empire, xii, xiii, 3, 4, 12-14, 16-19, 22, 38, 39, 43, 44, 56, 59, 62, 71, 85-88, 90-92, 94, 98, 100, 103, 107, 108, 125, 131-133, 136, 138, 143, 164-166, 179, 197, 199; Family Law, 85; jurists, 92; laws, 85-90, 94, 96, 99, 100, 103, 132, 188; *madrasah* system, 161; society, xiii

Padishah, 92
Pahang, 5, 9, 25, 49, 51-53, 64, 65, 196
Pakistan, 134, 139, 141, 153, 198
Palembang, 5, 6, 10
Palestine, 108
Pan-Malaysian Islamic Party (PAS), 189
Paris, 113, 236
Pasai, 2-4, 6, 35-38, 58, 60, 62, 63, 79
Pasha, 14, 107, 108, 110, 112, 134, 135, 162, 176, 198, 231
Patani, 2, 44-46
Pax Turcica, 198
Pedir, 37, 63
Pekojan, 11
Penghulu, 193
Perak, 4, 65, 202
Perikatan, 189
Perlak, 9, 35, 62
perpatih, 193, 207
Persia, 5, 29, 62
Persian, 6, 9, 28, 60, 61, 78, 83, 123, 162, 168, 176, 196
personal law, 100, 201
pesantrens, 6
pey akcha, 101
Philips, Nicholas, 137
Pidie, 37
Plato, 127
Pluralism, xiii
Pontianak, 10
Portugal, 15, 39, 62
Portuguese, 16, 37, 38, 40, 43, 50, 62, 63, 79, 80, 187, 194, 195, 198, 201, 211; and Dutch influence, 194; captured Malacca, 37
private law, 91
public good, 93, 99, 104
public law, 91, 94

qāḍī, 2, 67, 70-72, 76, 86, 88, 89, 91, 92, 108, 109, 114, 116, 118-125, 127-130, 132, 134, 136, 142, 143, 146, 148, 162
Qāḍī ʻaskar, 92, 109, 124
Qādiriyyah, 43, 63, 64
Qadızāde Efendi, 169
Qadri Pasha, xiii, 186, 197, 211
Qānūn, 146
Qānūnnāme, 93, 94
qāṣṣ, 118
qatʻ al-tarîq, 98
Qatar, 137, 138, 140, 151
qawāʻid, 155
Qawānīn al-Mulkiyyah li al-Dawlah al-ʻAliyyah, 103
qiṣāṣ, 98, 196
qiyās, 86, 88, 203
Qur'an, 42, 83, 85-89, 96, 98-100, 109, 115-117, 121, 126, 129, 144, 145, 148, 149, 154, 156-158, 164, 168, 179, 180, 189, 203, 205, 207

Raja Rum, 44, 83, 198
rasm al-qismah, 98
real estate, 101, 102
Red Sea, 63
reformer, 66
Reid, Anthony, 18, 29, 30, 48, 51,

52, 54, 78, 80, 81, 84, 209, 232, 233
Riddel, Peter G., 8, 27
Rightly Guided Caliphs, 118, 121, 142
Risalah Masailal Muhtadi li Ikhwanil Muhtadi, 32, 45, 38
Roman, empire, 88; law, 106
Rubʿ al-Khālī, 8
Rumi, Ismail ar-, 43
Rumi, Mustafa ar-, xii, 32, 33, 42, 46, 68
Ruqayyah Hanım, 20, 200
Russian, 5, 200

Saʿd b. Masʿūd, 119
Sabah, 140, 190
Safavid, 124
Sagoff, A.M. al-,12
Sagoff (family), 26, 30, 234
Sagoff, Syeikh Muhammad al-, 18, 19
ṣāḥib al-ḥaras, 118
ṣāḥib al-shurṭah, 118
Ṣalāḥ al-Dīn al-Ayyūbī, 123
Saljuk, 61, 88, 90, 198
Salmah b. ʿIkrimah, 119
Samarqand, 161
Samudra-Pasai, 35-37, 58, 62
Sanhouri, al-,135
Sarawak, 140, 190, 206
Saudi Arabia, 23, 139
Sayyid Abdul Aziz, 9
Sayyid Abdul Malik b. Alawi, 9
Sayyid Abdullah al-Qudsi, 9
Sayyid Abul Huda al-Sayyadi, 14
Sayyid Hussein al-Qadri, 10
Sayyid Muhammad b. Ahmad al-Idrus, 9
Sayyid Muhammad b. Hamid, 10
Sayyid Sultan Abdulaziz Shah, Mevlana, 35
Sayyid Uthman b. Syahab, 9, 10
secular, 100
Selçuk(s), 43, 160, 161, 198
Selim I, 14, 100, 124
Selim III, 100
Selim the Excellent, 98
Senois, 193
Servet Armağan, xiii
Seulimum, xii, 46, 56, 67, 70, 72, 74, 75
Şeyh Dergahı, 14
Shāfiʿī, 4, 124, 129, 154, 175, 194
Shāfiʿīs, 123
shahādah, 129, 130
Shaikh Abu'l Khair b. Shaikh Hajar, 35, 62
Shaikh Muhammad Jailani b. Hasan b. Muhammad, 35, 62
Shamsuddin Sumatranî, 35, 40, 57, 63
Shan Mehmed Efendi, 169
Shar'-i Sharif, 87
Sharʿiyyah Records, 96, 98, 99
Sharīʿah, xi, xiii, 14, 85-91, 93-101, 103, 105, 108, 109, 114, 115, 117, 119, 123, 125, 130, 132-134, 136-143, 146, 152, 165, 171, 173-175, 177, 184, 187, 191, 203-206, 211; decrees, 93; rules, 95, 97, 99

Sharī'ah al-Muḥammadiyyah, al-, 89
Shattariyya, 41, 57, 64, 67, 68, 70, 83
Shaykh al-Islām, 2, 14, 92, 107, 109, 124, 128, 163, 169
Shī'ah, 160; Ismā'īlī, 123
Shī'ī, 17
shi'r, 156
Shihi, 8
shūrā, 123
shurṭah, 138
shurūṭ, 155
Siak, 10
Sicily, 108
sijill, 125, 148
Sijillāt, 96
Sikhism, 188
Sind, 34
Singapore, 5, 7, 11-13, 16, 18, 19, 24, 26, 27, 29, 30, 45, 49, 51, 77, 80, 82, 84, 199, 206-210; Arab community in, 11, 12
Singapore Mutiny, 199
Singkilī, Abdurrauf b. Ali al-Cavī al-Fansurī al-, xii, 32, 35, 41, 42, 63, 68, 83
siyāsah, 131, 132
siyāsah shar'iyyah, 155
Southeast Asia, xi, xii, 5, 6, 8, 24, 29, 33-35, 37, 40, 43, 48-52, 56-62, 65, 67, 77, 78, 80-82, 196-199, 201, 207-209; economic attraction, 6
Sri Lanka, 5, 34
Sribuza, 5
Sriwijaya, 5
Straits Settlements, 11, 201, 202
Straw, Jack, 137
subashi(s), 91
Sudan, 136, 139, 152
Suez Canal, 5
Sūfi(s), 6, 34, 47, 49, 52, 57, 61, 63, 64, 66, 67, 76, 80, 200, 235; introduced Islam, 6
Sufism, 25, 42, 49, 58, 62, 70, 76, 80, 157, 198
Sulaymān b. 'Abd al-Mālik, 120, 143
Süleyman I, 14, 38, 90, 94, 95, 98, 124, 162-164
Süleyman the Lawgiver, see *Süleyman I*
Süleyman the Lawmaker, see *Süleyman I*
Süleyman the Magnificent, see *Süleyman I*
Süleymaniye Dār al-Ḥadīth, 165, 172
Sultanate, xii, 2, 4, 7, 12, 18, 32, 34, 35, 37, 39, 44, 50, 51, 81, 82, 194, 235
Sumatra, 4, 10, 34, 48-52, 54, 60, 62, 63, 65, 78, 80, 83, 84, 192, 198, 209
Sunnah, 86-89, 96, 109, 121, 126, 129, 154, 156, 158, 180, 203
Sunnī, 17, 76, 85, 102, 108, 124, 130, 159-161, 167, 180, 198
Supreme Court, 92
Swiss Civil Code, 125
Switzerland, 137, 150

Syaikh Davud b. Ismail b. Mustafa ar-Rumi, 43
Syed Mohamed b. Abdul Rahman al-Koff, 19
Syiah Kuala, Teungku, xii, 32, 43, 46, 47, 83; see also *Abdurrauf as-Singkilī*
Syria, 13, 29, 35, 108, 139

ta'bīr, 157
ṭabaqāt al-fuqahā', 155
tablīgh, 155, 162
Tafsīr, 42, 156, 170, 172
Taftazanī, 160
Taha Safiuddin, Sultan, 16
tahāruj, 97
taḥrīr, 156
Ṭā'if, 8
Tāj al-Dīn 'Abd al-Wahhāb b. al-A'azz, 124
Tanqīḥ, 171, 174, 177
Tanẓīmāt, xii, 85-87, 90, 94, 100-104, 109, 162, 179
Taoist, 188
ṭarīqah, 67, 68, 70, 83
taṣawwuf, 157
Taşköprülüzâde Ahmed İsamuddin Efendi, 156, 157
taṣwīr, 157
ta'zīr, 85, 90, 94, 95, 98, 99, 102, 197
temenggong, 193, 194
Terengganu, 197, 209
Thailand, 2, 40, 44-46, 151
theosophy, 6
Tibbets, 5
Timur, 161
Timurids, 161
Tioman, 5
Tionghoa, 40
Tiro, 67, 73, 78, 84
transparency, 187
Tuğrul Bey, 160
Tunisia, 134, 139
Tunku Chik, 43, 46
Turk Hukuk Tarihi, 112
Turkestan, 108
Turkey, 5, 7, 13, 15, 18, 19, 21, 22, 43, 102, 108, 132, 136, 139, 140, 144, 148, 150, 151, 153, 163, 169, 197
Turkish Civil Code, 106
Turkish, xi, xii, 15, 16, 18-20, 22, 27, 28, 30, 32, 33, 37-39, 43, 47, 51, 59-61, 68, 89, 92, 104, 106, 107, 110, 151, 152, 168, 176, 198, 200, 201
Turkistan, 160, 175
Turks, xii, 13, 28, 37, 43, 44, 60, 108, 160, 197-199

'ulamā', 1-3, 14, 15, 19, 21-23, 46, 58, 62-64, 68, 77, 117-119, 121, 124, 128, 142, 143, 157, 159, 160,
uleebalang, 72
ulū al-amr, 85, 90, 91, 93, 100, 101, 109
Uluğ Bey, 161
'Umar b. al-Khaṭṭāb, 118, 120, 121, 142
'Umar Hilmi Effendi, 98

umarā', 1, 2
Umayyad(s), 78, 119, 120, 142, 146, 161, 166, 231
ummah, 17, 117
UMNO, 20, 188, 200
Undang-undang, xiii, 186, 194, 197, 208
Ungku Abdul Aziz, 20, 200
Ungku Abdul Majid, 200
Ungku Abdulhamid, 20
United Kingdom, 137, 146
United States, 136, 137, 151, 236
University of Malaya, 20, 23, 30, 50, 200, 205, 209, 232, 236
uqūbāt, 90, 154
'urfī ḥuqūq, 94
uṣūl al-fiqh, xiii, 155-157, 174, 177
uṣūl al-ḥadīth, 156
Uthman Beg, 91

van Bruinessen, Martin, 59
Van Den Berg, 11
Victoria, Queen, 18
von Mehden, Fred R., 3

waḥdah al-wujūd, 64, 66
waḥy, 155, 166
Wali al-Amr, 93
waqf, 2, 159
West Indies, 8
westernization, 100, 131
Willer, Thomas F., 3
Windsted, 4
Wiqāyah, Al-, 175

Yahya Armajani, 13, 27
yamīn, 129
yasaqnamahs, 99
yaya, 95
Yemen, 5, 8, 28, 117, 139

ẓāhirī, 157
Zakāh, 176
Zanzibar, 139, 152, 235
zāwiyah, xii, 56-59, 61, 66-77, 159; to spread Islamic and scientific knowledge, 70
Zoroastrians, 120